#50 The Pacifists' Last Trace

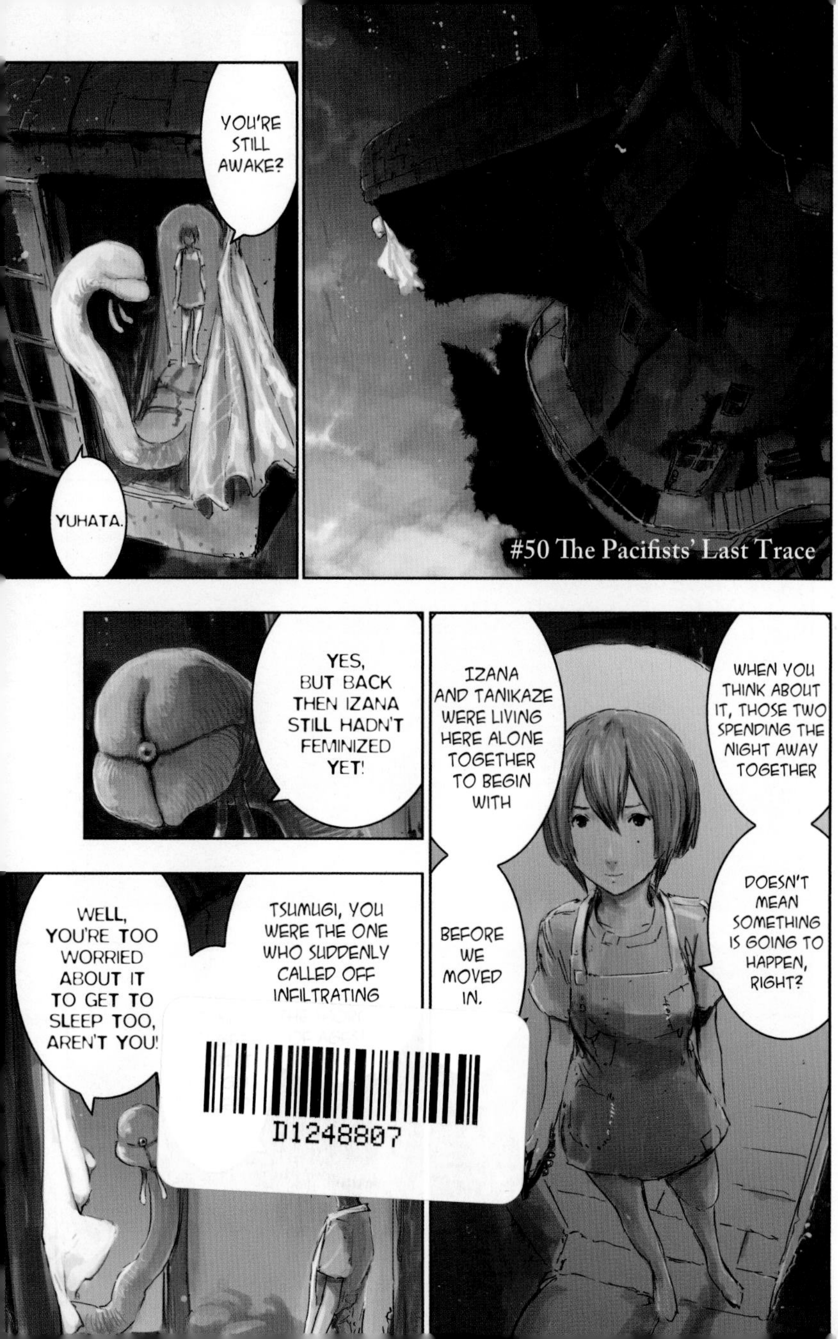
YOU'RE STILL AWAKE?
YUHATA.
WHEN YOU THINK ABOUT IT, THOSE TWO SPENDING THE NIGHT AWAY TOGETHER
DOESN'T MEAN SOMETHING IS GOING TO HAPPEN, RIGHT?
IZANA AND TANIKAZE WERE LIVING HERE ALONE TOGETHER TO BEGIN WITH
BEFORE WE MOVED IN.
YES, BUT BACK THEN IZANA STILL HADN'T FEMINIZED YET!
TSUMUGI, YOU WERE THE ONE WHO SUDDENLY CALLED OFF INFILTRATING
WELL, YOU'RE TOO WORRIED ABOUT IT TO GET TO SLEEP TOO, AREN'T YOU!

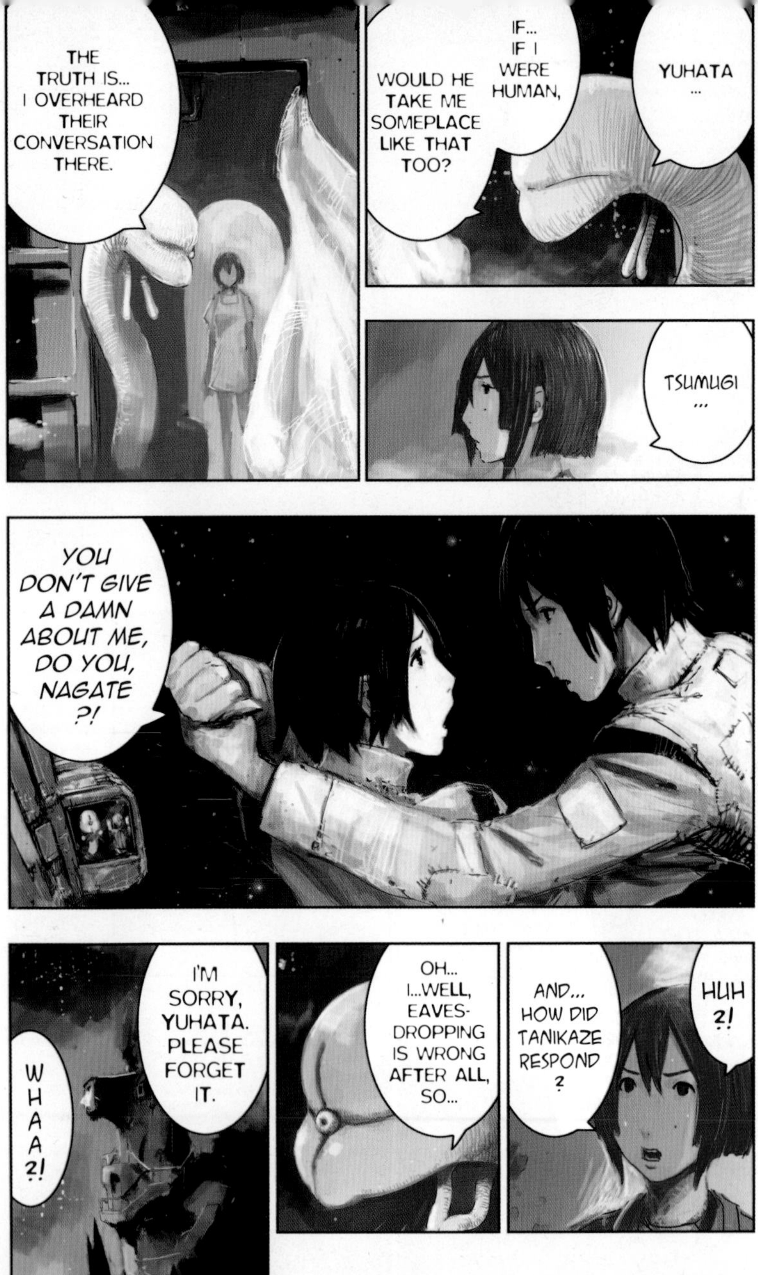
YUHATA ...
IF... IF I WERE HUMAN,
WOULD HE TAKE ME SOMEPLACE LIKE THAT TOO?
TSUMUGI ...
THE TRUTH IS... I OVERHEARD THEIR CONVERSATION THERE.
YOU DON'T GIVE A DAMN ABOUT ME, DO YOU, NAGATE ?!
HUH ?!
AND... HOW DID TANIKAZE RESPOND ?
OH... I...WELL, EAVES-DROPPING IS WRONG AFTER ALL, SO...
I'M SORRY, YUHATA. PLEASE FORGET IT.
WHAAA ?!

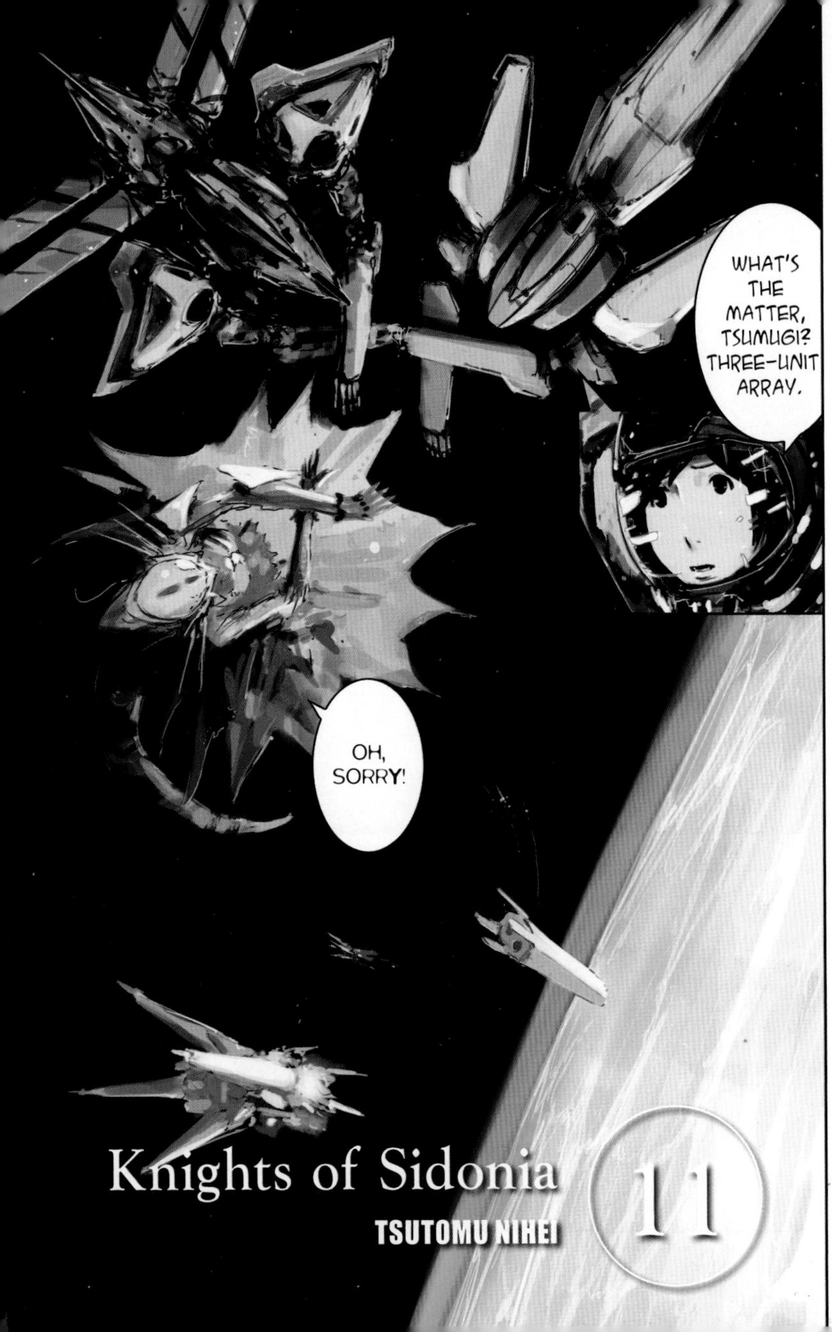
WHAT'S THE MATTER, TSUMUGI? THREE-UNIT ARRAY.
OH, SORRY!

Knights of Sidonia 11

TSUTOMU NIHEI

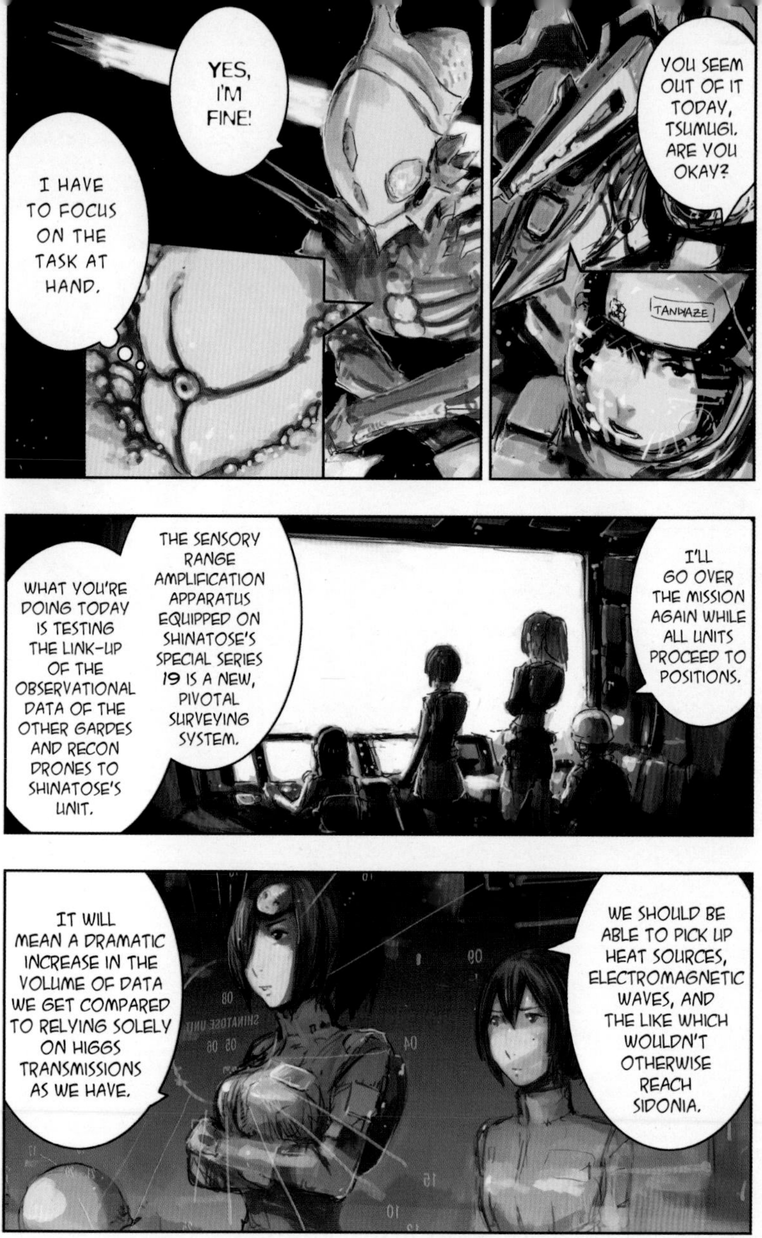
YOU SEEM OUT OF IT TODAY, TSUMUGI. ARE YOU OKAY?
YES, I'M FINE!
I HAVE TO FOCUS ON THE TASK AT HAND.
I'LL GO OVER THE MISSION AGAIN WHILE ALL UNITS PROCEED TO POSITIONS.
THE SENSORY RANGE AMPLIFICATION APPARATUS EQUIPPED ON SHINATOSE'S SPECIAL SERIES 19 IS A NEW, PIVOTAL SURVEYING SYSTEM.
WHAT YOU'RE DOING TODAY IS TESTING THE LINK-UP OF THE OBSERVATIONAL DATA OF THE OTHER GARDES AND RECON DRONES TO SHINATOSE'S UNIT.
WE SHOULD BE ABLE TO PICK UP HEAT SOURCES, ELECTROMAGNETIC WAVES, AND THE LIKE WHICH WOULDN'T OTHERWISE REACH SIDONIA.
IT WILL MEAN A DRAMATIC INCREASE IN THE VOLUME OF DATA WE GET COMPARED TO RELYING SOLELY ON HIGGS TRANSMISSIONS AS WE HAVE.

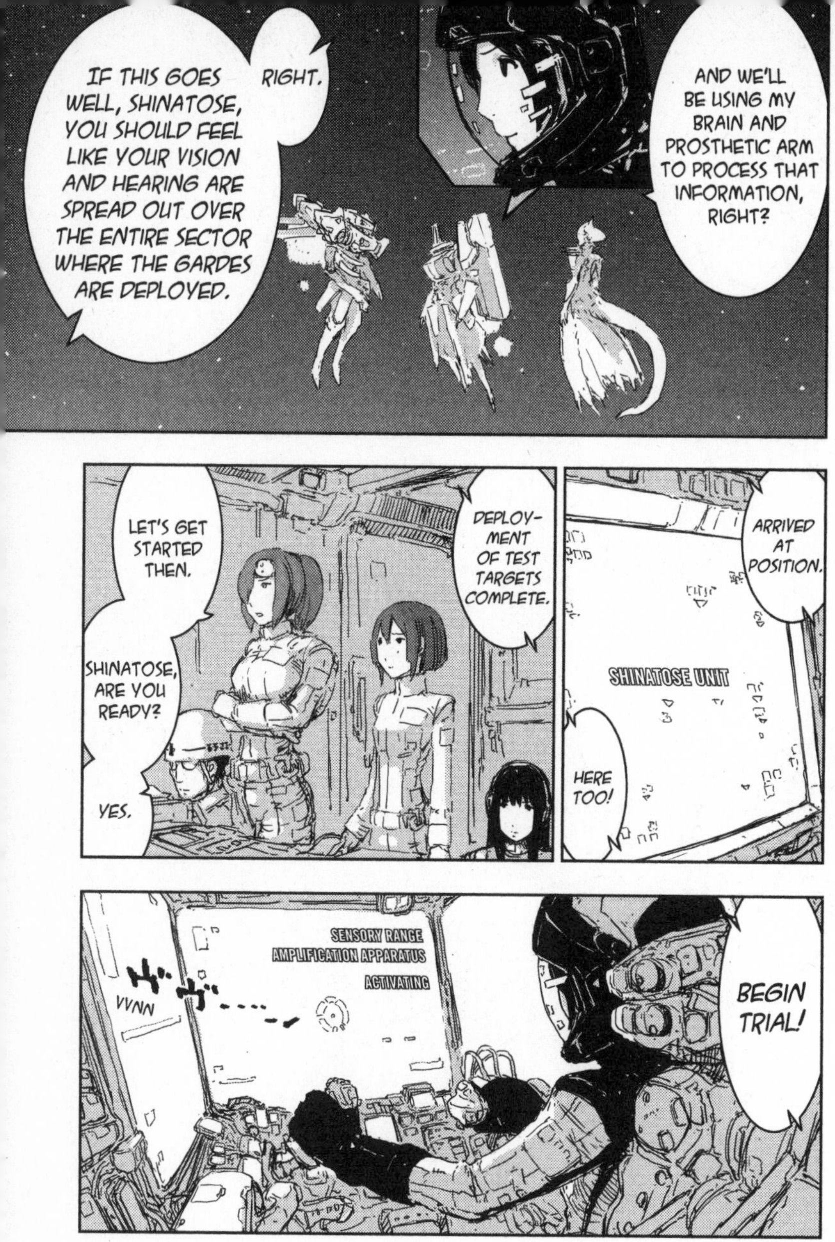
IF THIS GOES WELL, SHINATOSE, YOU SHOULD FEEL LIKE YOUR VISION AND HEARING ARE SPREAD OUT OVER THE ENTIRE SECTOR WHERE THE GARDES ARE DEPLOYED.
RIGHT.
AND WE'LL BE USING MY BRAIN AND PROSTHETIC ARM TO PROCESS THAT INFORMATION, RIGHT?
LET'S GET STARTED THEN.
DEPLOY-MENT OF TEST TARGETS COMPLETE.
SHINATOSE, ARE YOU READY?
YES.
ARRIVED AT POSITION.
SHINATOSE UNIT
HERE TOO!
SENSORY RANGE
AMPLIFICATION APPARATUS
ACTIVATING
VVNN
BEGIN TRIAL!

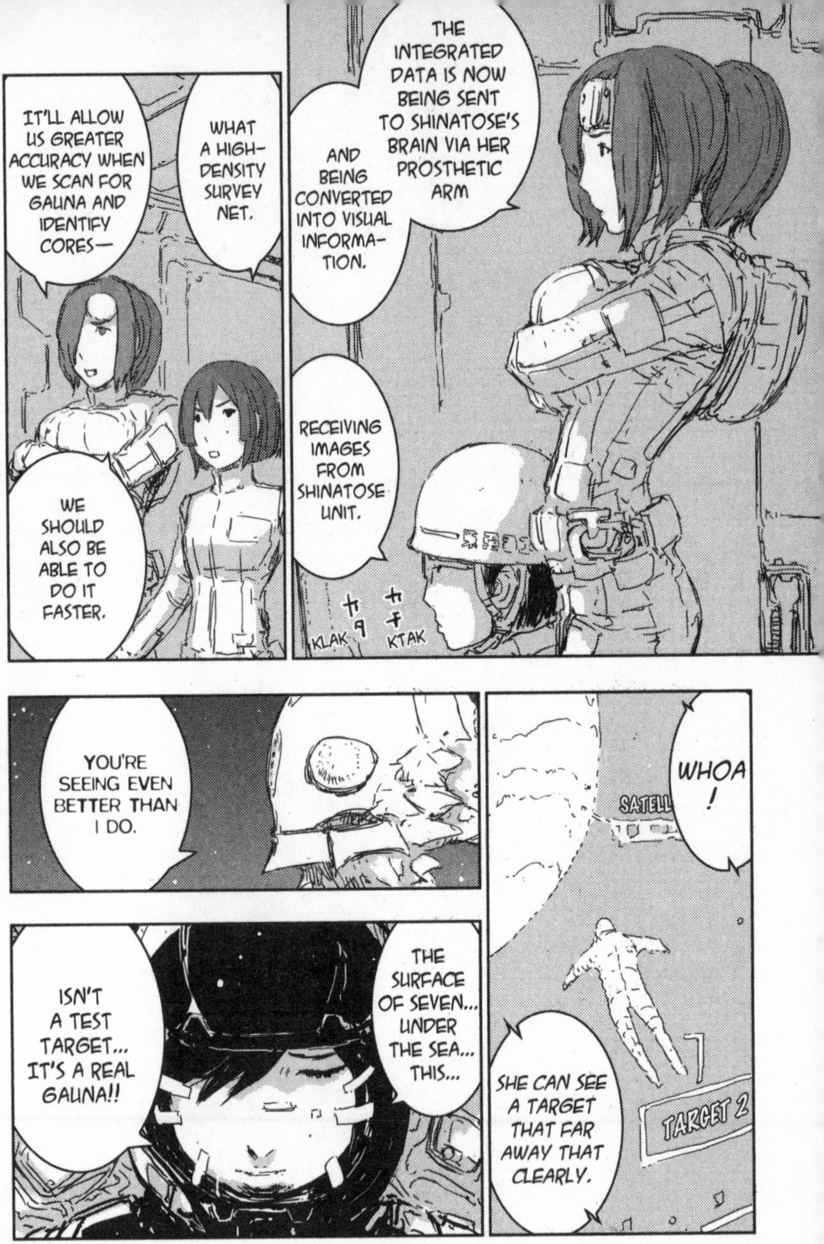
THE INTEGRATED DATA IS NOW BEING SENT TO SHINATOSE'S BRAIN VIA HER PROSTHETIC ARM
AND BEING CONVERTED INTO VISUAL INFORMA-TION.
RECEIVING IMAGES FROM SHINATOSE UNIT.
KLAK
KTAK
WHAT A HIGH-DENSITY SURVEY NET.
IT'LL ALLOW US GREATER ACCURACY WHEN WE SCAN FOR GAUNA AND IDENTIFY CORES—
WE SHOULD ALSO BE ABLE TO DO IT FASTER.
WHOA!
SATELL
TARGET 2
SHE CAN SEE A TARGET THAT FAR AWAY THAT CLEARLY.
YOU'RE SEEING EVEN BETTER THAN I DO.
THE SURFACE OF SEVEN... UNDER THE SEA... THIS...
ISN'T A TEST TARGET... IT'S A REAL GAUNA!!

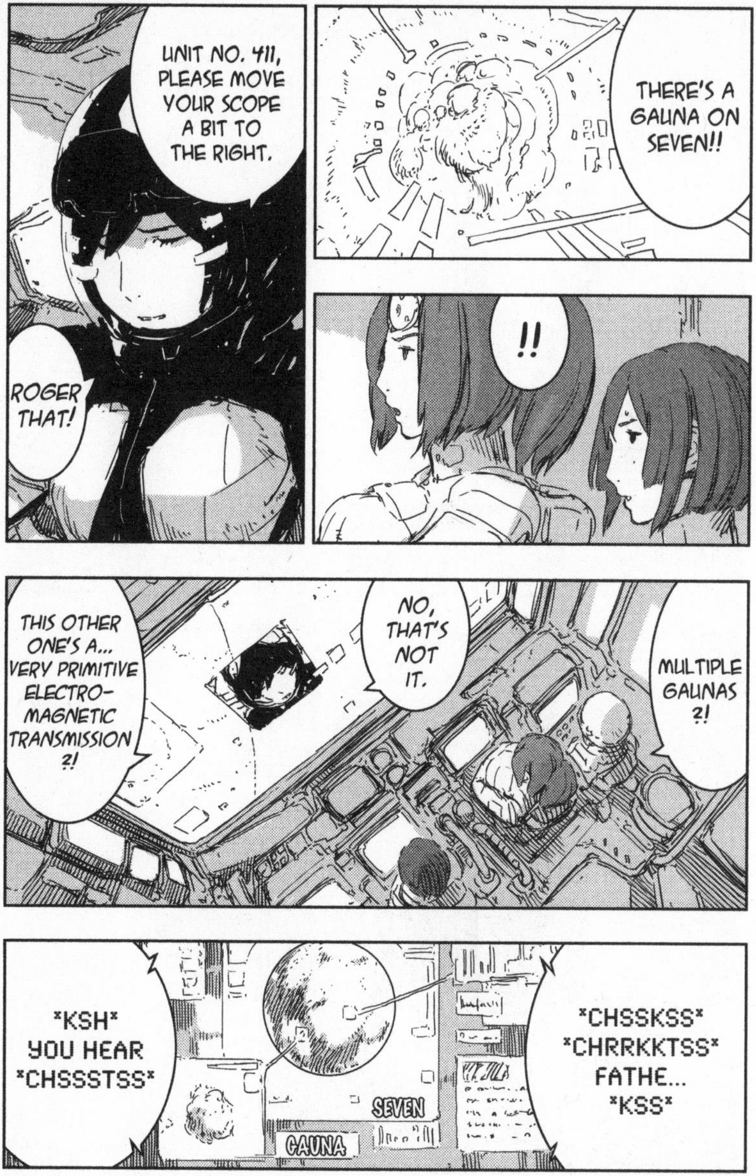
THERE'S A GAUNA ON SEVEN!!
!!
UNIT NO. 411, PLEASE MOVE YOUR SCOPE A BIT TO THE RIGHT.
ROGER THAT!
MULTIPLE GAUNAS ?!
NO, THAT'S NOT IT.
THIS OTHER ONE'S A... VERY PRIMITIVE ELECTRO-MAGNETIC TRANSMISSION ?!
CHSSKSS *CHRRKKTSS* FATHE... *KSS*
SEVEN
GAUNA
KSH YOU HEAR *CHSSSTSS*

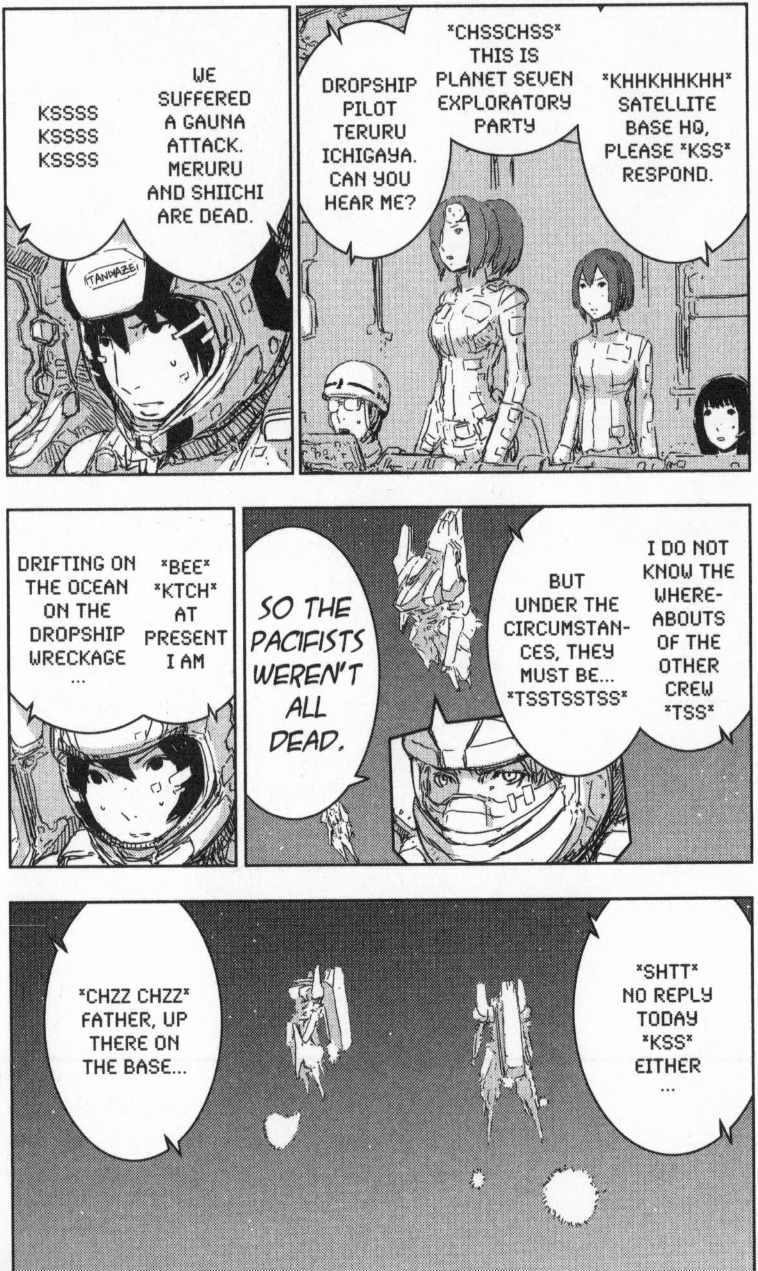
KHHKHHKHH SATELLITE BASE HQ, PLEASE *KSS* RESPOND.
CHSSCHSS THIS IS PLANET SEVEN EXPLORATORY PARTY
DROPSHIP PILOT TERURU ICHIGAYA. CAN YOU HEAR ME?
WE SUFFERED A GAUNA ATTACK. MERURU AND SHIICHI ARE DEAD.
KSSSS KSSSS KSSSS
TANIKAZE
I DO NOT KNOW THE WHERE-ABOUTS OF THE OTHER CREW *TSS*
BUT UNDER THE CIRCUMSTAN-CES, THEY MUST BE... *TSSTSSTSS*
SO THE PACIFISTS WEREN'T ALL DEAD.
BEE *KTCH* AT PRESENT I AM
DRIFTING ON THE OCEAN ON THE DROPSHIP WRECKAGE ...
SHTT NO REPLY TODAY *KSS* EITHER ...
CHZZ CHZZ FATHER, UP THERE ON THE BASE...

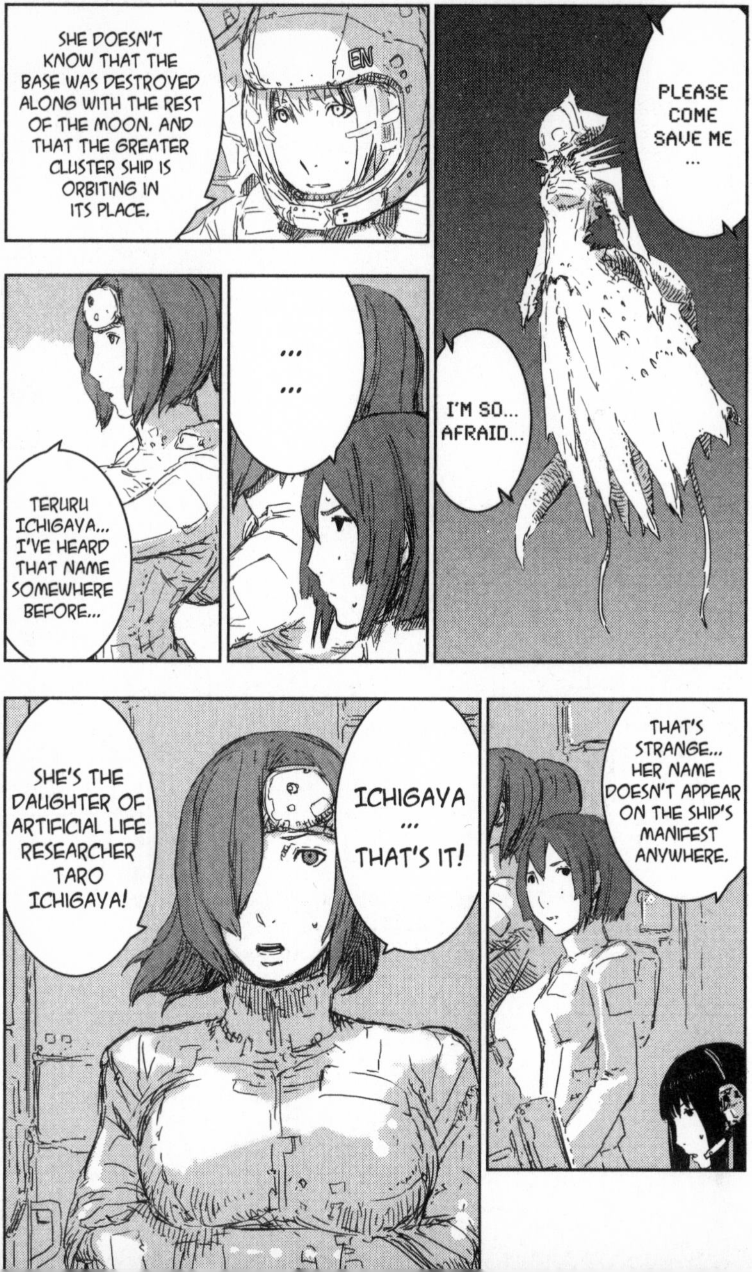
PLEASE COME SAVE ME ...
I'M SO... AFRAID...
SHE DOESN'T KNOW THAT THE BASE WAS DESTROYED ALONG WITH THE REST OF THE MOON. AND THAT THE GREATER CLUSTER SHIP IS ORBITING IN ITS PLACE.
... ...
TERURU ICHIGAYA... I'VE HEARD THAT NAME SOMEWHERE BEFORE...
THAT'S STRANGE... HER NAME DOESN'T APPEAR ON THE SHIP'S MANIFEST ANYWHERE.
ICHIGAYA ... THAT'S IT!
SHE'S THE DAUGHTER OF ARTIFICIAL LIFE RESEARCHER TARO ICHIGAYA!

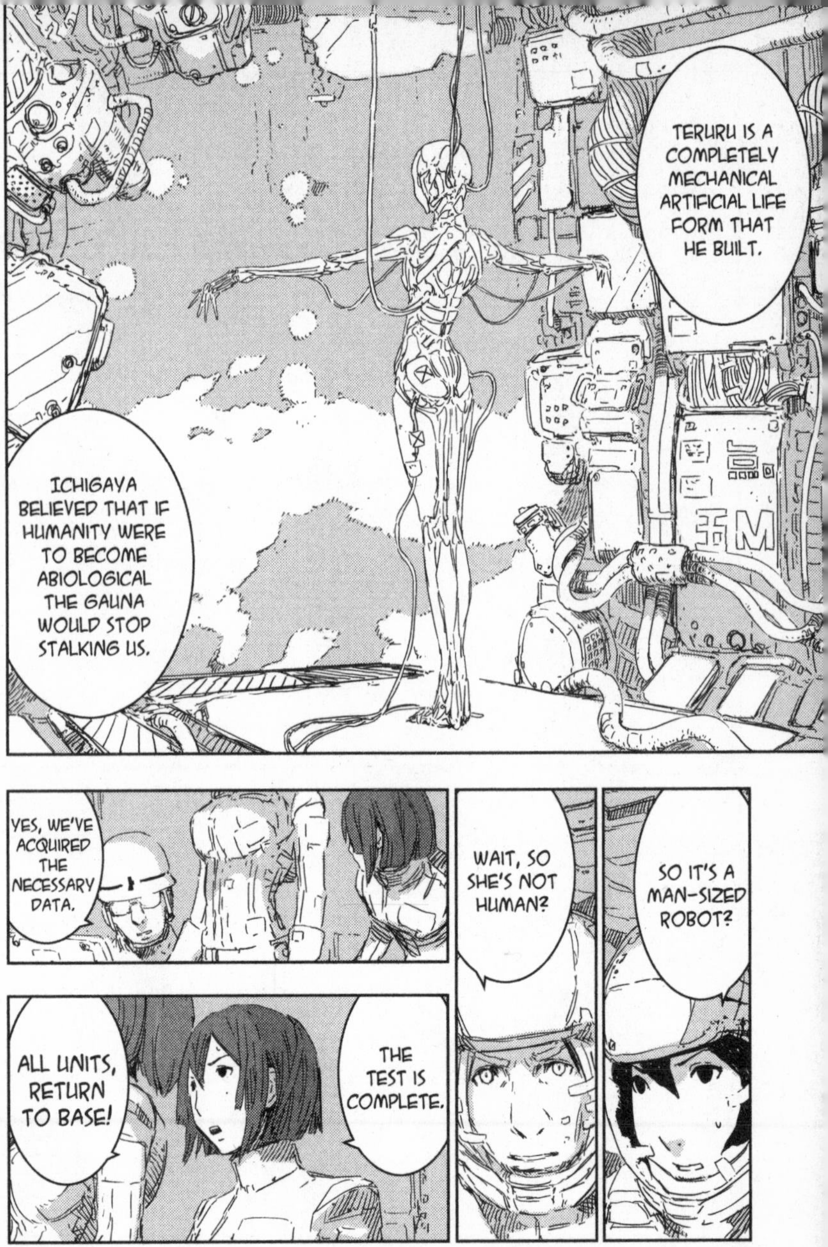
TERURU IS A COMPLETELY MECHANICAL ARTIFICIAL LIFE FORM THAT HE BUILT.
ICHIGAYA BELIEVED THAT IF HUMANITY WERE TO BECOME ABIOLOGICAL THE GAUNA WOULD STOP STALKING US.
SO IT'S A MAN-SIZED ROBOT?
WAIT, SO SHE'S NOT HUMAN?
YES, WE'VE ACQUIRED THE NECESSARY DATA.
THE TEST IS COMPLETE.
ALL UNITS, RETURN TO BASE!

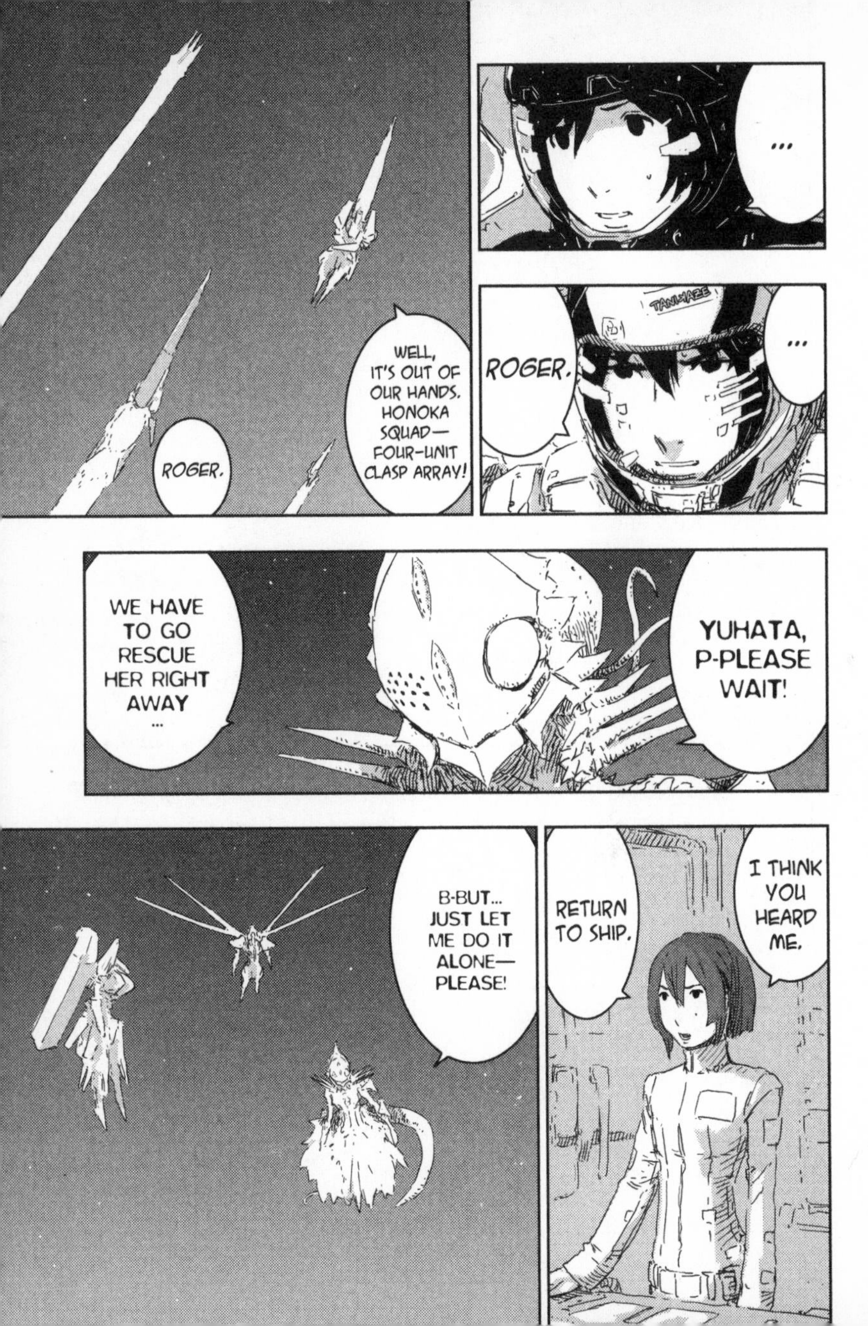
...
...
ROGER.
WELL, IT'S OUT OF OUR HANDS. HONOKA SQUAD—FOUR-UNIT CLASP ARRAY!
ROGER.
YUHATA, P-PLEASE WAIT!
WE HAVE TO GO RESCUE HER RIGHT AWAY...
I THINK YOU HEARD ME.
RETURN TO SHIP.
B-BUT... JUST LET ME DO IT ALONE—PLEASE!

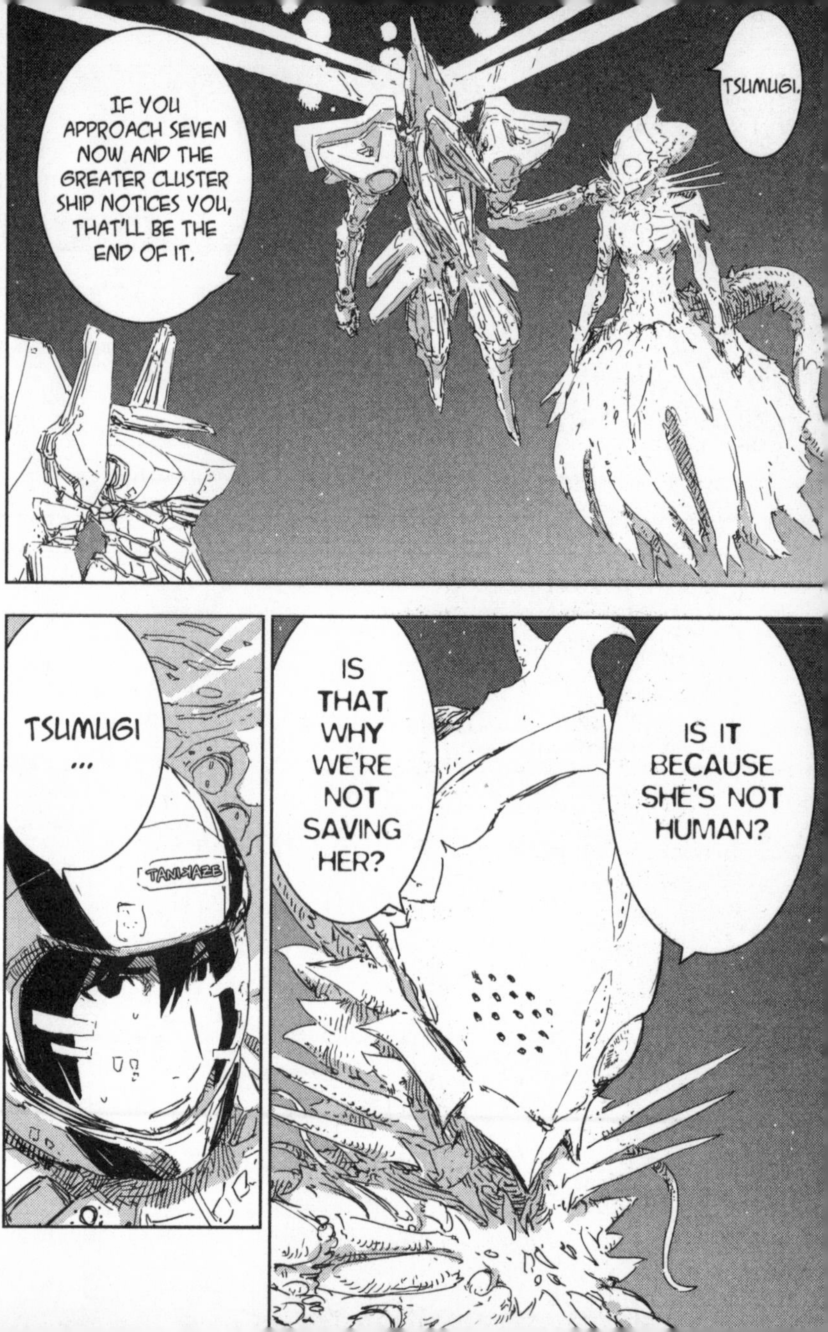
TSUMUGI.
IF YOU APPROACH SEVEN NOW AND THE GREATER CLUSTER SHIP NOTICES YOU, THAT'LL BE THE END OF IT.
IS IT BECAUSE SHE'S NOT HUMAN?
IS THAT WHY WE'RE NOT SAVING HER?
TSUMUGI ...
TANIKAZE

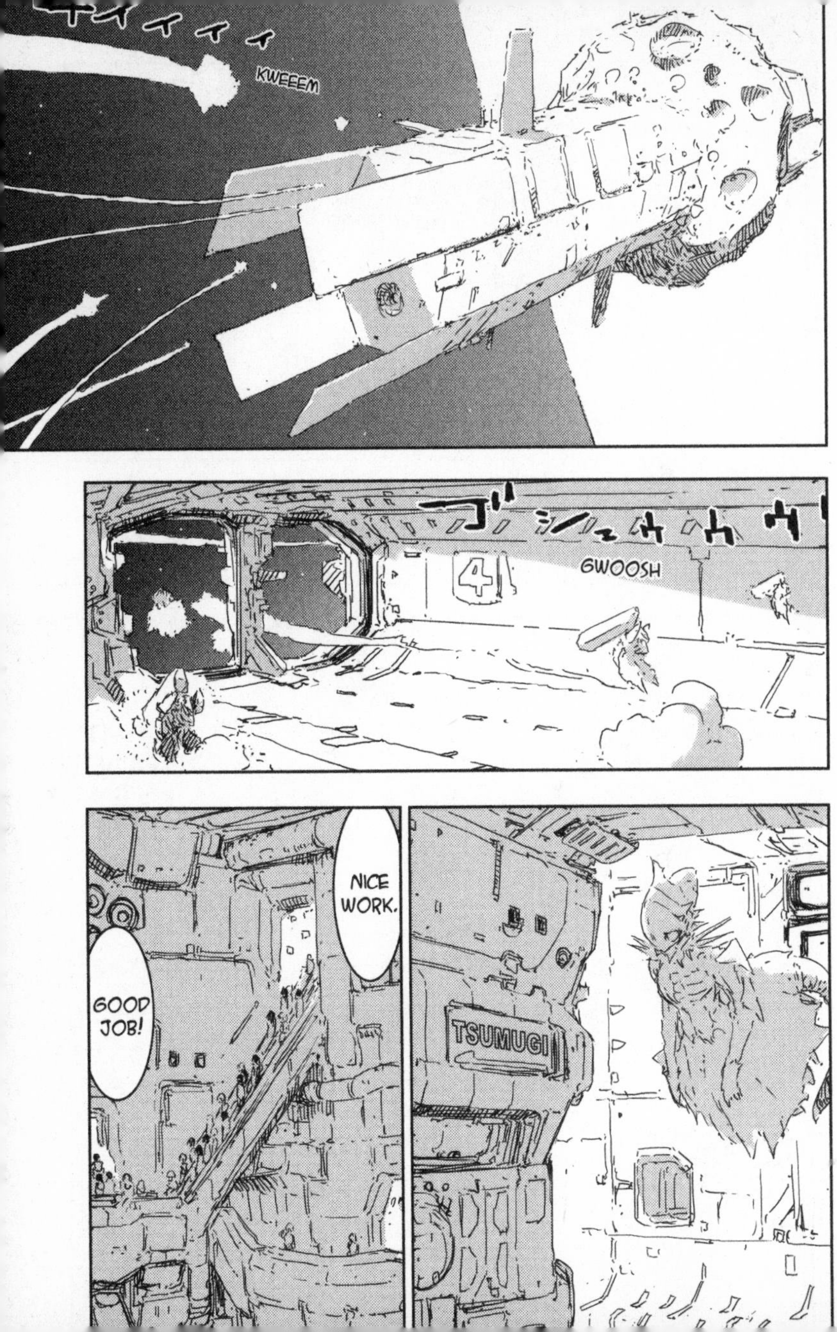

イイイイ
KWEEEM
ゴシュゥゥゥ
GWOOSH
4
TSUMUGI
NICE WORK.
GOOD JOB!

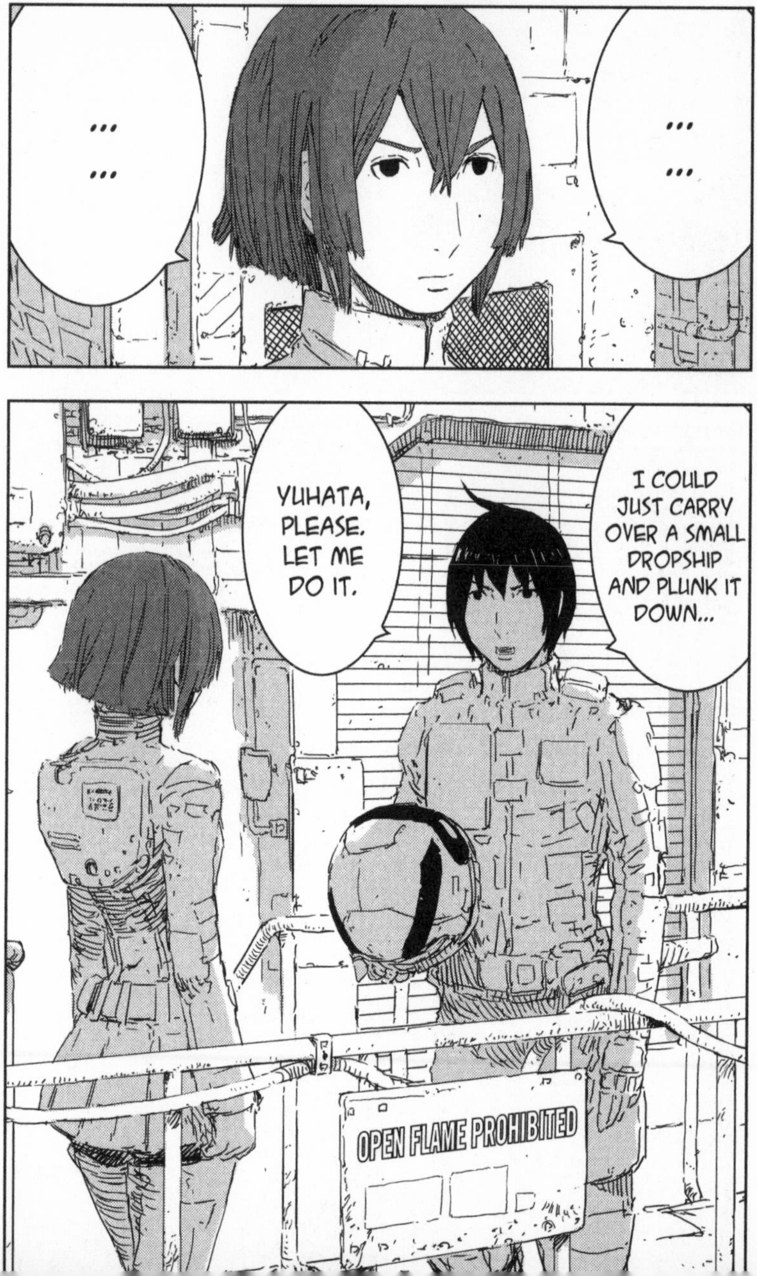
... ...
... ...
I COULD JUST CARRY OVER A SMALL DROPSHIP AND PLUNK IT DOWN...
YUHATA, PLEASE. LET ME DO IT.
OPEN FLAME PROHIBITED

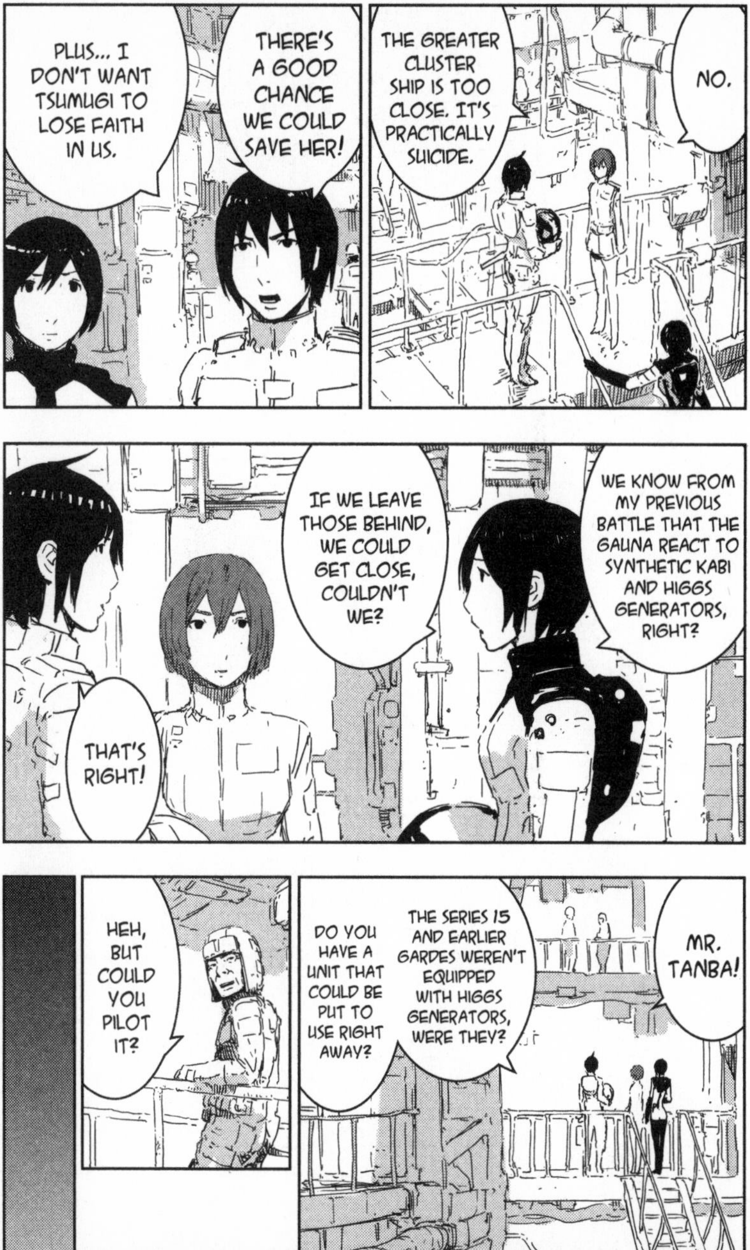
NO.
THE GREATER CLUSTER SHIP IS TOO CLOSE. IT'S PRACTICALLY SUICIDE.
THERE'S A GOOD CHANCE WE COULD SAVE HER!
PLUS... I DON'T WANT TSUMUGI TO LOSE FAITH IN US.
WE KNOW FROM MY PREVIOUS BATTLE THAT THE GAUNA REACT TO SYNTHETIC KABI AND HIGGS GENERATORS, RIGHT?
IF WE LEAVE THOSE BEHIND, WE COULD GET CLOSE, COULDN'T WE?
THAT'S RIGHT!
MR. TANBA!
THE SERIES 15 AND EARLIER GARDES WEREN'T EQUIPPED WITH HIGGS GENERATORS, WERE THEY?
DO YOU HAVE A UNIT THAT COULD BE PUT TO USE RIGHT AWAY?
HEH, BUT COULD YOU PILOT IT?

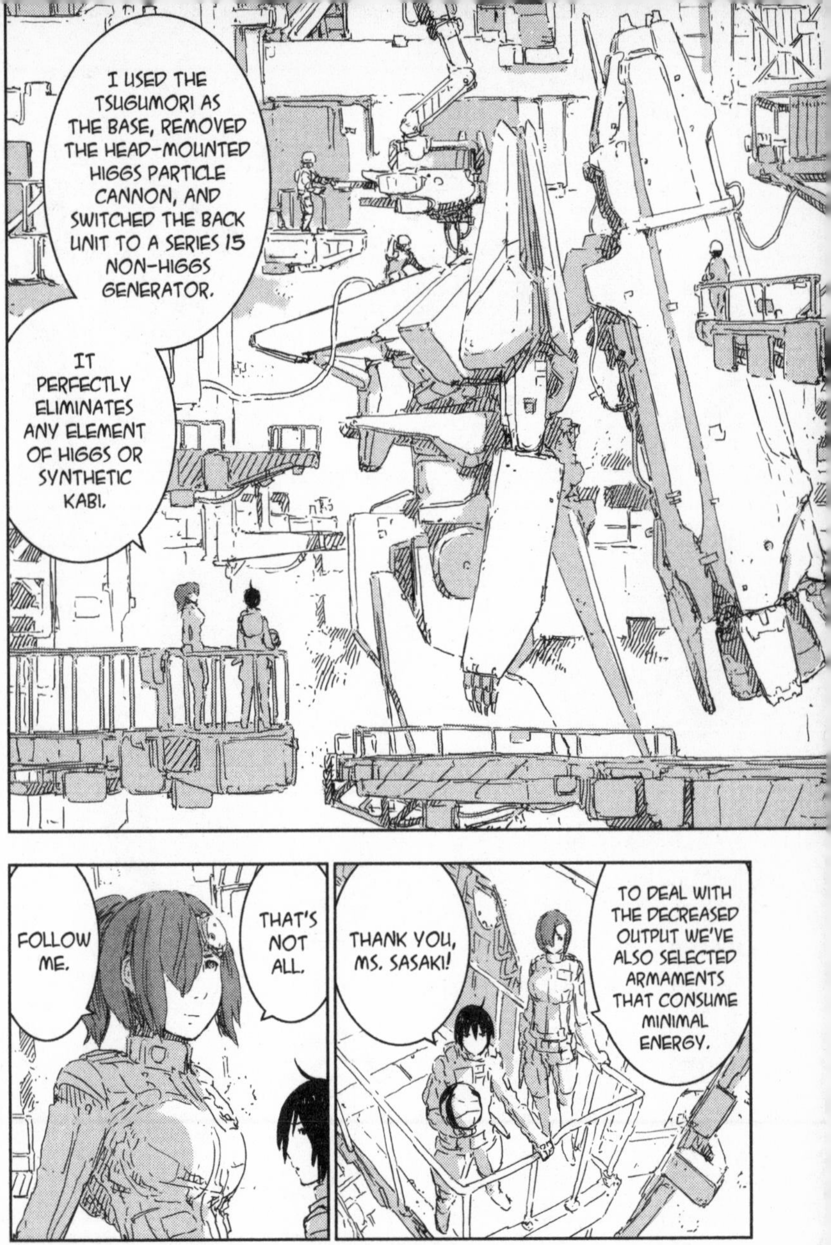

I USED THE TSUGUMORI AS THE BASE, REMOVED THE HEAD-MOUNTED HIGGS PARTICLE CANNON, AND SWITCHED THE BACK UNIT TO A SERIES 15 NON-HIGGS GENERATOR.
IT PERFECTLY ELIMINATES ANY ELEMENT OF HIGGS OR SYNTHETIC KABI.
TO DEAL WITH THE DECREASED OUTPUT WE'VE ALSO SELECTED ARMAMENTS THAT CONSUME MINIMAL ENERGY.
THANK YOU, MS. SASAKI!
THAT'S NOT ALL.
FOLLOW ME.

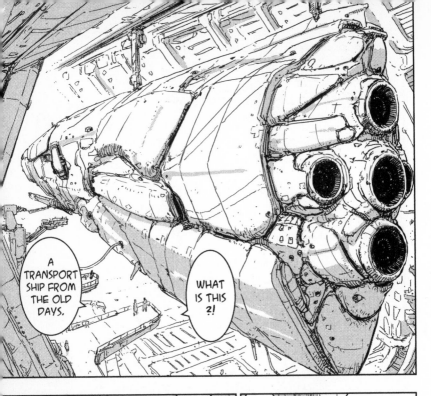

WHAT IS THIS ?!
A TRANSPORT SHIP FROM THE OLD DAYS.
WE CAN'T LET A LONE GARDE WITH AN OLD-FASHIONED ENGINE LUG A DROPSHIP, CAN WE?
HOW IS IT, SHINA-TOSE?
YES. I THINK I COULD HANDLE IT.

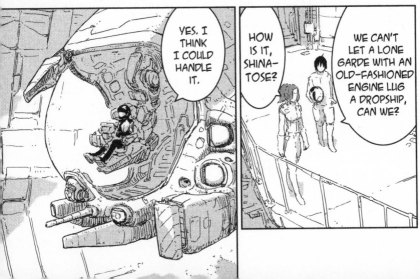

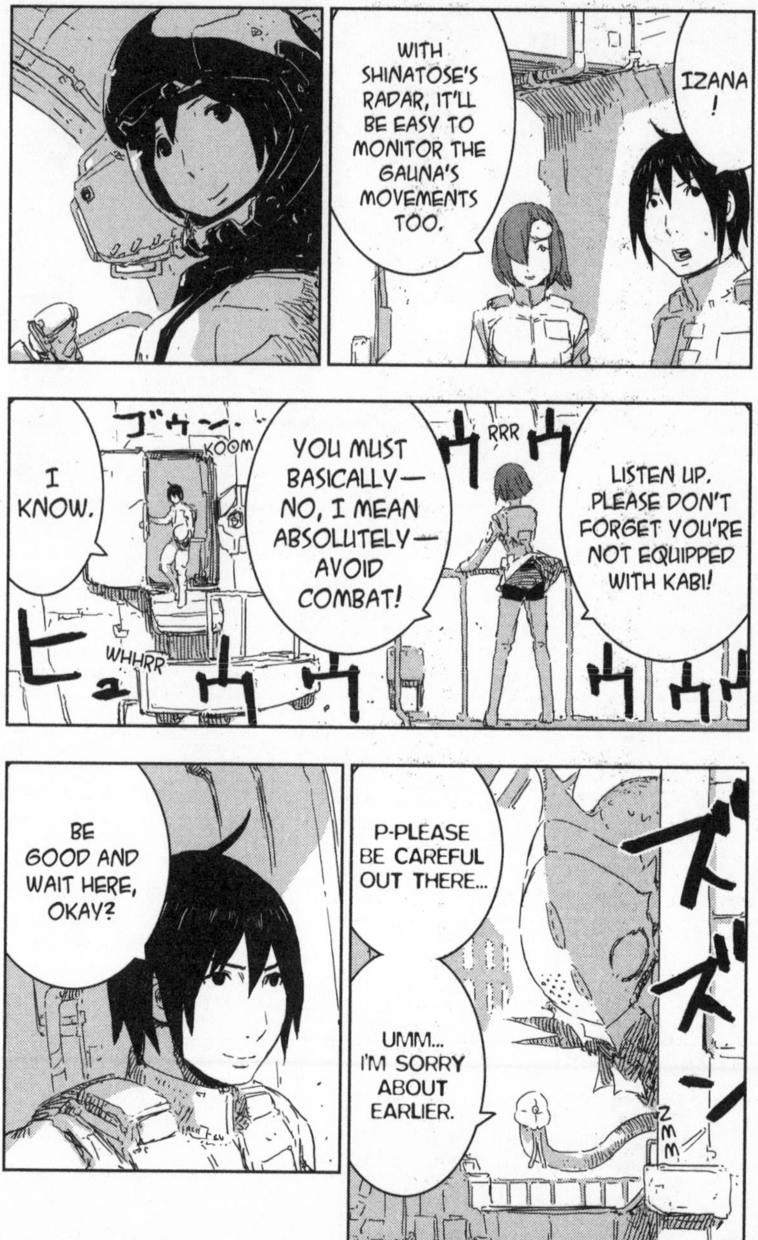
IZANA!
WITH SHINATOSE'S RADAR, IT'LL BE EASY TO MONITOR THE GAUNA'S MOVEMENTS TOO.
RRR
LISTEN UP. PLEASE DON'T FORGET YOU'RE NOT EQUIPPED WITH KABI!
YOU MUST BASICALLY—NO, I MEAN ABSOLUTELY—AVOID COMBAT!
KOOM
I KNOW.
WHHRR
ZMM
P-PLEASE BE CAREFUL OUT THERE...
UMM... I'M SORRY ABOUT EARLIER.
BE GOOD AND WAIT HERE, OKAY?

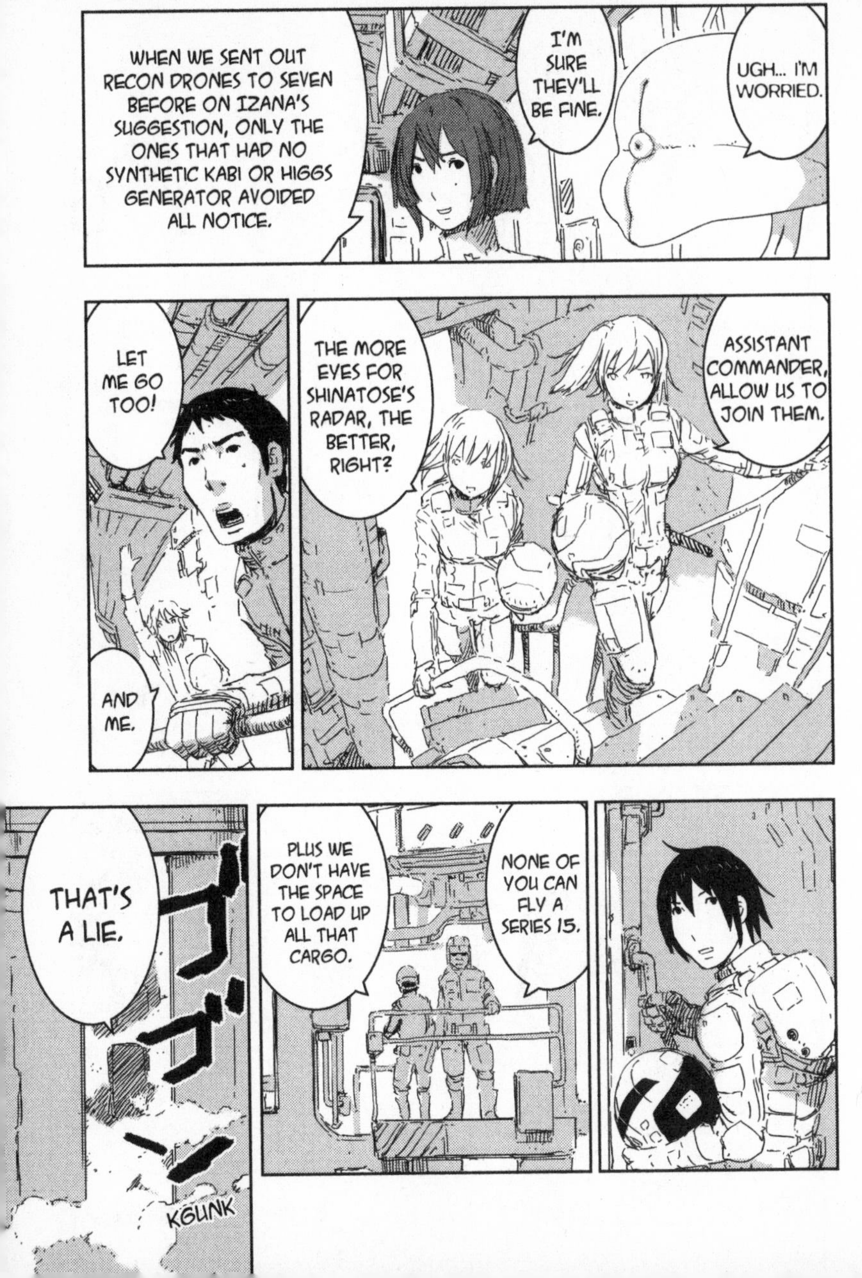
UGH... I'M WORRIED.
I'M SURE THEY'LL BE FINE.
WHEN WE SENT OUT RECON DRONES TO SEVEN BEFORE ON IZANA'S SUGGESTION, ONLY THE ONES THAT HAD NO SYNTHETIC KABI OR HIGGS GENERATOR AVOIDED ALL NOTICE.
ASSISTANT COMMANDER, ALLOW US TO JOIN THEM.
THE MORE EYES FOR SHINATOSE'S RADAR, THE BETTER, RIGHT?
LET ME GO TOO!
AND ME.
NONE OF YOU CAN FLY A SERIES 15.
PLUS WE DON'T HAVE THE SPACE TO LOAD UP ALL THAT CARGO.
THAT'S A LIE.
KGUNK

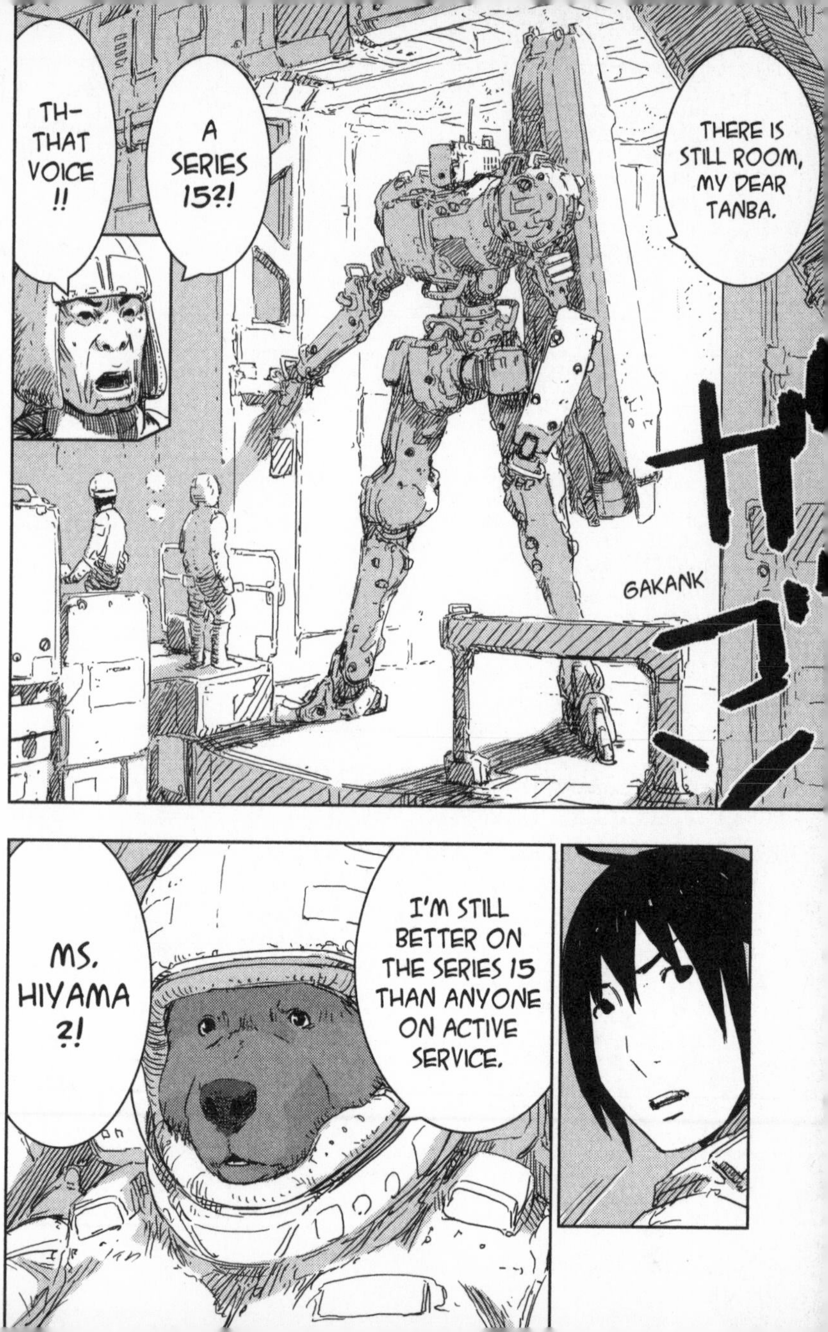
THERE IS STILL ROOM, MY DEAR TANBA.
A SERIES 15?!
TH-THAT VOICE!!
GAKANK
I'M STILL BETTER ON THE SERIES 15 THAN ANYONE ON ACTIVE SERVICE.
MS. HIYAMA?!

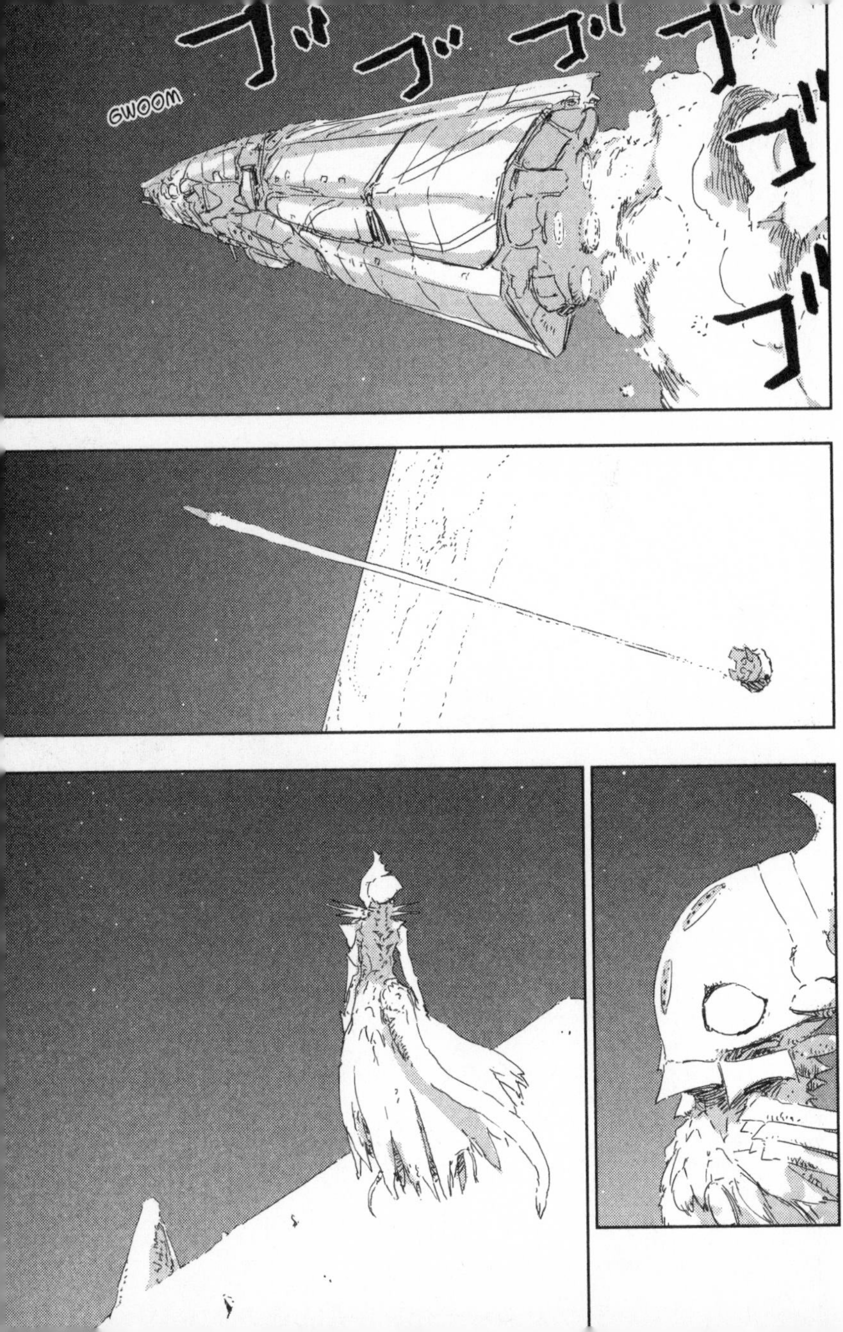
ゴゴゴゴゴゴ
GWOOM

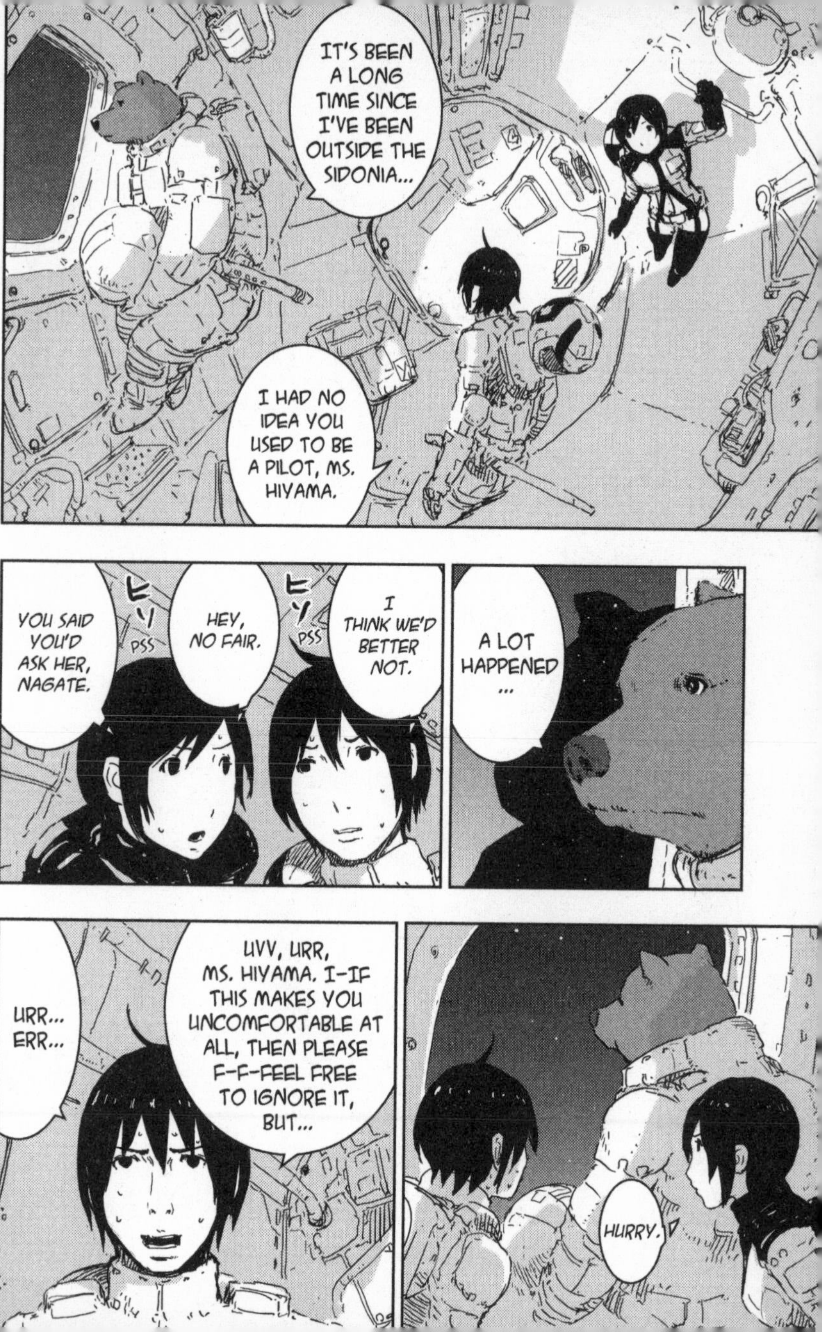
IT'S BEEN A LONG TIME SINCE I'VE BEEN OUTSIDE THE SIDONIA...
I HAD NO IDEA YOU USED TO BE A PILOT, MS. HIYAMA.
A LOT HAPPENED ...
I THINK WE'D BETTER NOT.
ヒソ PSS
HEY, NO FAIR.
ヒソ PSS
YOU SAID YOU'D ASK HER, NAGATE.
HURRY.
UVV, URR, MS. HIYAMA. I-IF THIS MAKES YOU UNCOMFORTABLE AT ALL, THEN PLEASE F-F-FEEL FREE TO IGNORE IT, BUT...
URR... ERR...

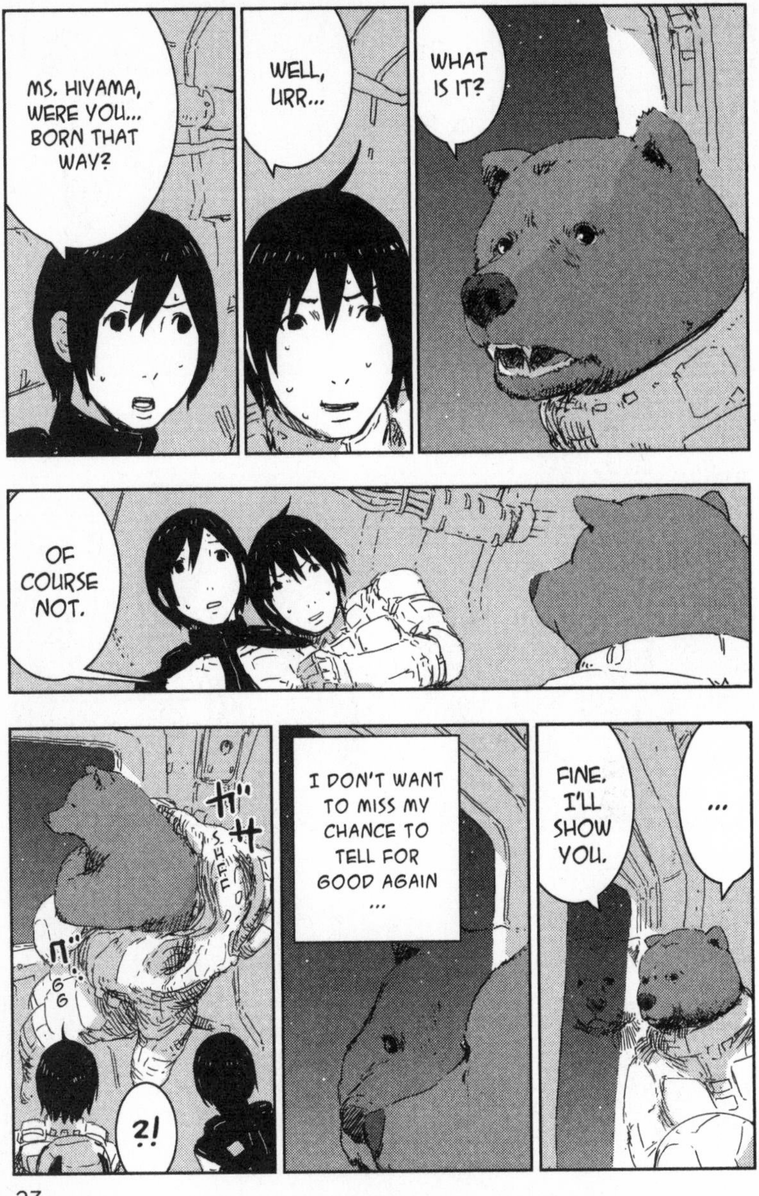
WHAT IS IT?
WELL, URR...
MS. HIYAMA, WERE YOU... BORN THAT WAY?
OF COURSE NOT.
...
FINE. I'LL SHOW YOU.
I DON'T WANT TO MISS MY CHANCE TO TELL FOR GOOD AGAIN ...
ガッ
S.HFF
GG
?!

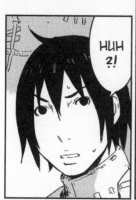

NA-GATE.
PART THE FUR ALONG MY SPINE.
HUH ?!
ファサ…
FWSS
E- EXCUSE ME...
WH-WHAT IS...THIS?
MY HIDE IS A LIFE-SUPPORT SYSTEM. MY REAL BODY IS INSIDE.
IF I DITCHED THIS, I'D DIE.
パキ
CLIK

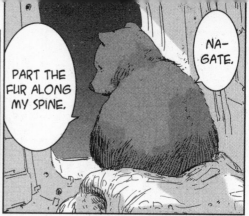

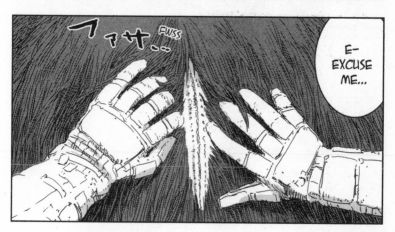

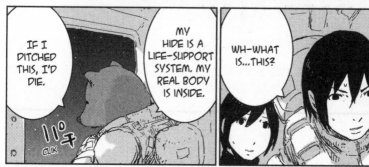

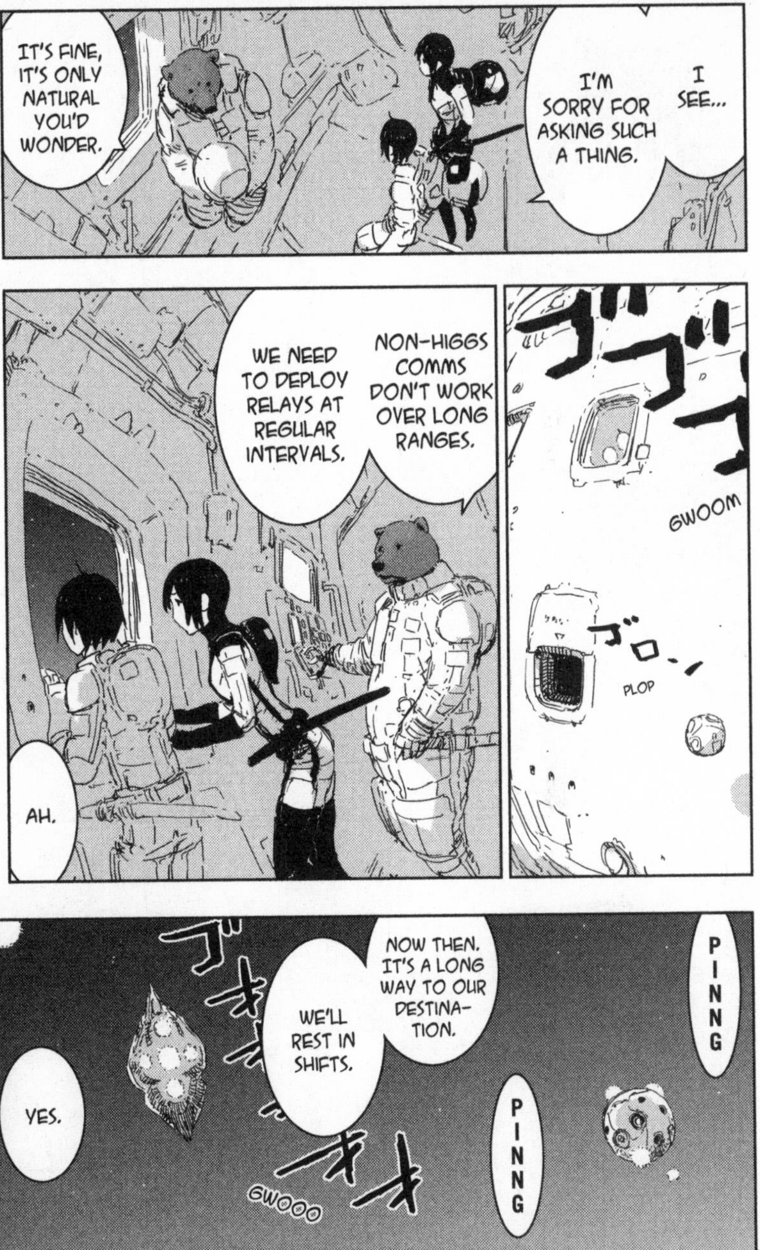

I SEE...
I'M SORRY FOR ASKING SUCH A THING.
IT'S FINE, IT'S ONLY NATURAL YOU'D WONDER.
GWOOM
PLOP
NON-HIGGS COMMS DON'T WORK OVER LONG RANGES.
WE NEED TO DEPLOY RELAYS AT REGULAR INTERVALS.
AH.
PINNG
PINNG
NOW THEN. IT'S A LONG WAY TO OUR DESTINATION.
WE'LL REST IN SHIFTS.
YES.
GWOOO

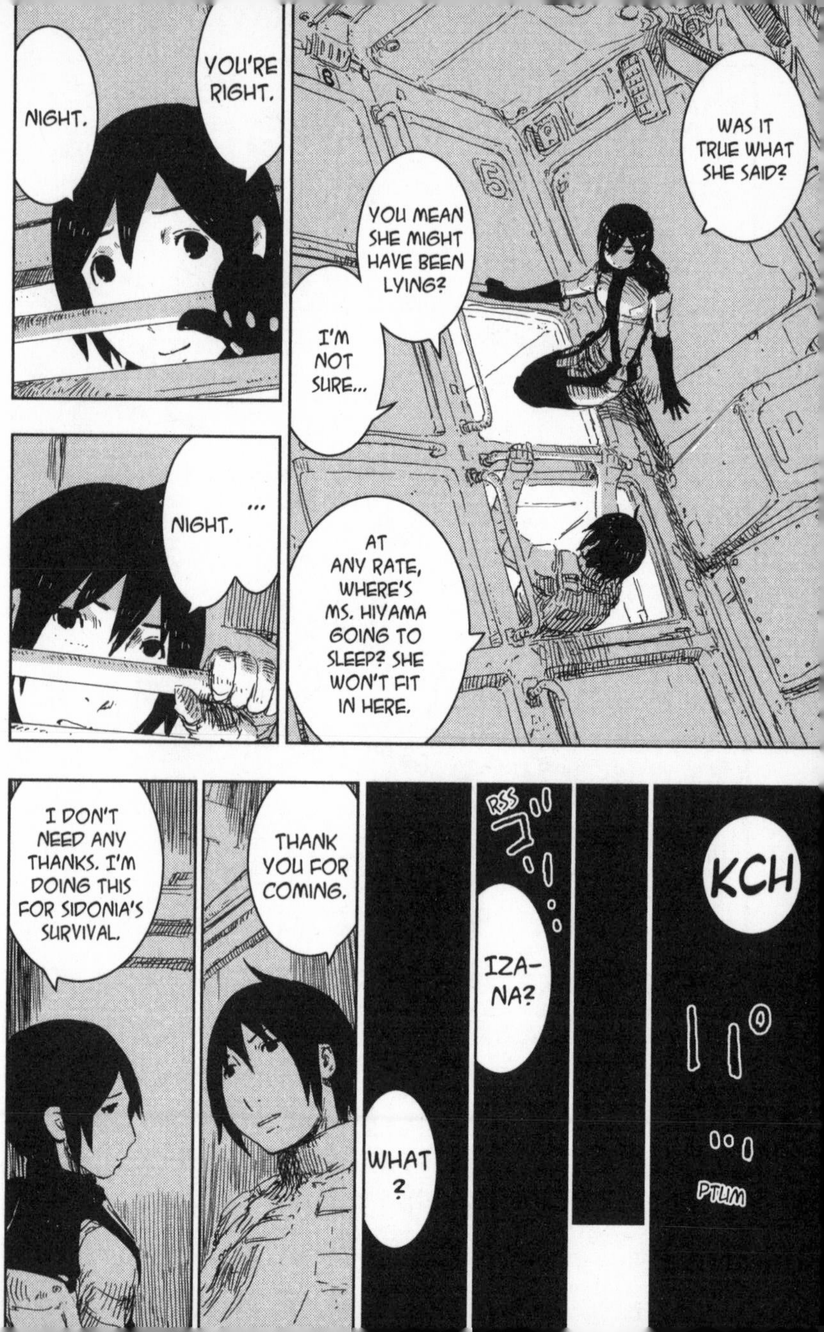
WAS IT TRUE WHAT SHE SAID?
YOU MEAN SHE MIGHT HAVE BEEN LYING?
I'M NOT SURE...
AT ANY RATE, WHERE'S MS. HIYAMA GOING TO SLEEP? SHE WON'T FIT IN HERE.
YOU'RE RIGHT.
NIGHT.
...NIGHT.
KCH
PTUM
RSS
IZANA?
WHAT?
THANK YOU FOR COMING.
I DON'T NEED ANY THANKS. I'M DOING THIS FOR SIDONIA'S SURVIVAL.

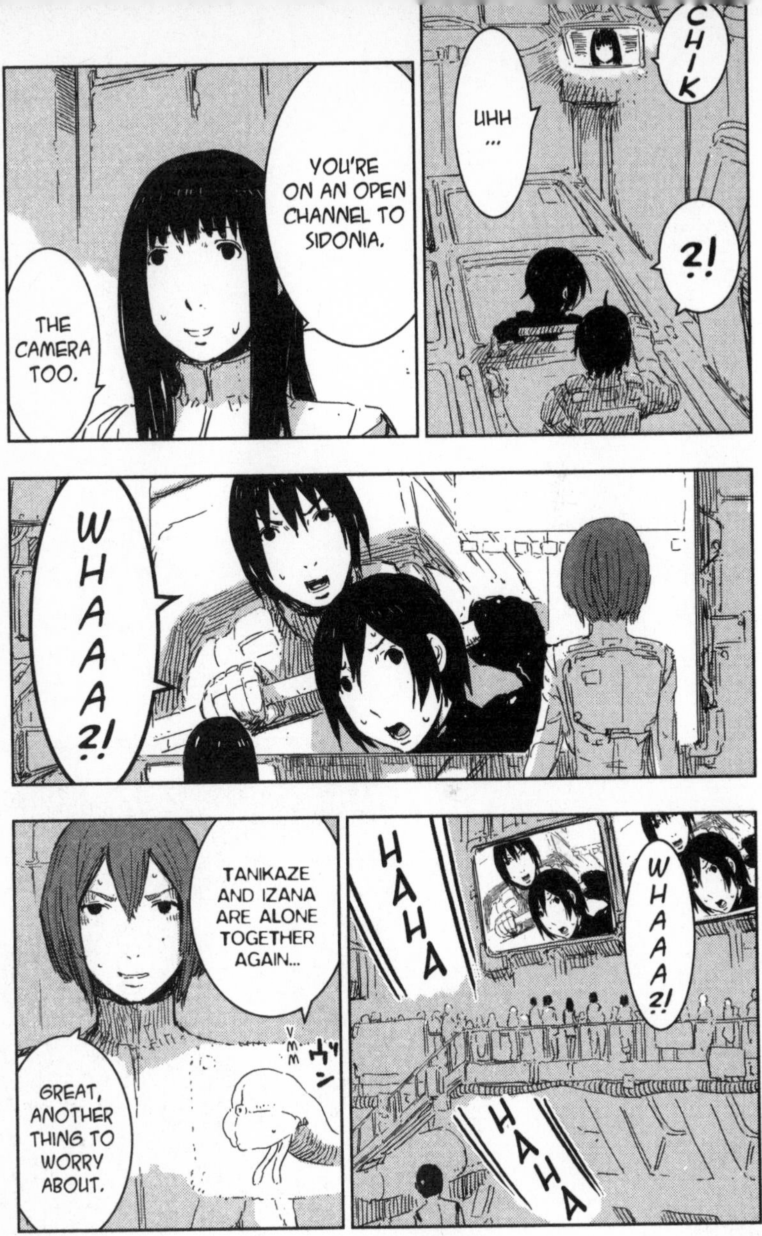
CHIK
UHH ...
?!
YOU'RE ON AN OPEN CHANNEL TO SIDONIA.
THE CAMERA TOO.
WHAAAA?!
HAHA
WHAAAA?!
HAHA
TANIKAZE AND IZANA ARE ALONE TOGETHER AGAIN...
VMM ヴン
GREAT, ANOTHER THING TO WORRY ABOUT.

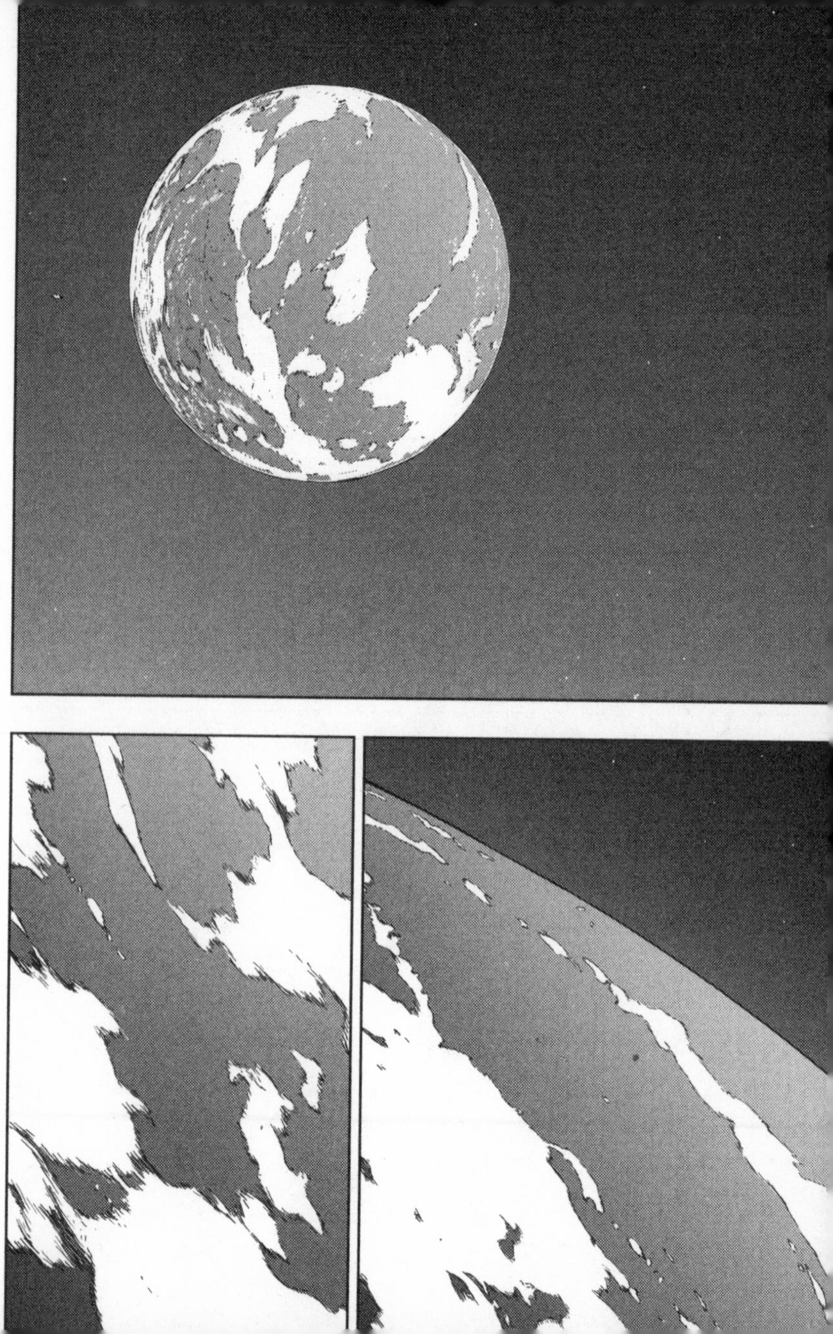

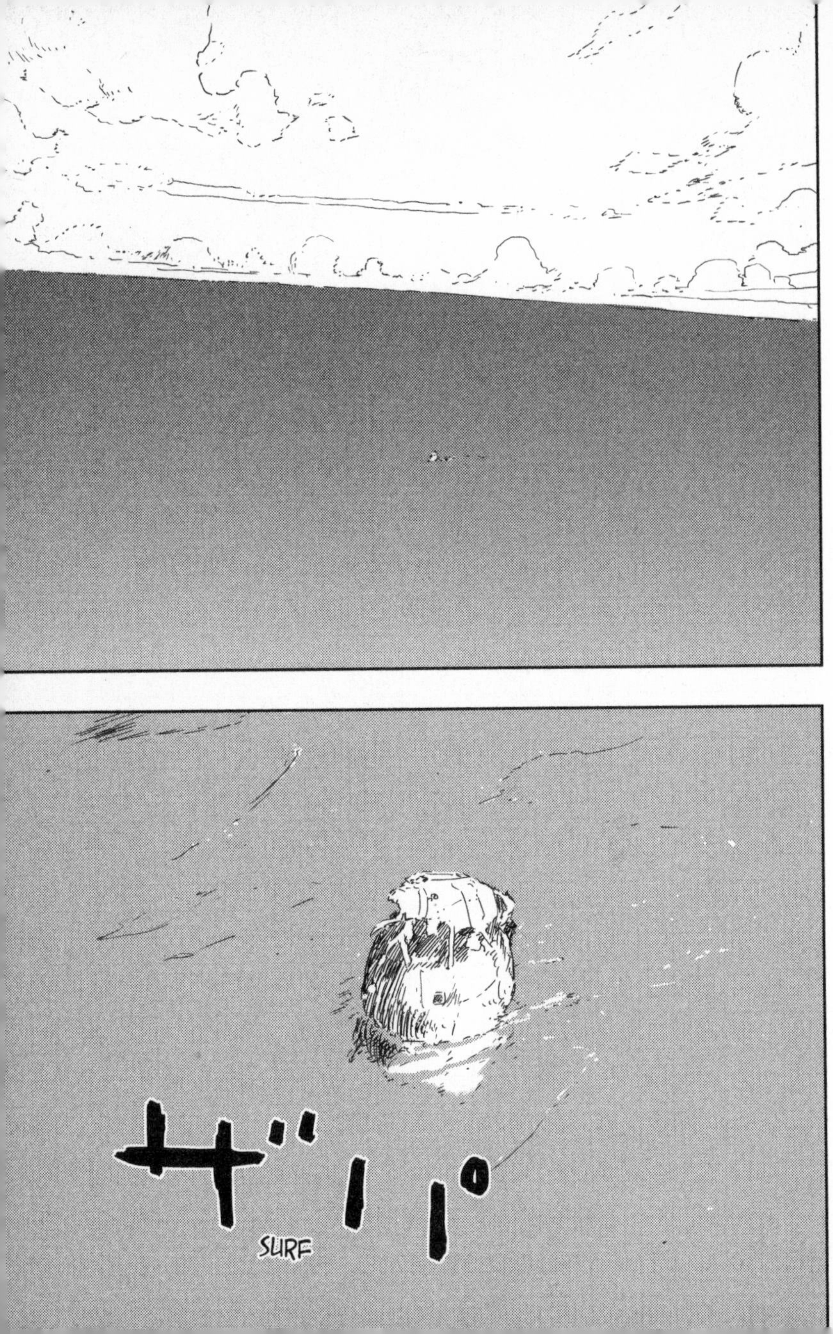
ザバ
SURF

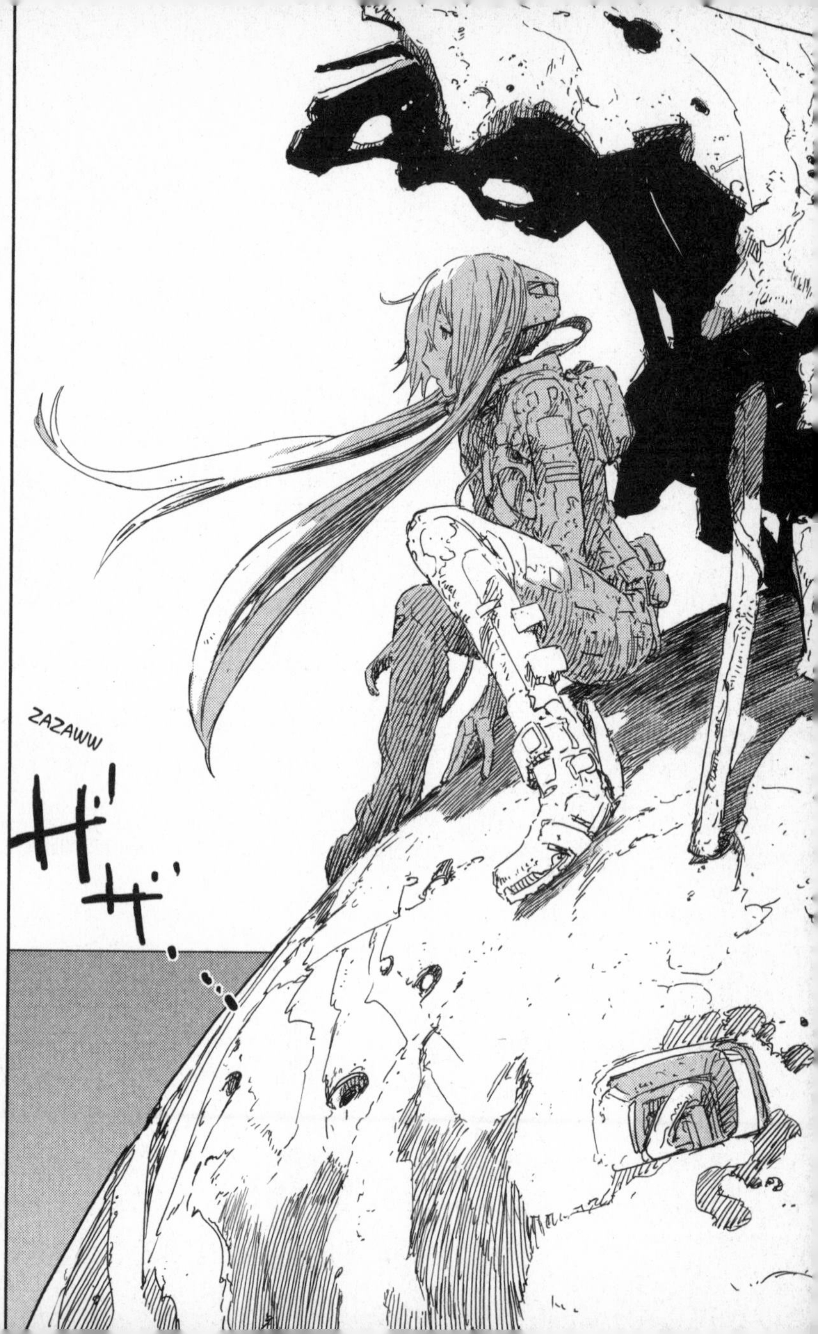
ZAZAWW
ザザ…

Chapter 50: END

シドニアの騎士

KNIGHTS OF SIDONIA

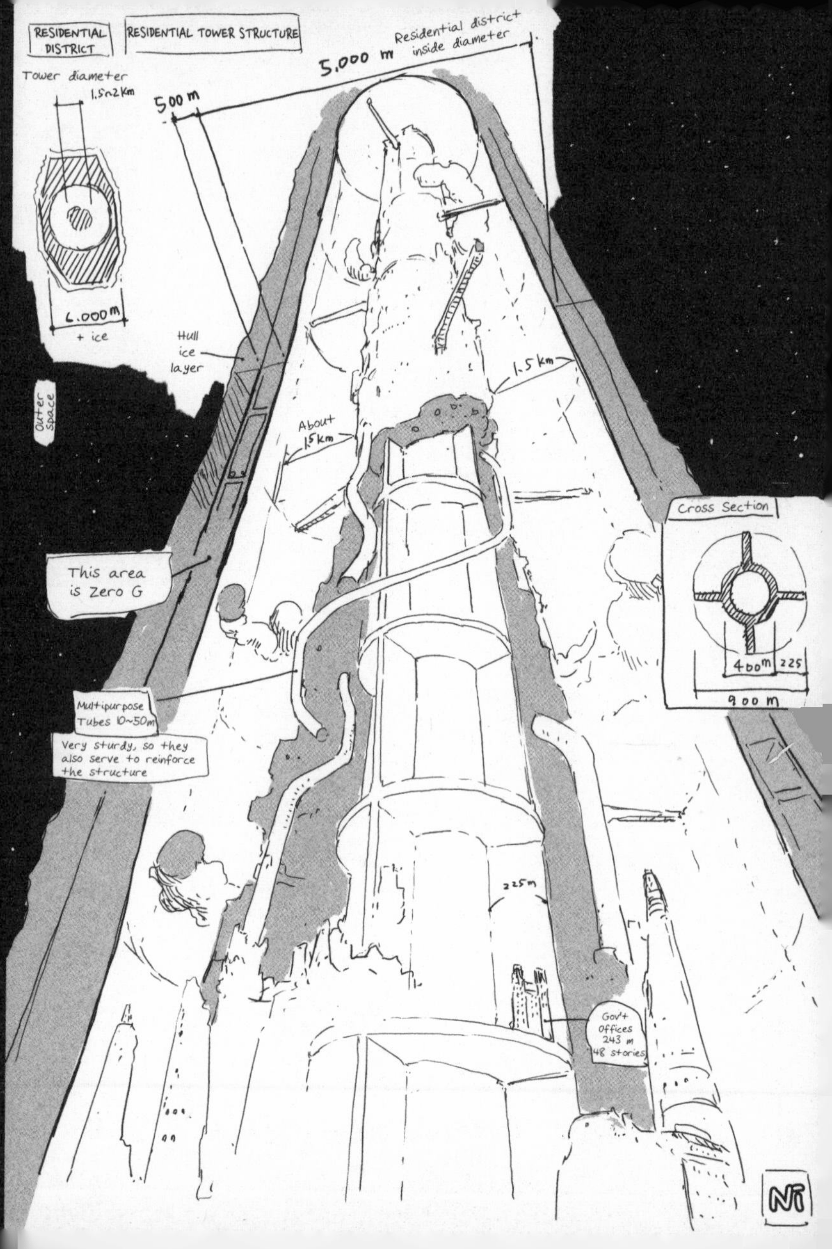

RESIDENTIAL DISTRICT
RESIDENTIAL TOWER STRUCTURE
5,000 m Residential district inside diameter
500 m
Tower diameter
1.5~2 km
6,000 m
+ ice
Hull ice layer
Outer space
1.5 km
About 1.5 km
This area is Zero G
Cross Section
400 m
225
900 m
Multipurpose Tubes 10~50 m
Very sturdy, so they also serve to reinforce the structure
225 m
Gov't Offices 243 m 48 stories

Chapter 51: The Survivor's Rescue

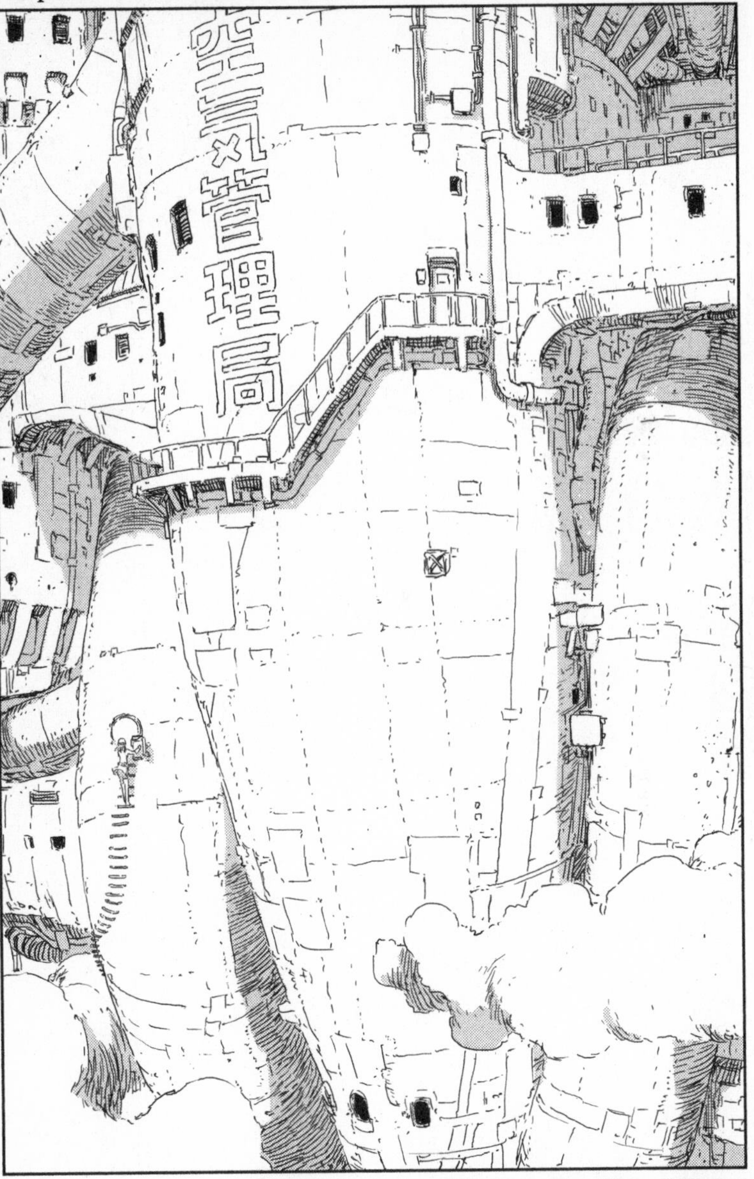
空気管理局

One Hundred Sights of Sidonia Part Thirty-Eight:
Air Regulation Bureau

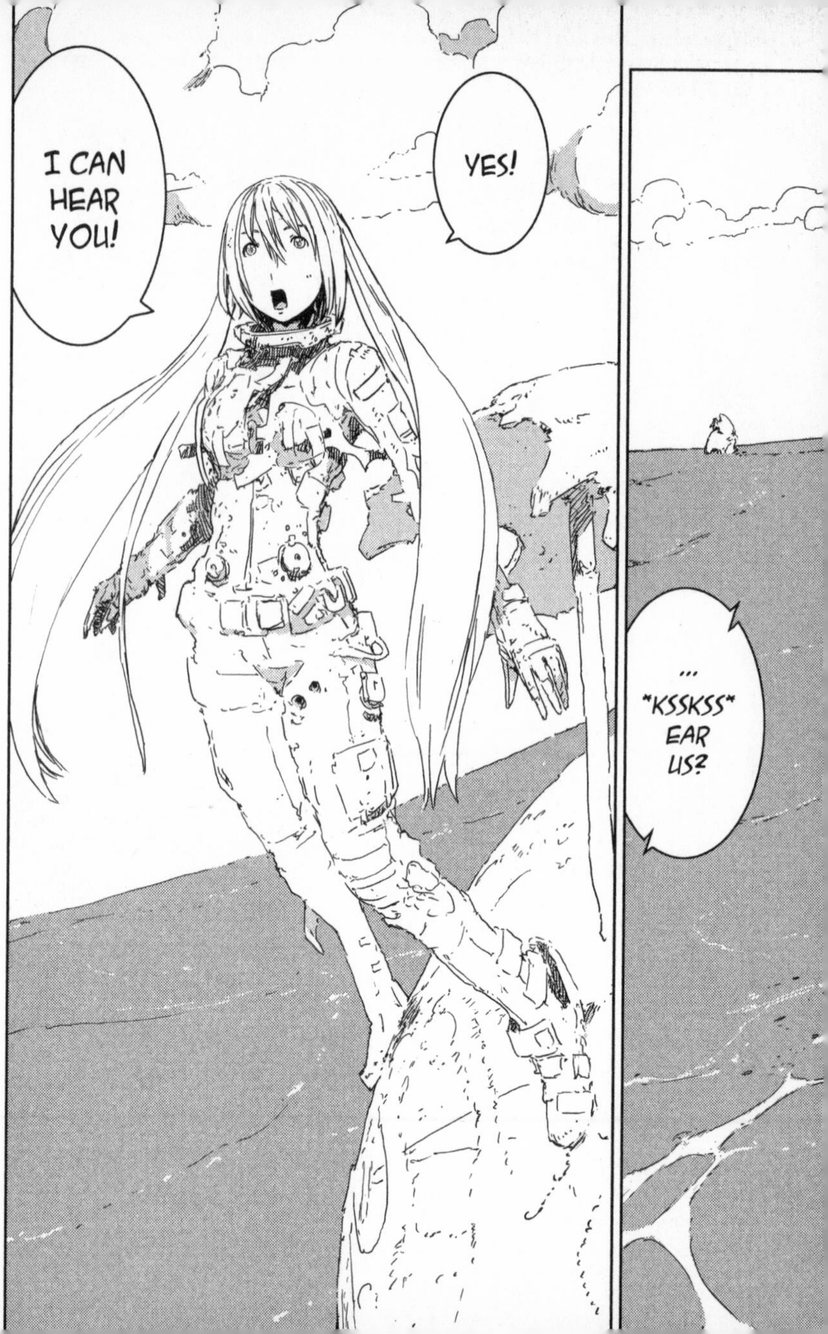
... *KSSKSS* EAR US?
YES!
I CAN HEAR YOU!

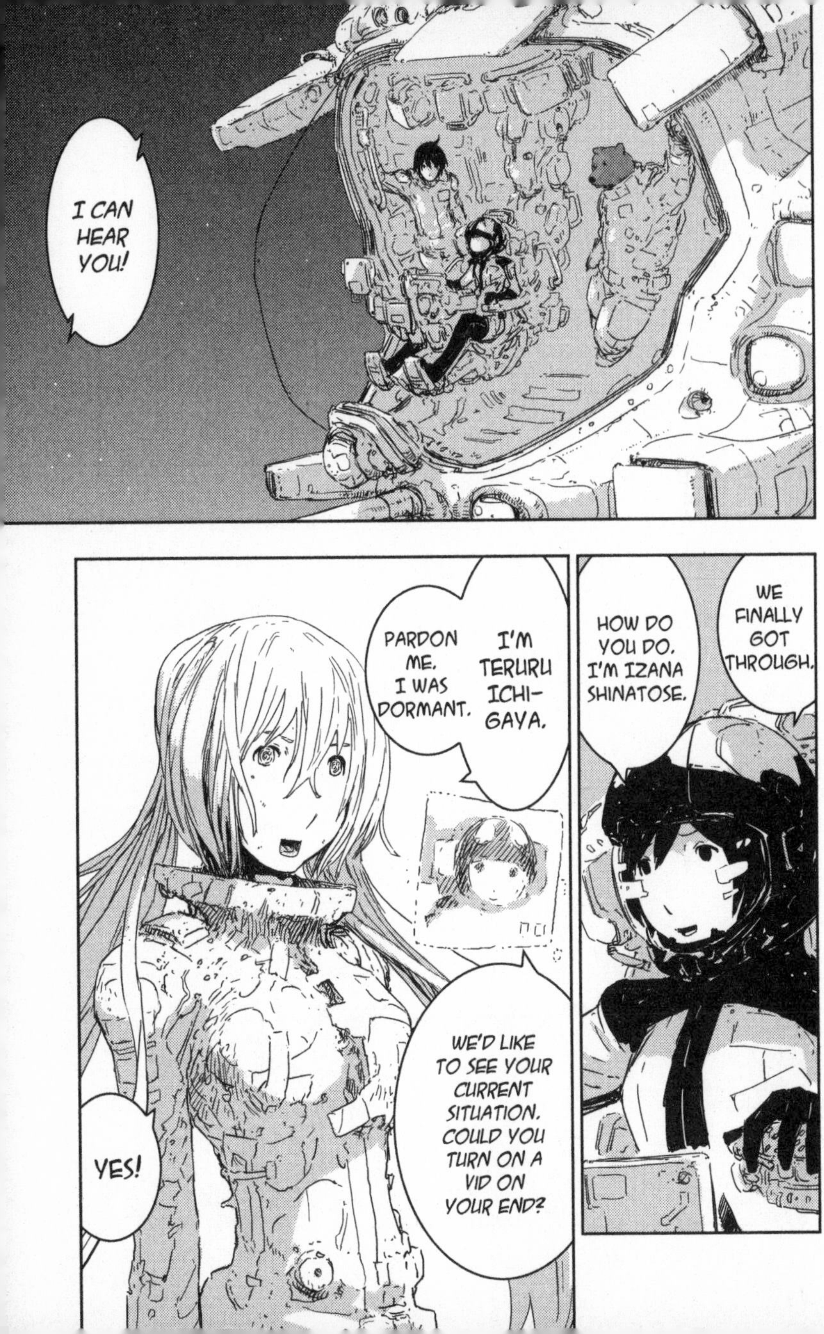
I CAN HEAR YOU!
WE FINALLY GOT THROUGH.
HOW DO YOU DO. I'M IZANA SHINATOSE.
I'M TERURU ICHI-GAYA.
PARDON ME. I WAS DORMANT.
WE'D LIKE TO SEE YOUR CURRENT SITUATION. COULD YOU TURN ON A VID ON YOUR END?
YES!

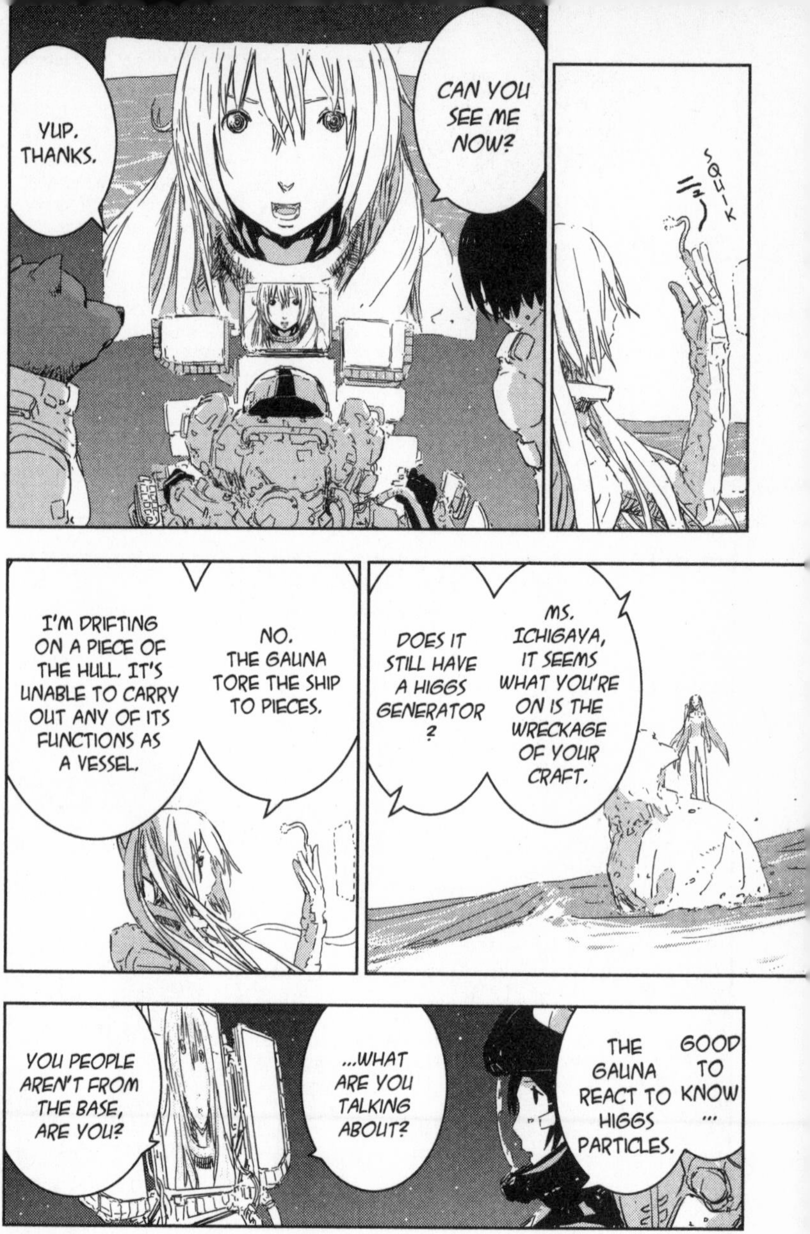
SQUIK
CAN YOU SEE ME NOW?
YUP. THANKS.
MS. ICHIGAYA, IT SEEMS WHAT YOU'RE ON IS THE WRECKAGE OF YOUR CRAFT.
DOES IT STILL HAVE A HIGGS GENERATOR?
NO. THE GAUNA TORE THE SHIP TO PIECES.
I'M DRIFTING ON A PIECE OF THE HULL. IT'S UNABLE TO CARRY OUT ANY OF ITS FUNCTIONS AS A VESSEL.
GOOD TO KNOW...
THE GAUNA REACT TO HIGGS PARTICLES.
...WHAT ARE YOU TALKING ABOUT?
YOU PEOPLE AREN'T FROM THE BASE, ARE YOU?

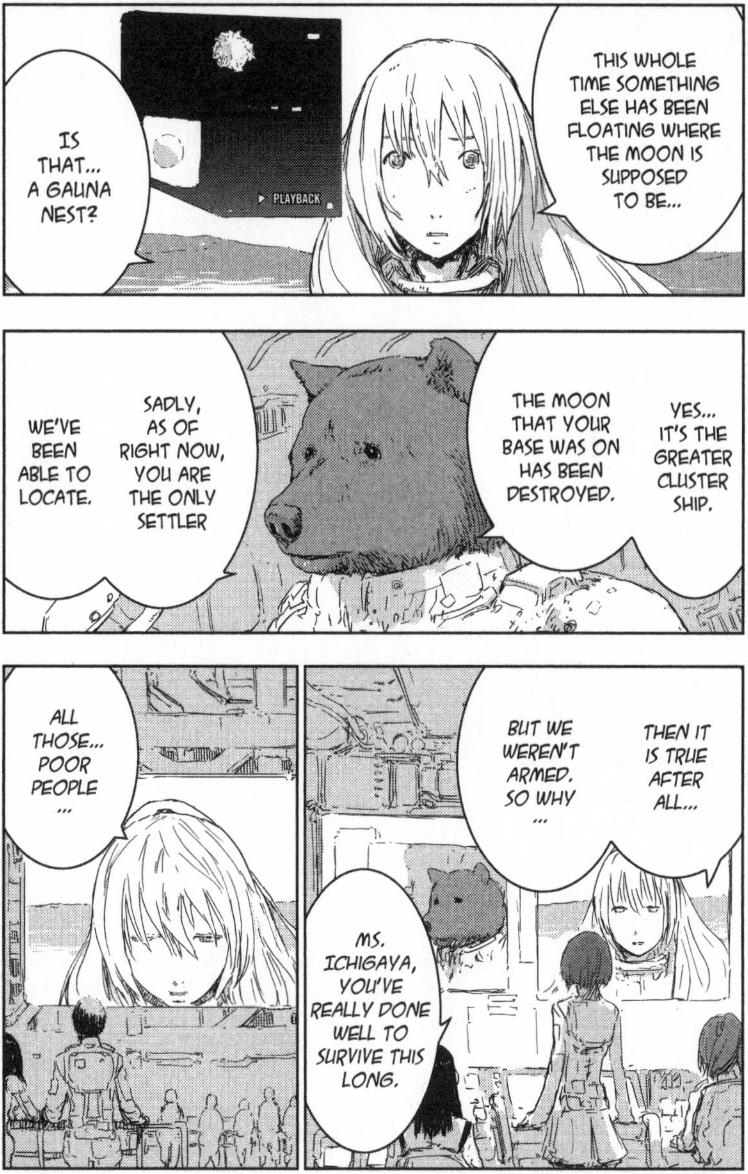

PLAYBACK
THIS WHOLE TIME SOMETHING ELSE HAS BEEN FLOATING WHERE THE MOON IS SUPPOSED TO BE...
IS THAT... A GAUNA NEST?
YES... IT'S THE GREATER CLUSTER SHIP.
THE MOON THAT YOUR BASE WAS ON HAS BEEN DESTROYED.
SADLY, AS OF RIGHT NOW, YOU ARE THE ONLY SETTLER
WE'VE BEEN ABLE TO LOCATE.
THEN IT IS TRUE AFTER ALL...
BUT WE WEREN'T ARMED. SO WHY ...
MS. ICHIGAYA, YOU'VE REALLY DONE WELL TO SURVIVE THIS LONG.
ALL THOSE... POOR PEOPLE ...

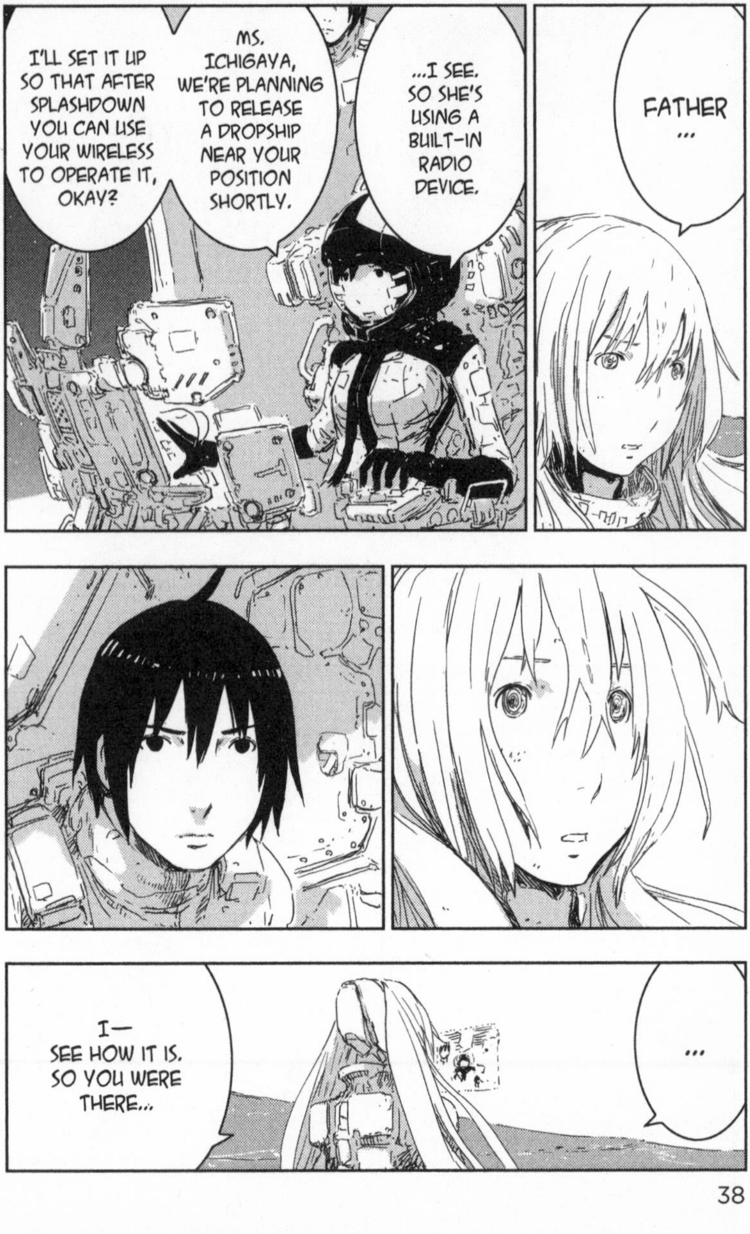
FATHER ...
...I SEE. SO SHE'S USING A BUILT-IN RADIO DEVICE.
MS. ICHIGAYA, WE'RE PLANNING TO RELEASE A DROPSHIP NEAR YOUR POSITION SHORTLY.
I'LL SET IT UP SO THAT AFTER SPLASHDOWN YOU CAN USE YOUR WIRELESS TO OPERATE IT, OKAY?
...
I— SEE HOW IT IS. SO YOU WERE THERE...

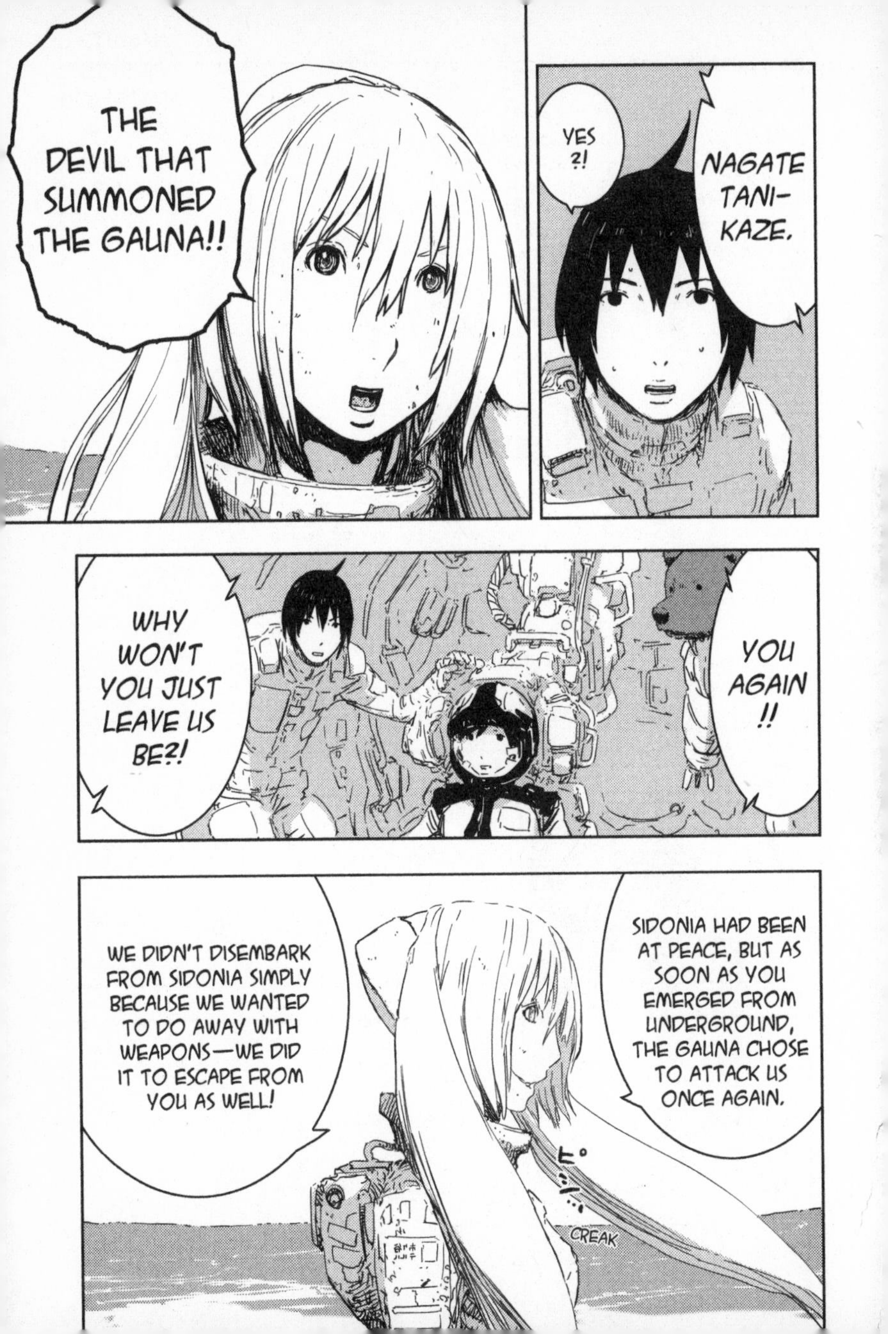
NAGATE TANI-KAZE.
YES?!
THE DEVIL THAT SUMMONED THE GAUNA!!
YOU AGAIN!!
WHY WON'T YOU JUST LEAVE US BE?!
SIDONIA HAD BEEN AT PEACE, BUT AS SOON AS YOU EMERGED FROM UNDERGROUND, THE GAUNA CHOSE TO ATTACK US ONCE AGAIN.
WE DIDN'T DISEMBARK FROM SIDONIA SIMPLY BECAUSE WE WANTED TO DO AWAY WITH WEAPONS—WE DID IT TO ESCAPE FROM YOU AS WELL!
CREAK

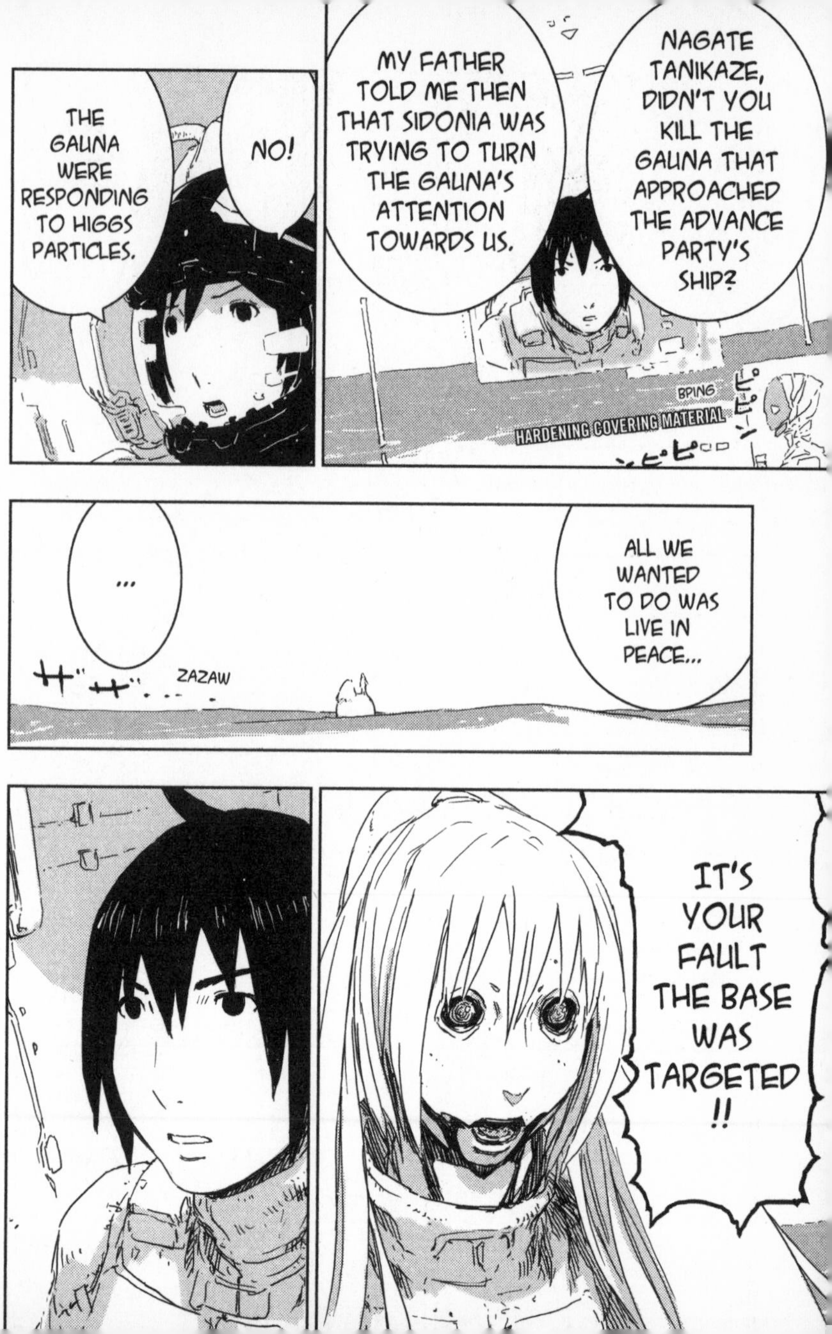
NAGATE TANIKAZE, DIDN'T YOU KILL THE GAUNA THAT APPROACHED THE ADVANCE PARTY'S SHIP?
MY FATHER TOLD ME THEN THAT SIDONIA WAS TRYING TO TURN THE GAUNA'S ATTENTION TOWARDS US.
BPING
HARDENING COVERING MATERIAL
NO!
THE GAUNA WERE RESPONDING TO HIGGS PARTICLES.
ALL WE WANTED TO DO WAS LIVE IN PEACE...
...
ZAZAW
IT'S YOUR FAULT THE BASE WAS TARGETED!!

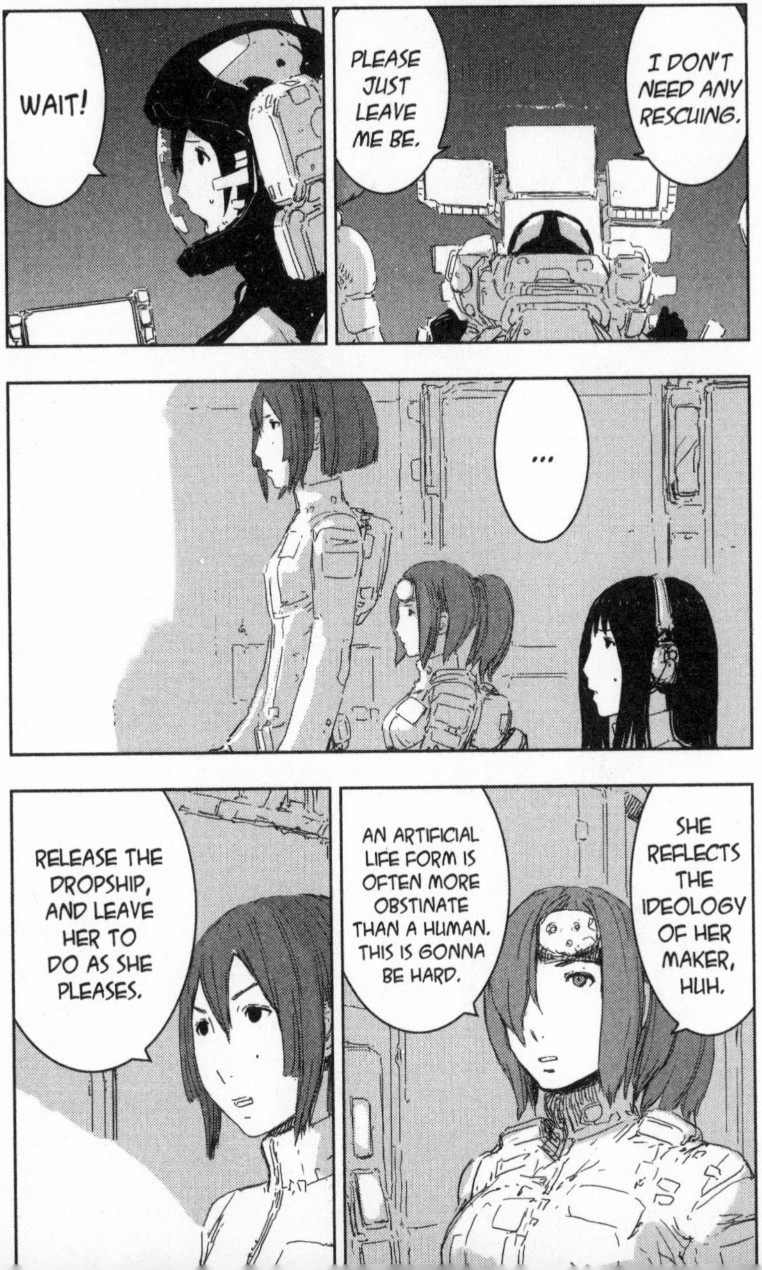
WAIT!
PLEASE JUST LEAVE ME BE.
I DON'T NEED ANY RESCUING.
...
RELEASE THE DROPSHIP, AND LEAVE HER TO DO AS SHE PLEASES.
AN ARTIFICIAL LIFE FORM IS OFTEN MORE OBSTINATE THAN A HUMAN. THIS IS GONNA BE HARD.
SHE REFLECTS THE IDEOLOGY OF HER MAKER, HUH.

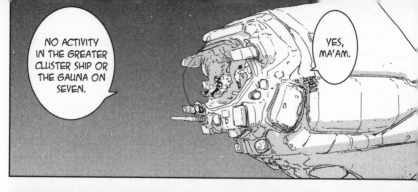

NO ACTIVITY IN THE GREATER CLUSTER SHIP OR THE GAUNA ON SEVEN.

YES, MA'AM.

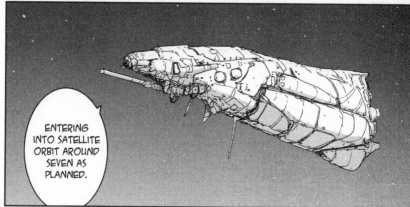

ENTERING INTO SATELLITE ORBIT AROUND SEVEN AS PLANNED.

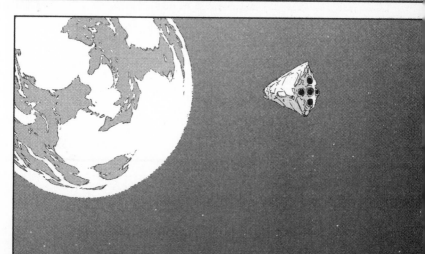

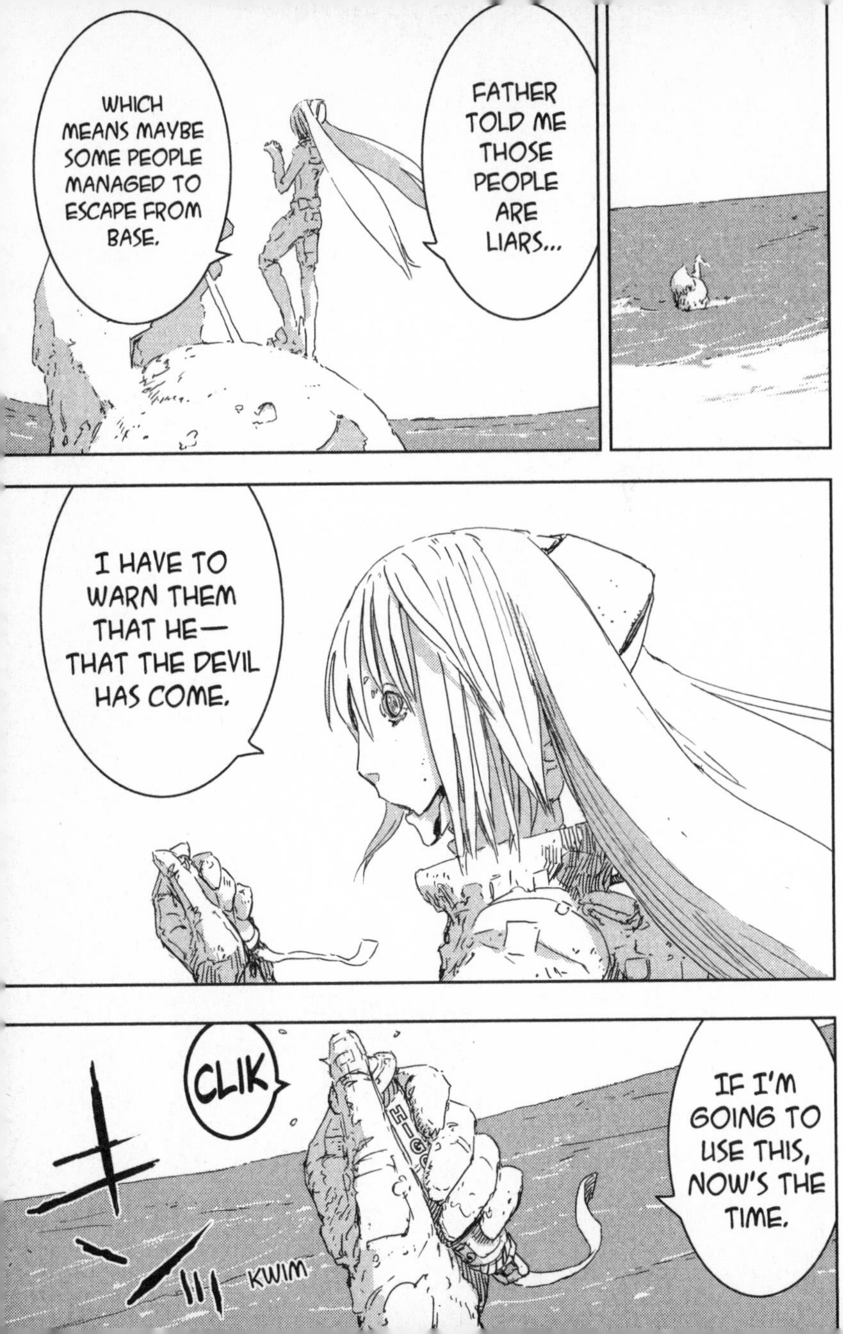
FATHER TOLD ME THOSE PEOPLE ARE LIARS...
WHICH MEANS MAYBE SOME PEOPLE MANAGED TO ESCAPE FROM BASE.
I HAVE TO WARN THEM THAT HE— THAT THE DEVIL HAS COME.
IF I'M GOING TO USE THIS, NOW'S THE TIME.
CLIK
KWIM

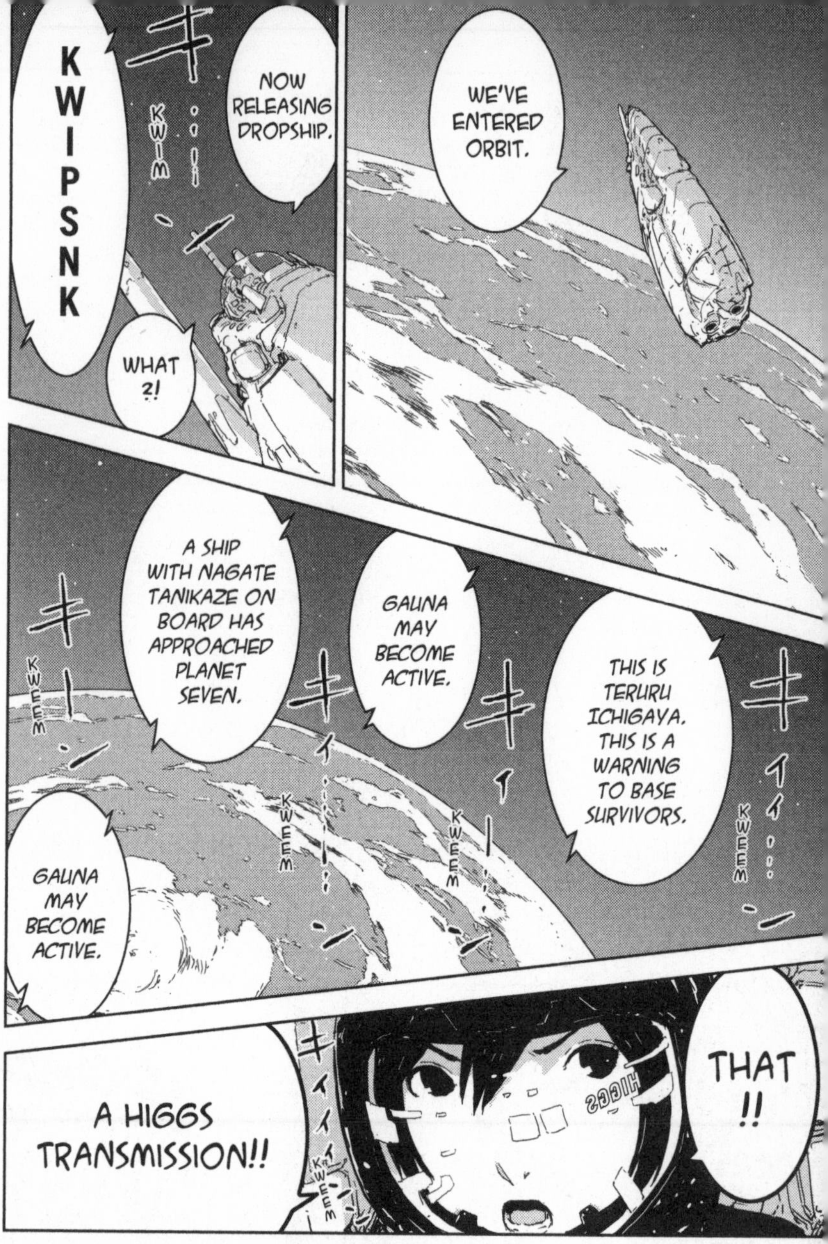
WE'VE ENTERED ORBIT.
NOW RELEASING DROPSHIP.
KWIM
KWIPSNK
WHAT ?!
THIS IS TERURU ICHIGAYA. THIS IS A WARNING TO BASE SURVIVORS.
KWEEM
GAUNA MAY BECOME ACTIVE.
KWEEM
A SHIP WITH NAGATE TANIKAZE ON BOARD HAS APPROACHED PLANET SEVEN.
KWEEM
KWEEM
GAUNA MAY BECOME ACTIVE.
THAT !!
HIGGS
A HIGGS TRANSMISSION!!
KWEEM

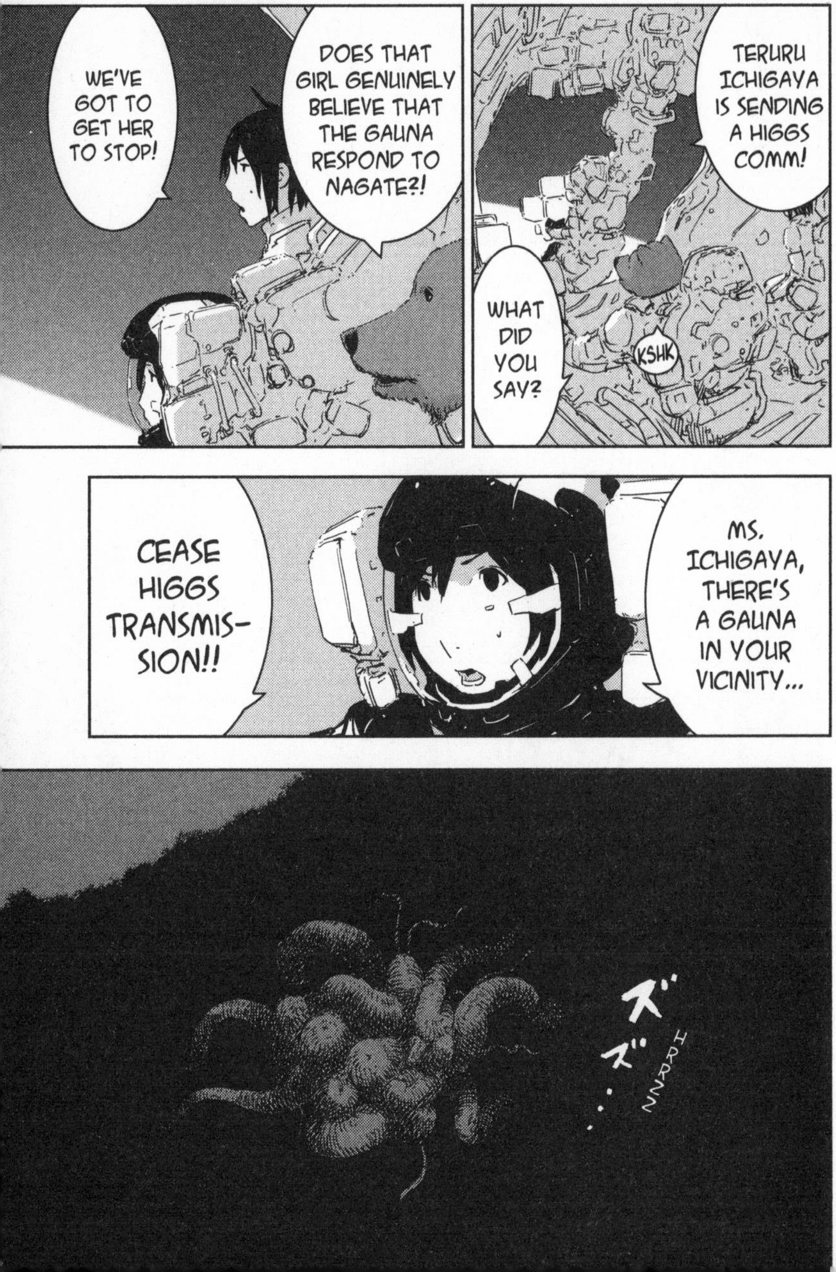
TERURU ICHIGAYA IS SENDING A HIGGS COMM!
WHAT DID YOU SAY?
KSHK
DOES THAT GIRL GENUINELY BELIEVE THAT THE GAUNA RESPOND TO NAGATE?!
WE'VE GOT TO GET HER TO STOP!
MS. ICHIGAYA, THERE'S A GAUNA IN YOUR VICINITY...
CEASE HIGGS TRANSMISSION!!
ズズ…
HRRZZ

SPOOOSH

DVSHH

!

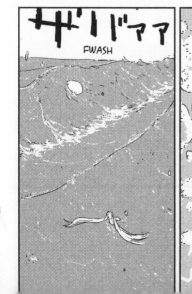
FWASH

WHAMM

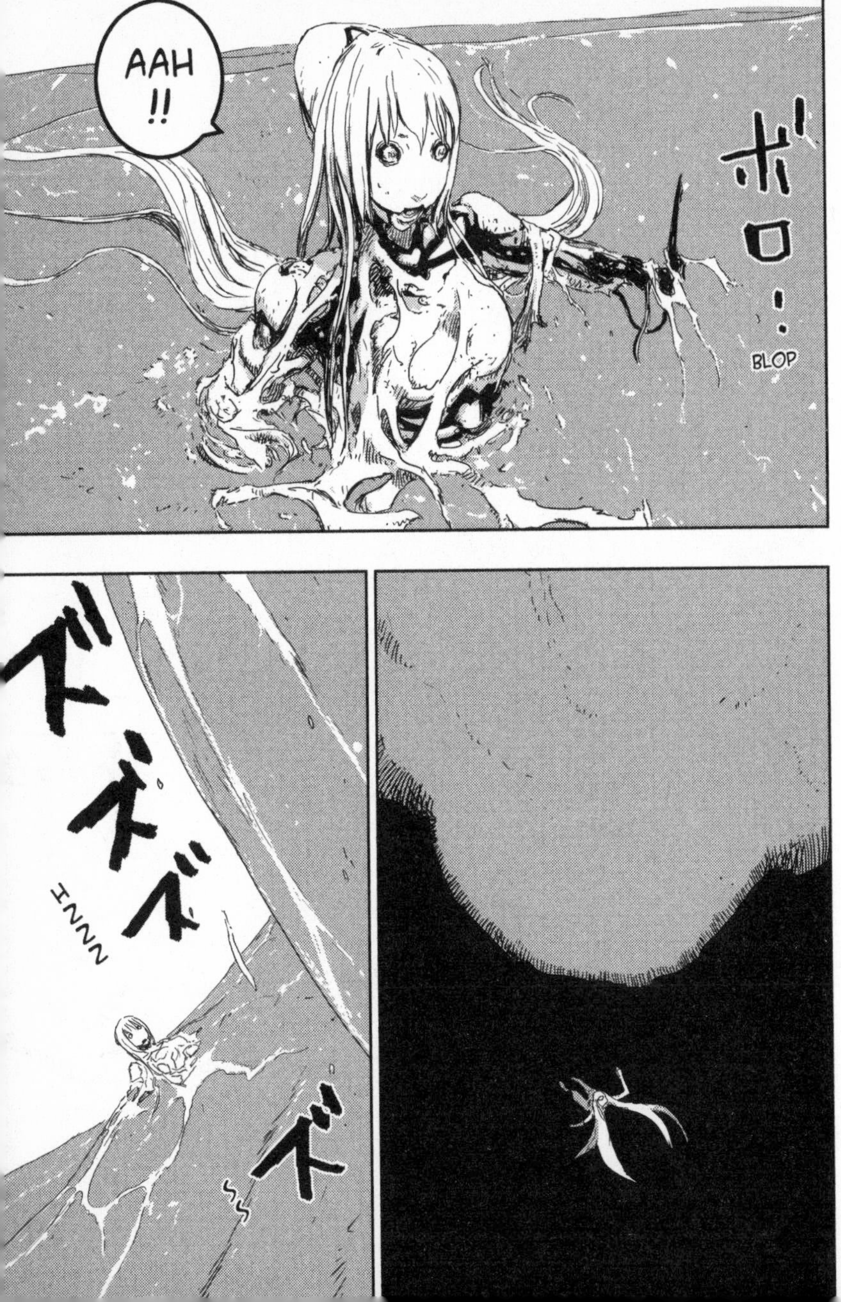
ボロ・・
BLOP
AAH !!
ズズズ
INNN
ズ

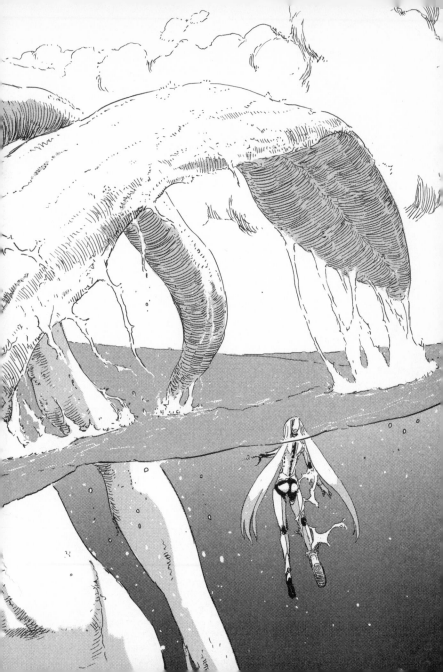

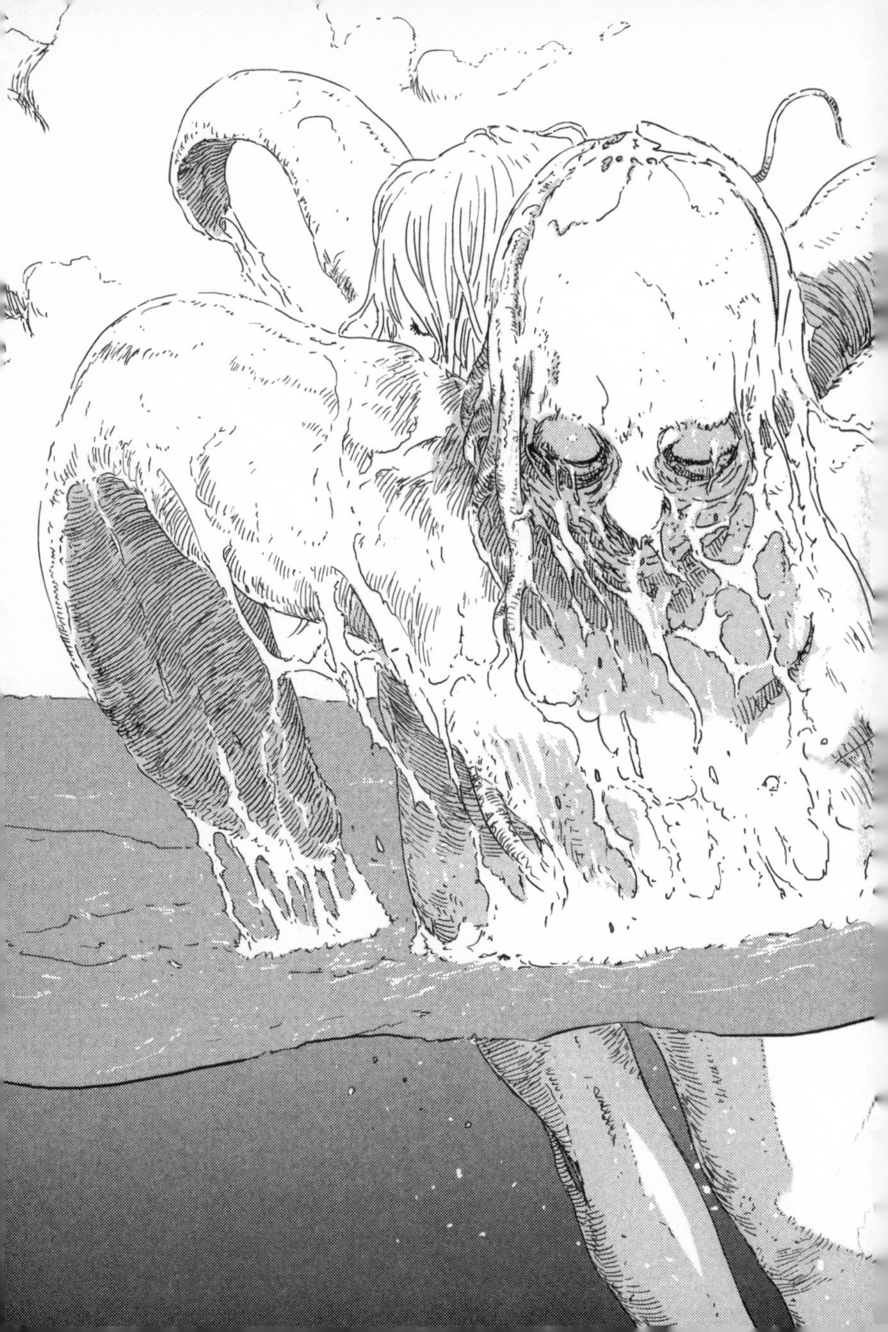

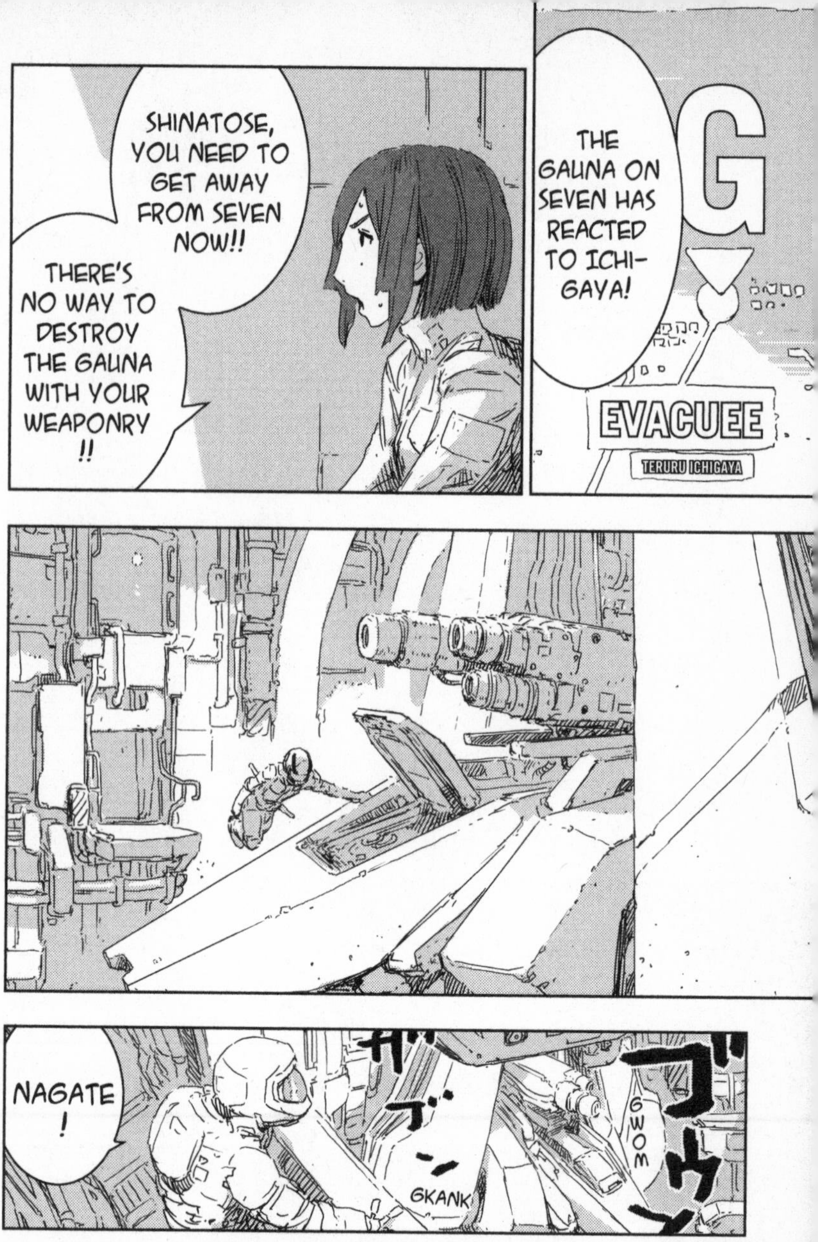
THE GAUNA ON SEVEN HAS REACTED TO ICHI-GAYA!
G
EVACUEE
TERURU ICHIGAYA
SHINATOSE, YOU NEED TO GET AWAY FROM SEVEN NOW!!
THERE'S NO WAY TO DESTROY THE GAUNA WITH YOUR WEAPONRY !!
GWOM
GKANK
NAGATE !

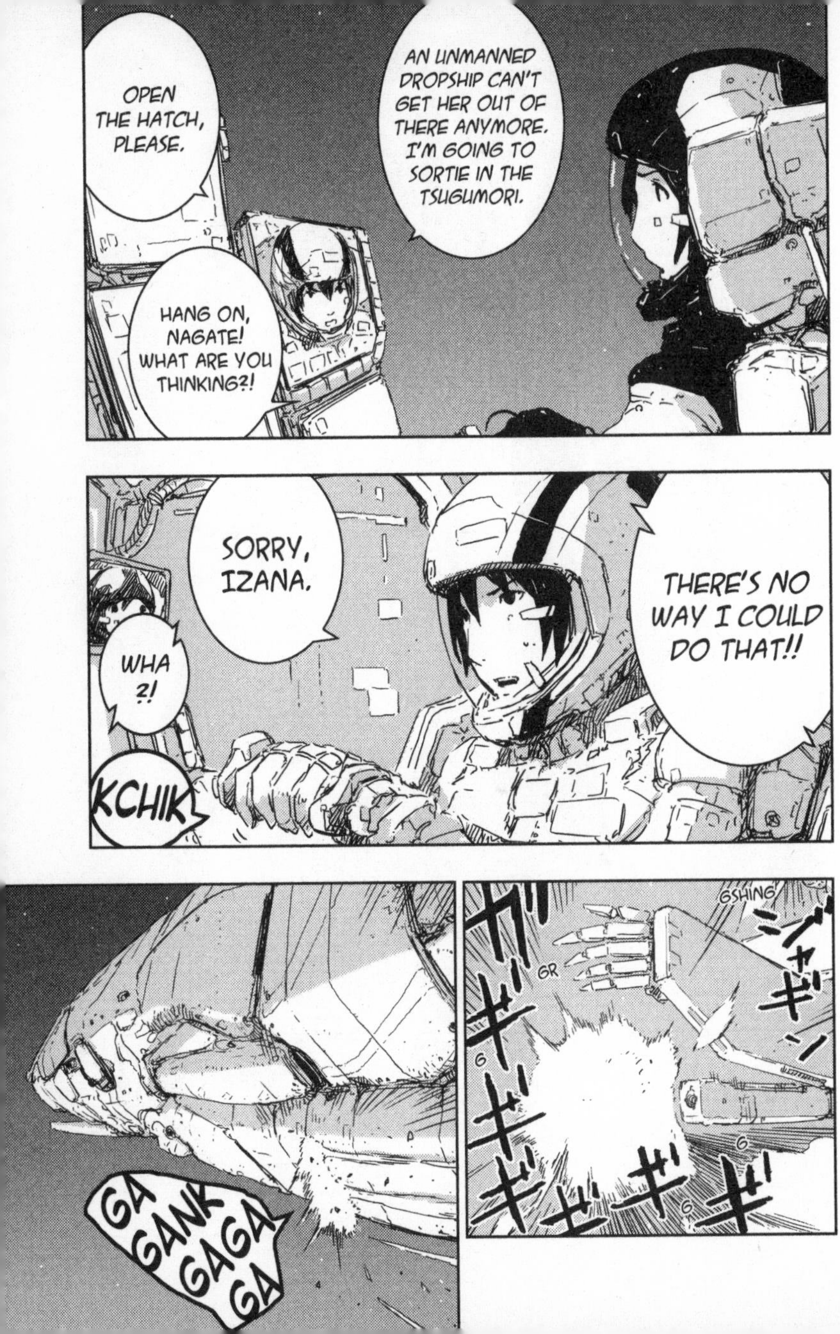
AN UNMANNED DROPSHIP CAN'T GET HER OUT OF THERE ANYMORE. I'M GOING TO SORTIE IN THE TSUGUMORI.
OPEN THE HATCH, PLEASE.
HANG ON, NAGATE! WHAT ARE YOU THINKING?!
THERE'S NO WAY I COULD DO THAT!!
SORRY, IZANA.
WHA ?!
KCHIK
GSHING
GR
GA GANK GAGA GA

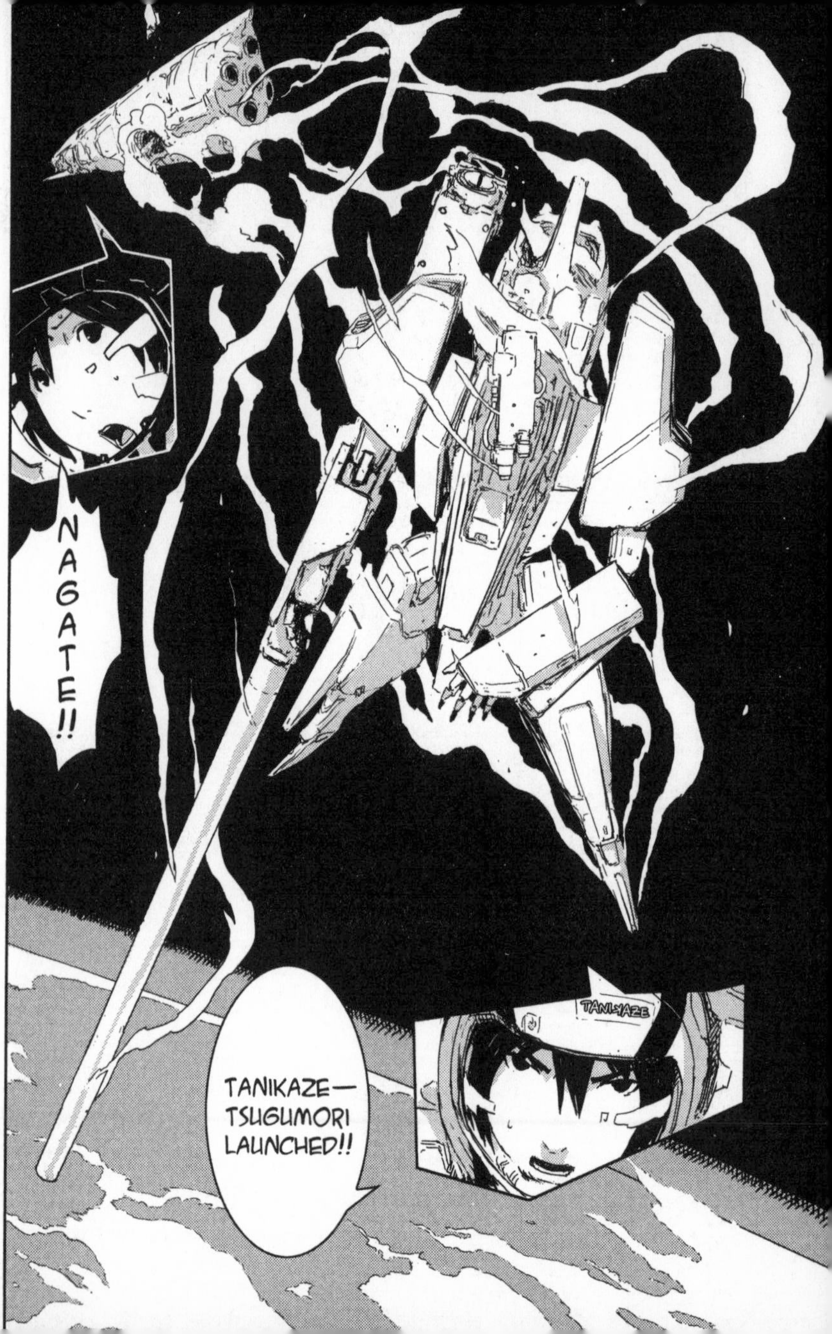
NAGATE!!
TANIKAZE
TANIKAZE—
TSUGUMORI
LAUNCHED!!

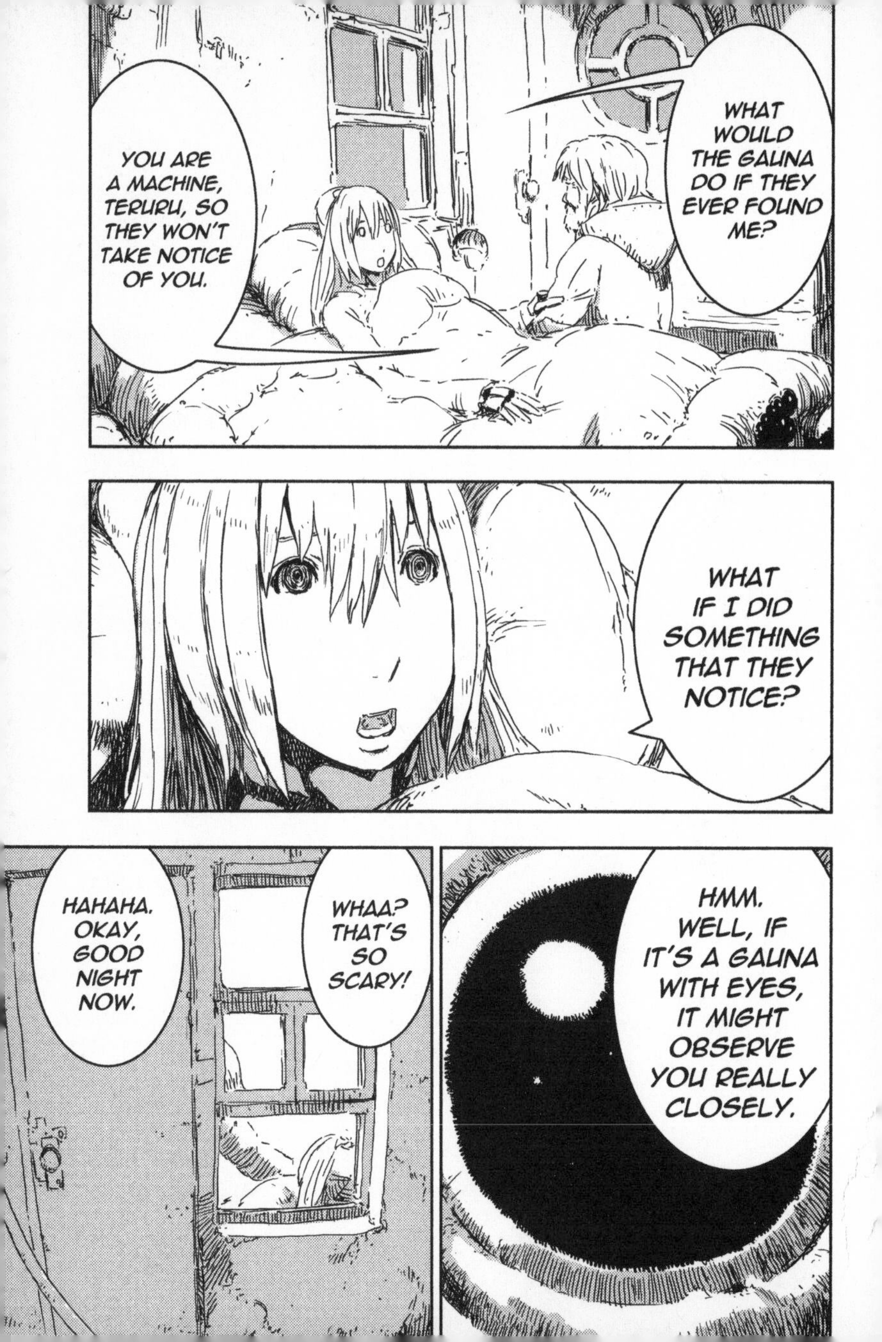
WHAT WOULD THE GAUNA DO IF THEY EVER FOUND ME?
YOU ARE A MACHINE, TERURU, SO THEY WON'T TAKE NOTICE OF YOU.
WHAT IF I DID SOMETHING THAT THEY NOTICE?
HMM. WELL, IF IT'S A GAUNA WITH EYES, IT MIGHT OBSERVE YOU REALLY CLOSELY.
WHAA? THAT'S SO SCARY!
HAHAHA. OKAY, GOOD NIGHT NOW.

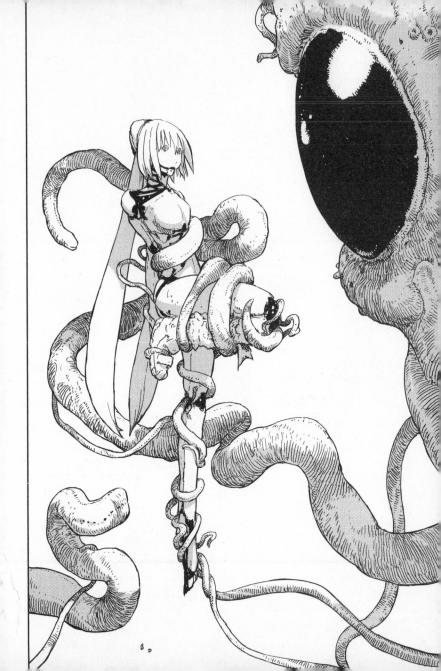

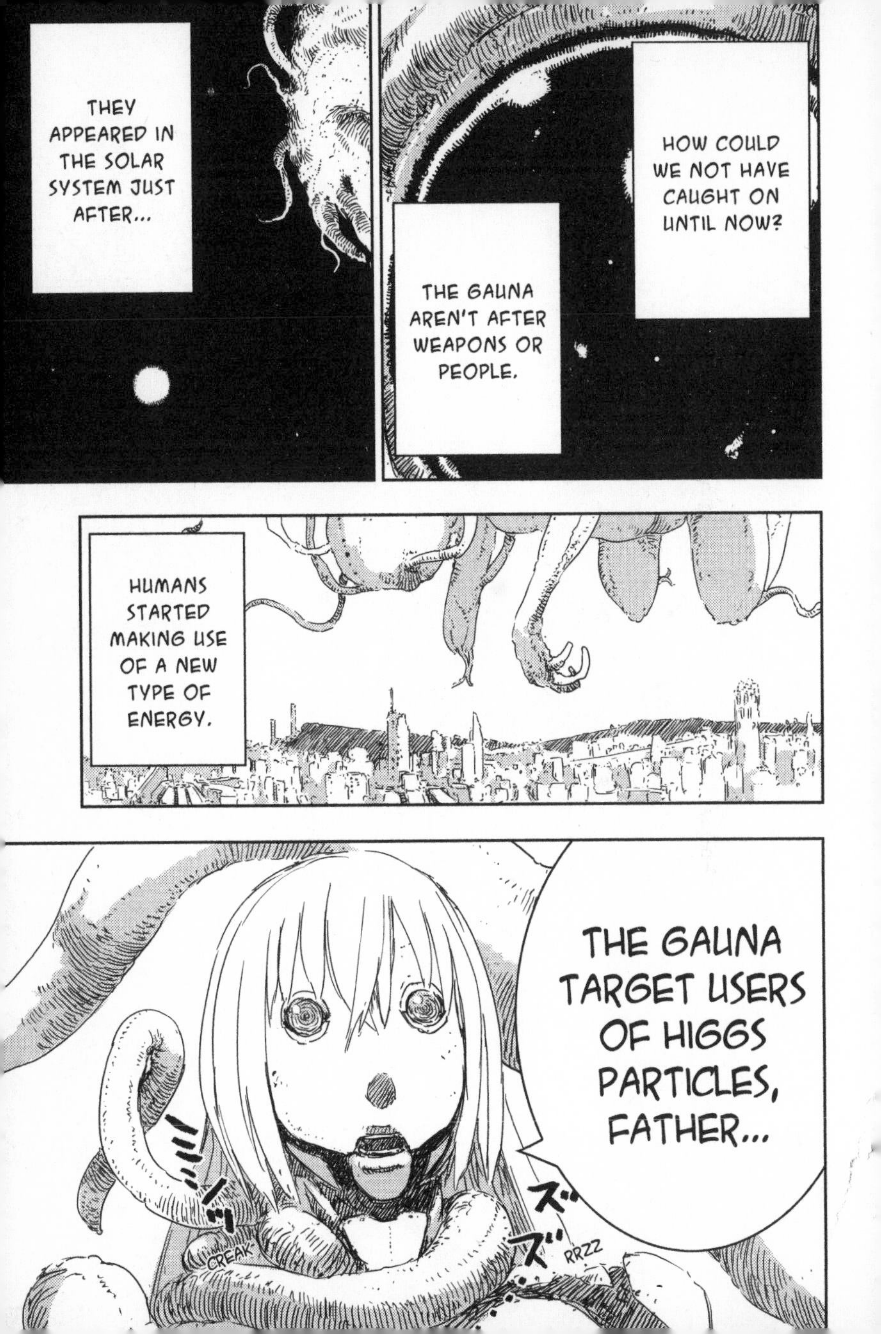
HOW COULD WE NOT HAVE CAUGHT ON UNTIL NOW?
THE GAUNA AREN'T AFTER WEAPONS OR PEOPLE.
THEY APPEARED IN THE SOLAR SYSTEM JUST AFTER...
HUMANS STARTED MAKING USE OF A NEW TYPE OF ENERGY.
THE GAUNA TARGET USERS OF HIGGS PARTICLES, FATHER...
RRZZ
CREAK

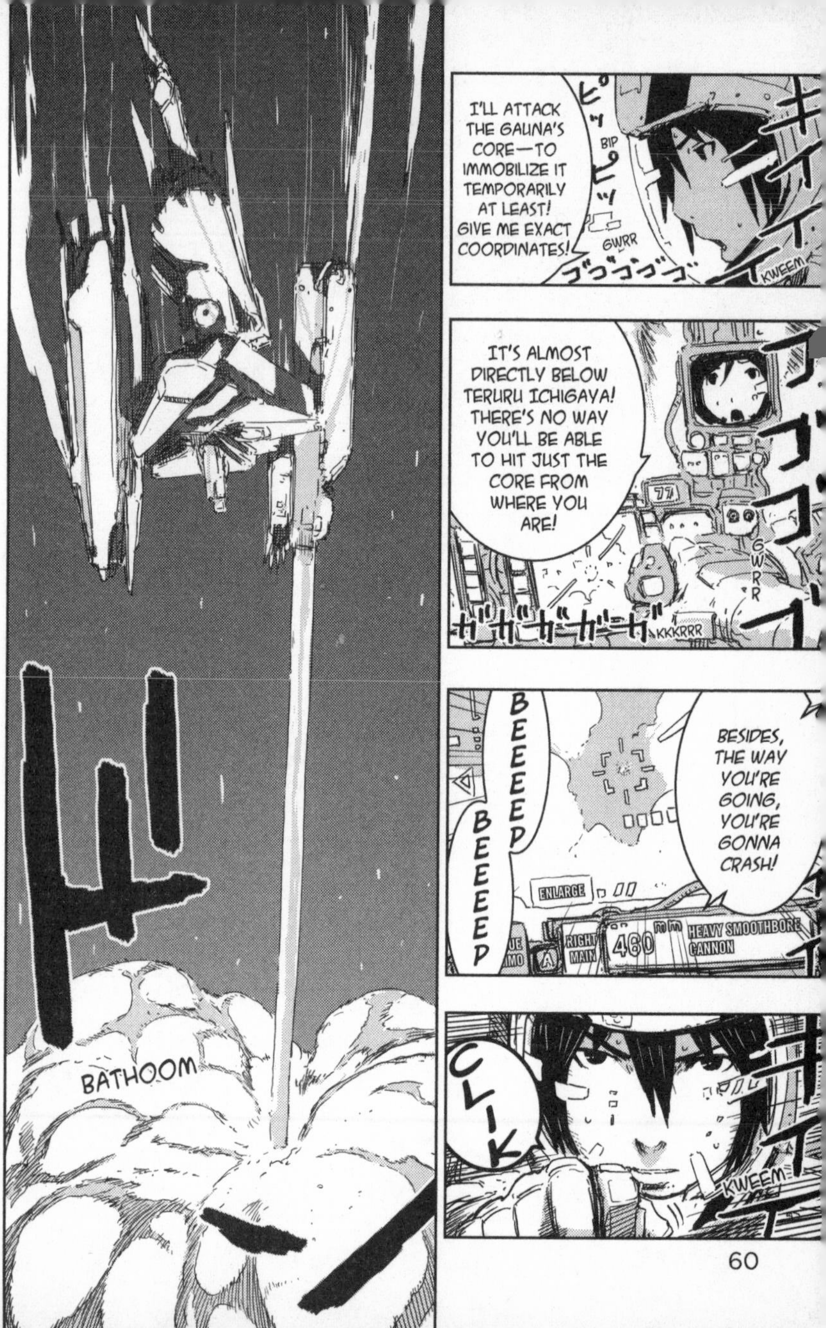
I'LL ATTACK THE GAUNA'S CORE—TO IMMOBILIZE IT TEMPORARILY AT LEAST! GIVE ME EXACT COORDINATES!
BIP
GWRR
KWEEM
IT'S ALMOST DIRECTLY BELOW TERURU ICHIGAYA! THERE'S NO WAY YOU'LL BE ABLE TO HIT JUST THE CORE FROM WHERE YOU ARE!
GWRR
KKKRRR
BESIDES, THE WAY YOU'RE GOING, YOU'RE GONNA CRASH!
BEEEEEP
BEEEEEP
ENLARGE
RIGHT MAIN
460 mm HEAVY SMOOTHBORE CANNON
CLIK
KWEEM
BATHOOM

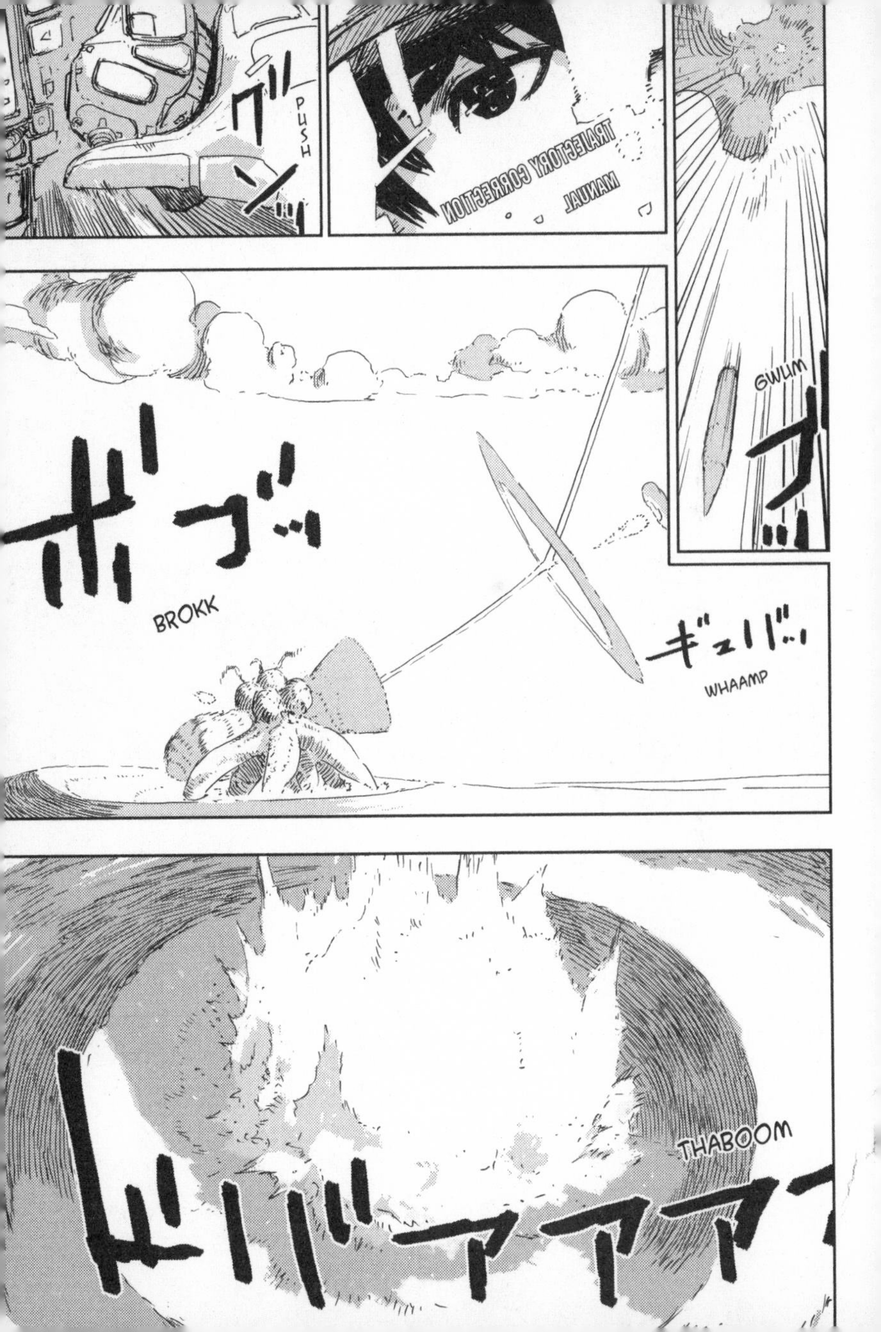
GWUM
TRAJECTORY CORRECTION
MANUAL
PUSH
ギュバッ
WHAAMP
ボゴッ
BROKK
THABOOM
ドバァァァ

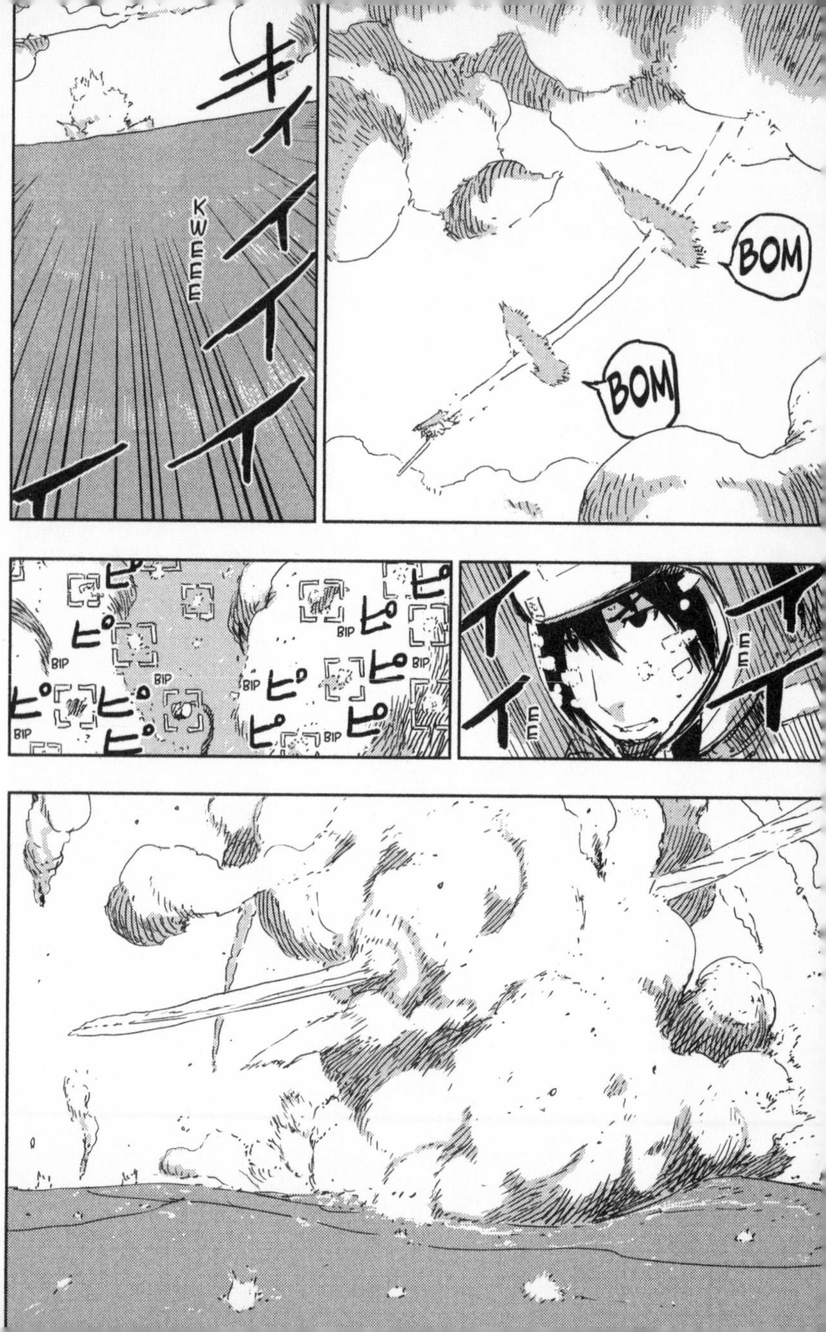
BOM
BOM
キイイイイ
KWEEE
イイ
EEE
イ
EE
ピピ
BIP
ピピ
BIP
ピピ
BIP
ピピ
BIP
ピピピ
BIP
ピ
BIP

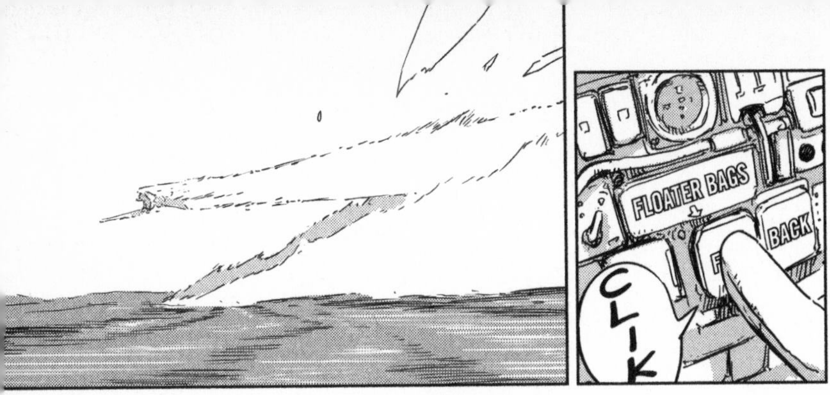
FLOATER BAGS
BACK
CLIK

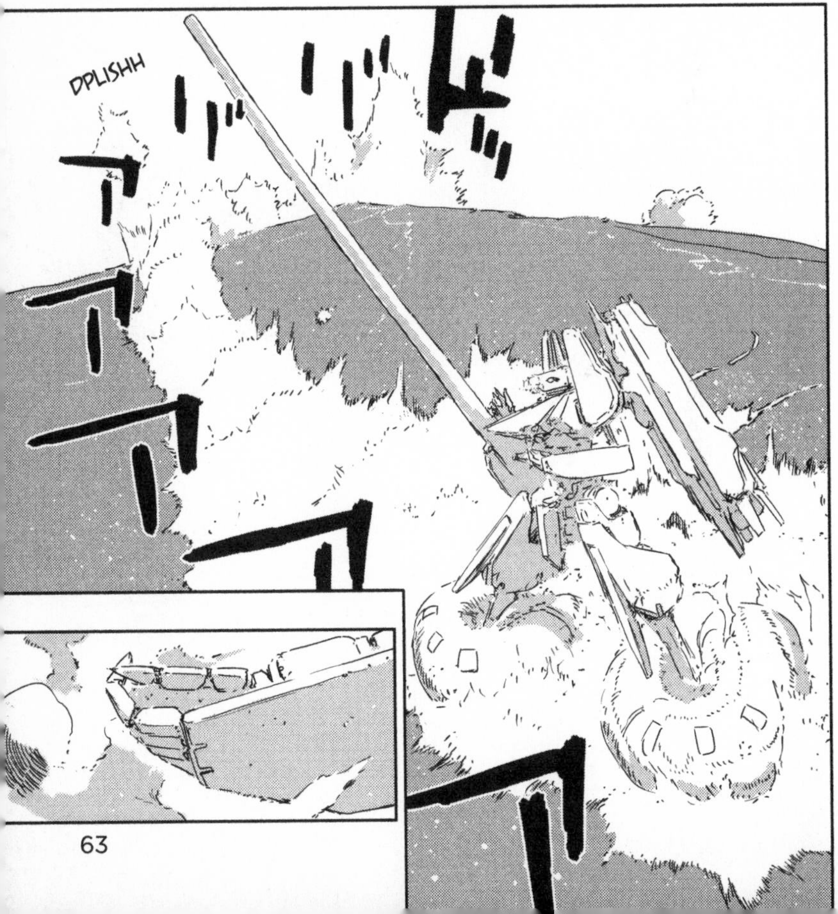
DPLISHH

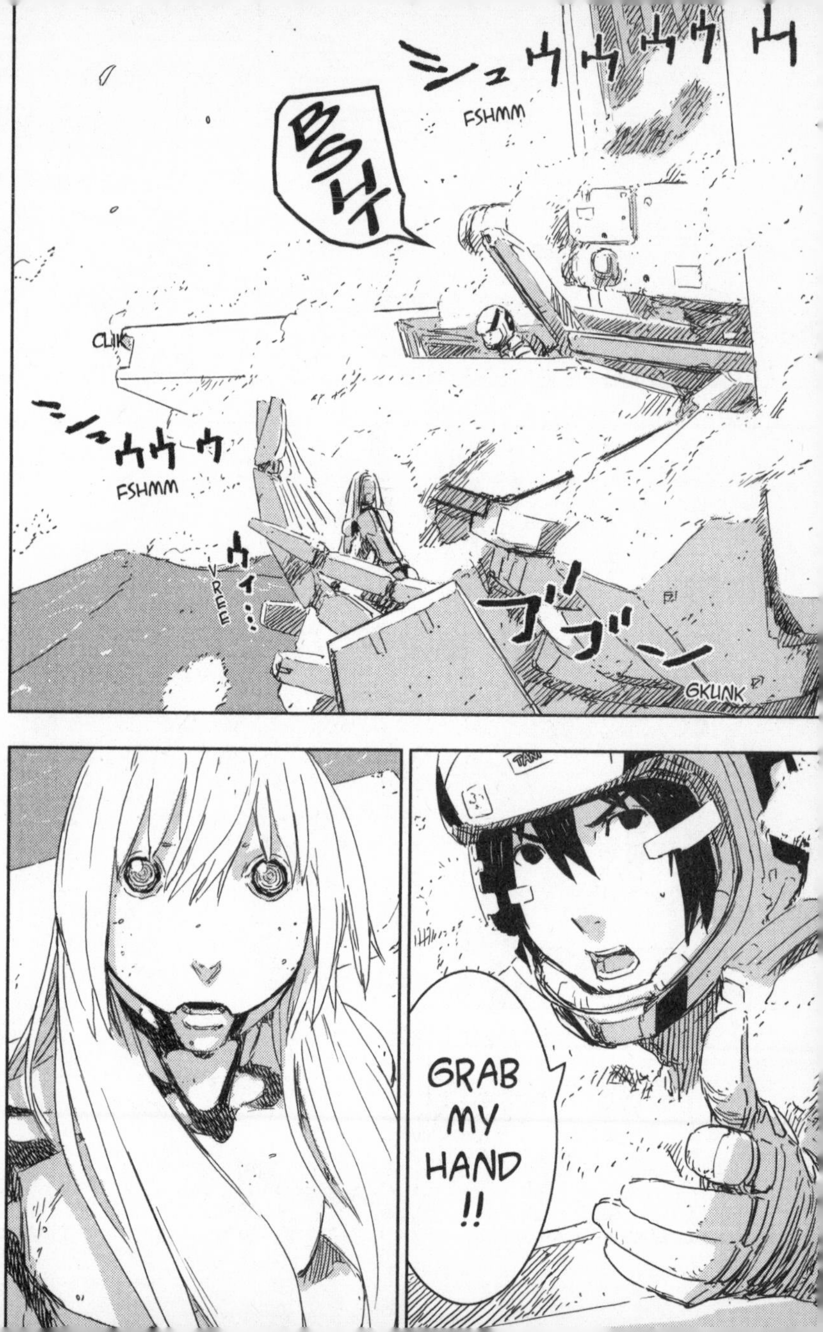
FSHMM
BSHT
CLIK
FSHMM
VREE
GKUNK
GRAB MY HAND !!

THE PLACENTA IS REGENERATING! HURRY!!

BLUP

WHUM

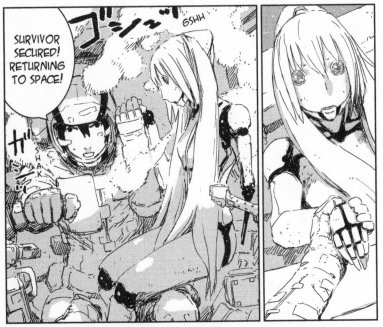

SURVIVOR SECURED! RETURNING TO SPACE!

GSHH

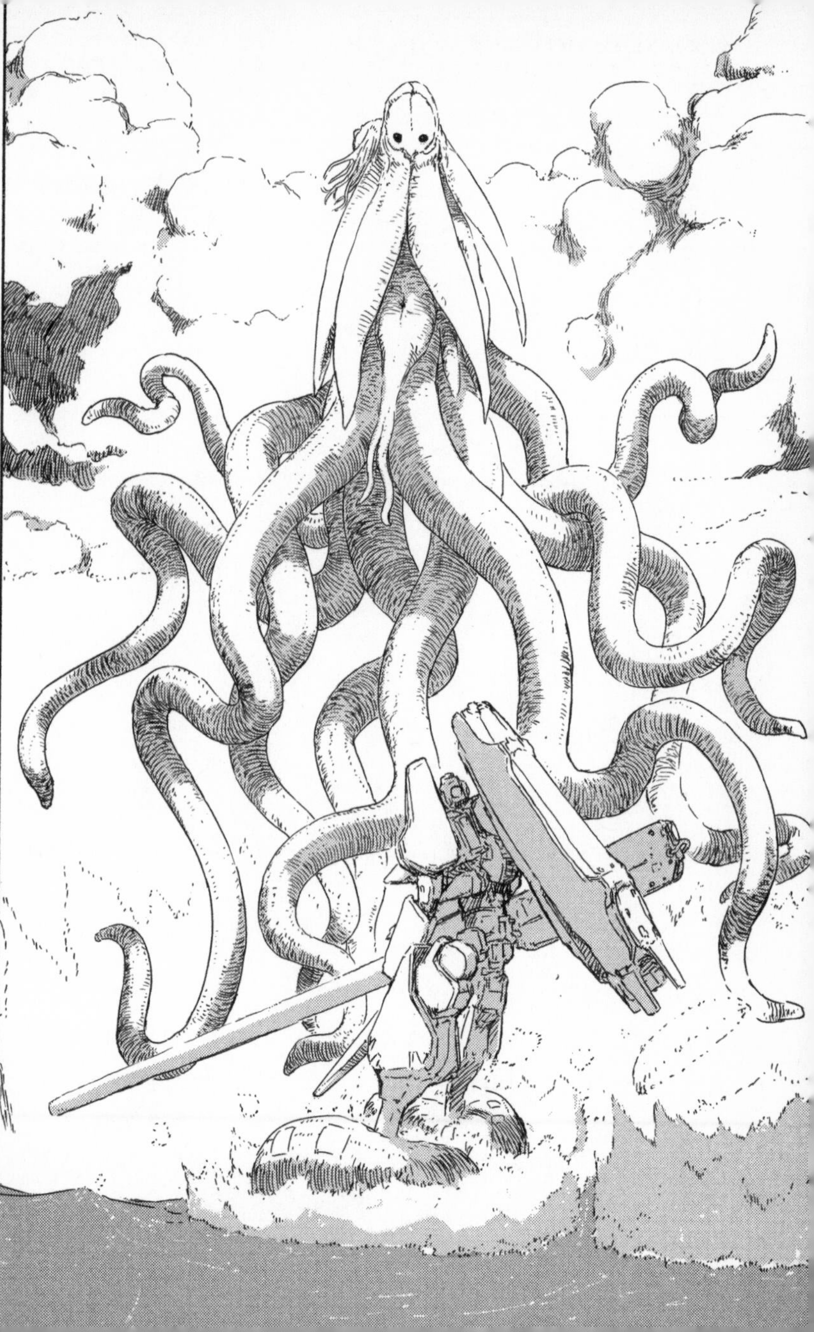

Chapter 51: END

Chapter 52: Lalah Hiyama's Exertions

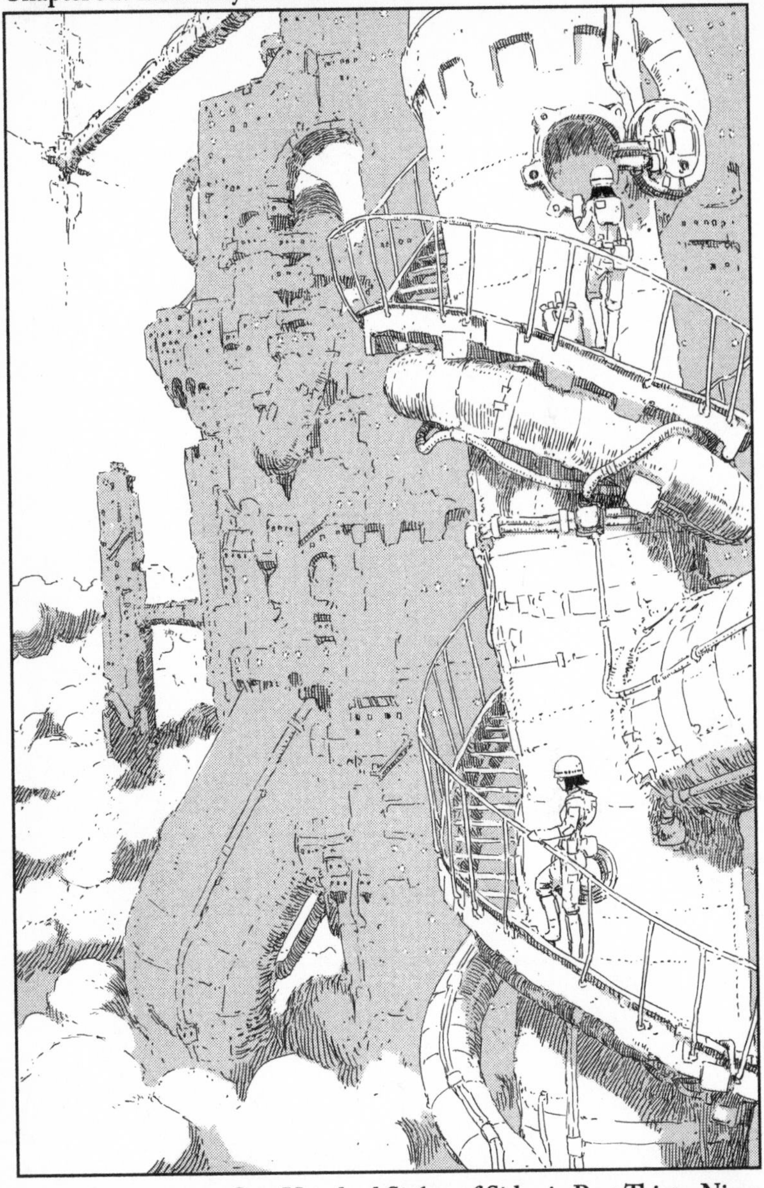

One Hundred Sights of Sidonia Part Thirty-Nine:
West 1483-34-4 Multipurpose Tubing Access Hatch

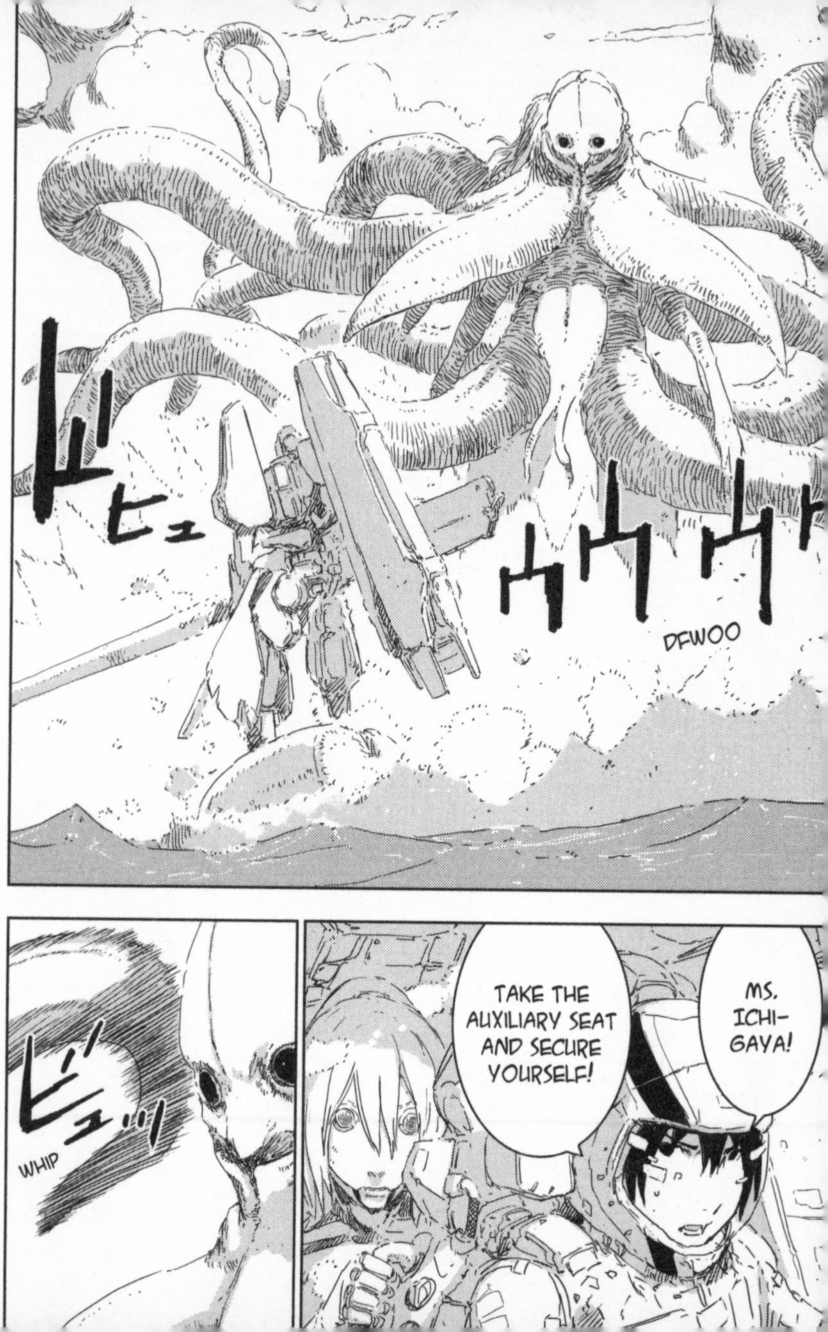
ドヒュ
DFWOO
MS. ICHI-GAYA!
TAKE THE AUXILIARY SEAT AND SECURE YOURSELF!
ビュッ
WHIP

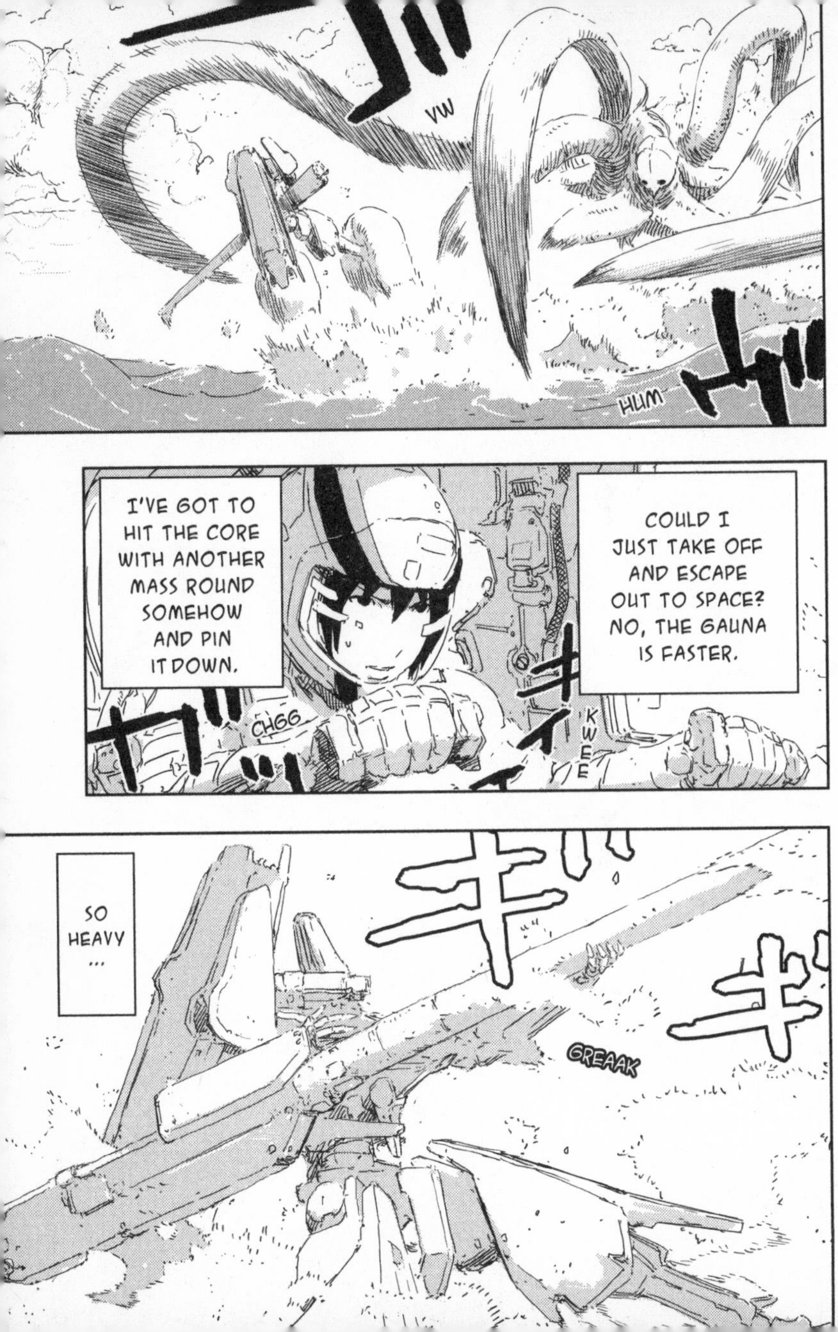
VW
HUM
COULD I JUST TAKE OFF AND ESCAPE OUT TO SPACE? NO, THE GAUNA IS FASTER.
I'VE GOT TO HIT THE CORE WITH ANOTHER MASS ROUND SOMEHOW AND PIN IT DOWN.
KWEE
CHGG
SO HEAVY ...
GREAAK

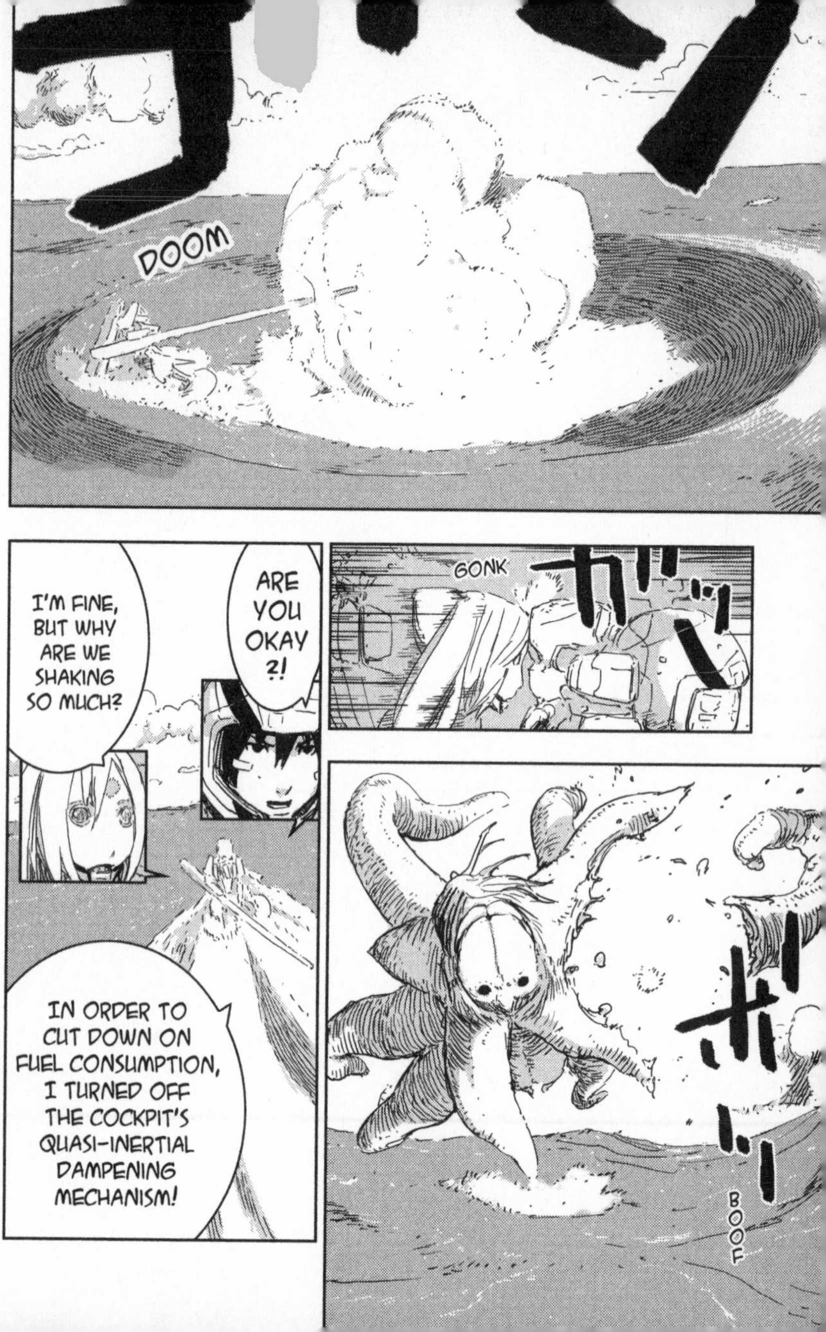
DOOM
GONK
BOOF
ARE YOU OKAY ?!
I'M FINE, BUT WHY ARE WE SHAKING SO MUCH?
IN ORDER TO CUT DOWN ON FUEL CONSUMPTION, I TURNED OFF THE COCKPIT'S QUASI-INERTIAL DAMPENING MECHANISM!

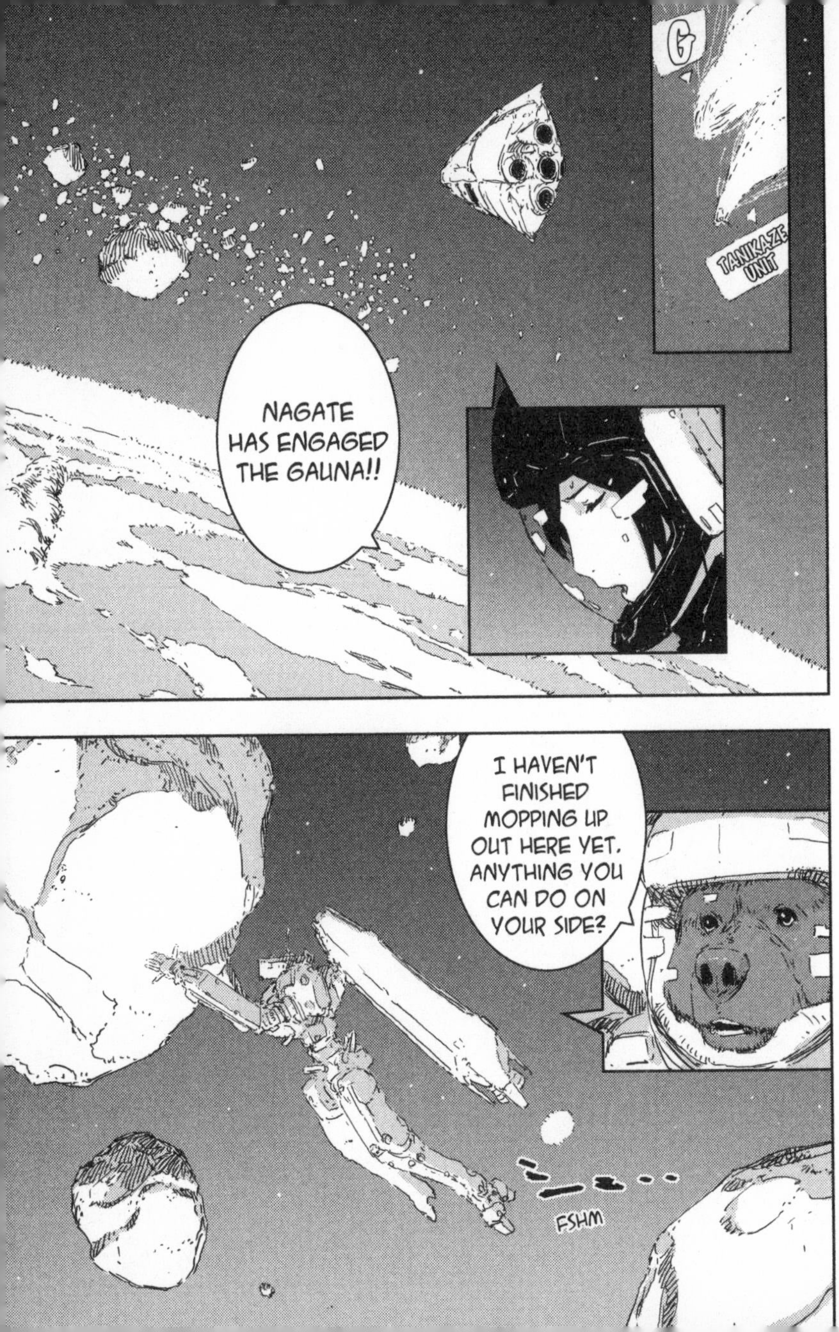
G
TANIKAZE UNIT
NAGATE HAS ENGAGED THE GAUNA!!
I HAVEN'T FINISHED MOPPING UP OUT HERE YET. ANYTHING YOU CAN DO ON YOUR SIDE?
FSHM

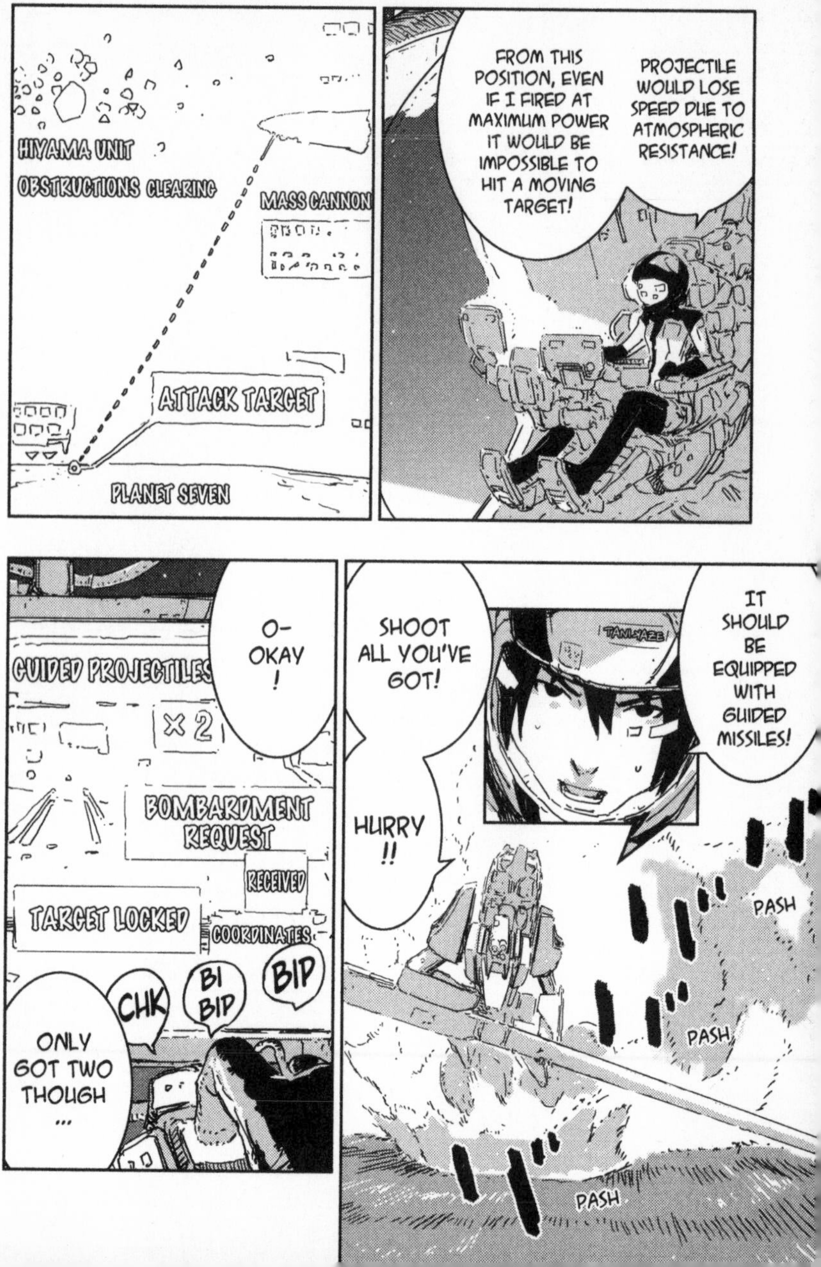

FROM THIS POSITION, EVEN IF I FIRED AT MAXIMUM POWER IT WOULD BE IMPOSSIBLE TO HIT A MOVING TARGET!
PROJECTILE WOULD LOSE SPEED DUE TO ATMOSPHERIC RESISTANCE!
HIYAMA UNIT
OBSTRUCTIONS CLEARING
MASS CANNON
ATTACK TARGET
PLANET SEVEN
IT SHOULD BE EQUIPPED WITH GUIDED MISSILES!
SHOOT ALL YOU'VE GOT!
HURRY !!
PASH
PASH
PASH
O-OKAY !
GUIDED PROJECTILES
× 2
BOMBARDMENT REQUEST
RECEIVED
TARGET LOCKED
COORDINATES
BIP
BI BIP
CHK
ONLY GOT TWO THOUGH ...

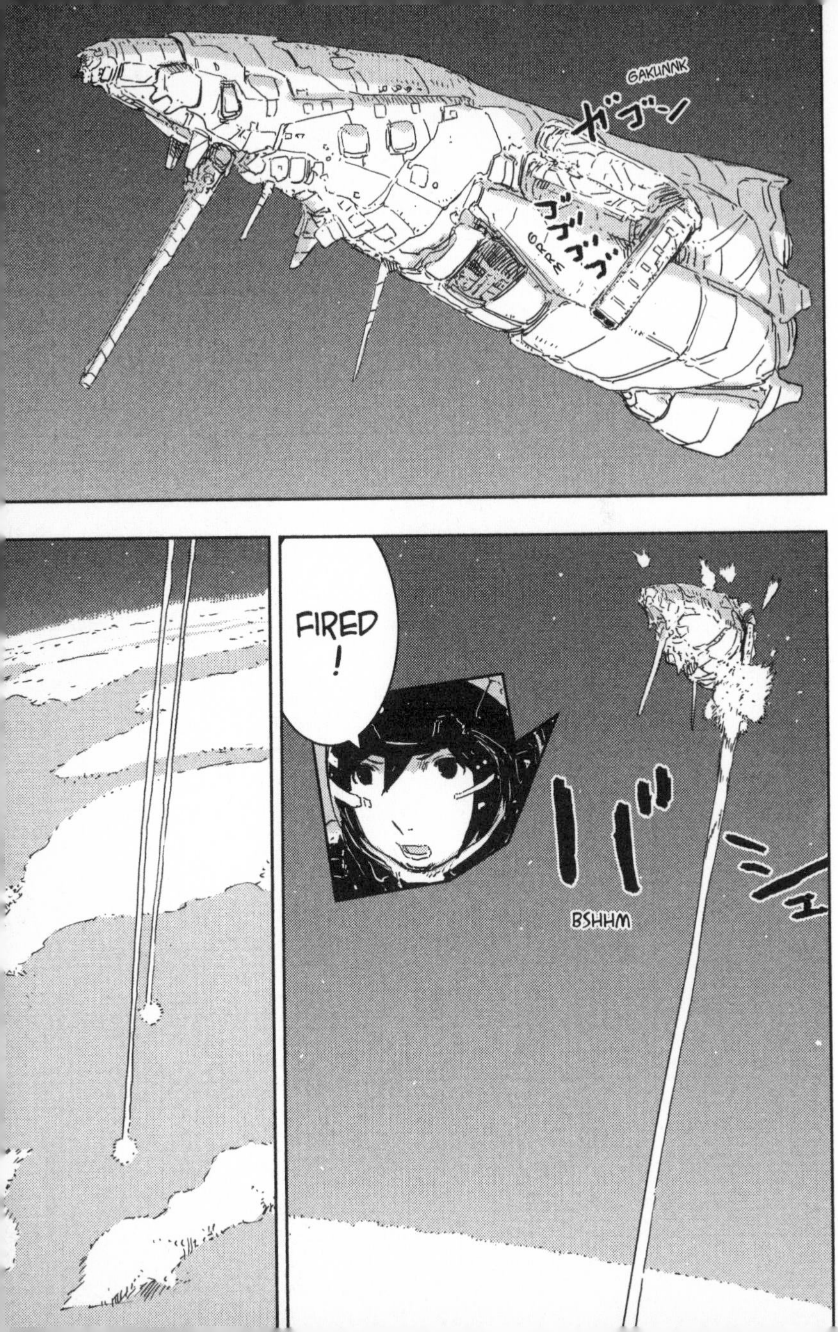
GAKUNNK
ゴゴゴゴ
GRRM
FIRED
!
BSHHM

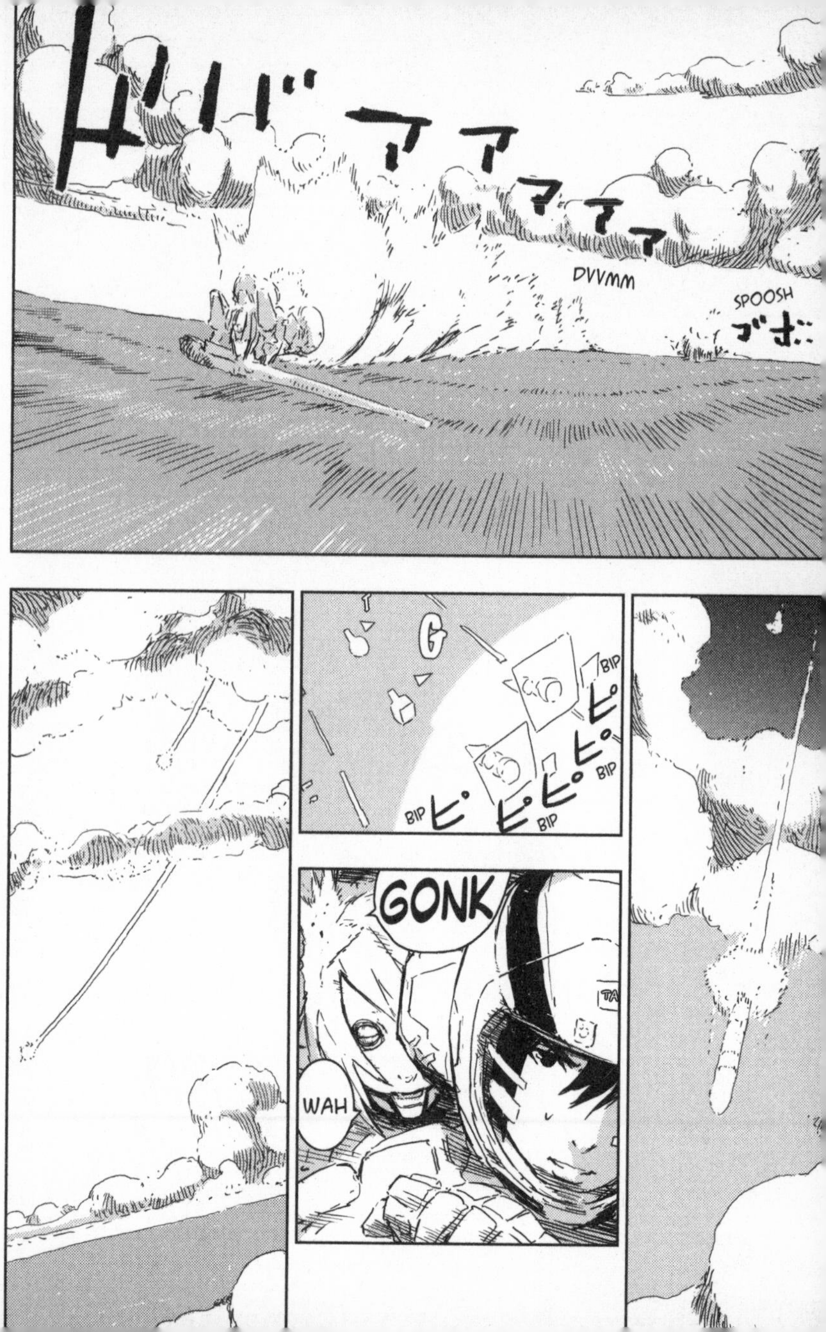
DVVMM
SPOOSH
G
BIP
BIP
BIP
BIP
GONK
WAH

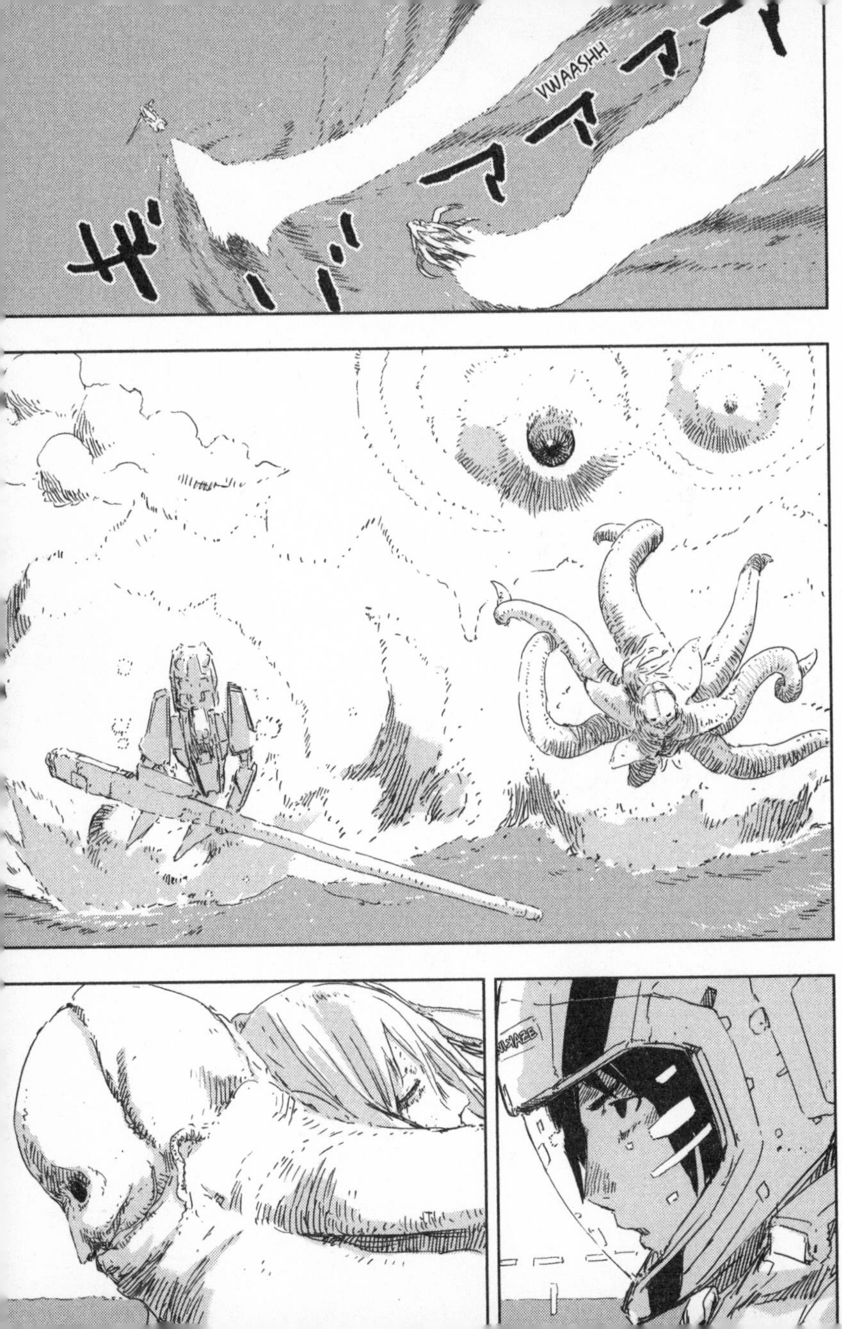
VWAASHH

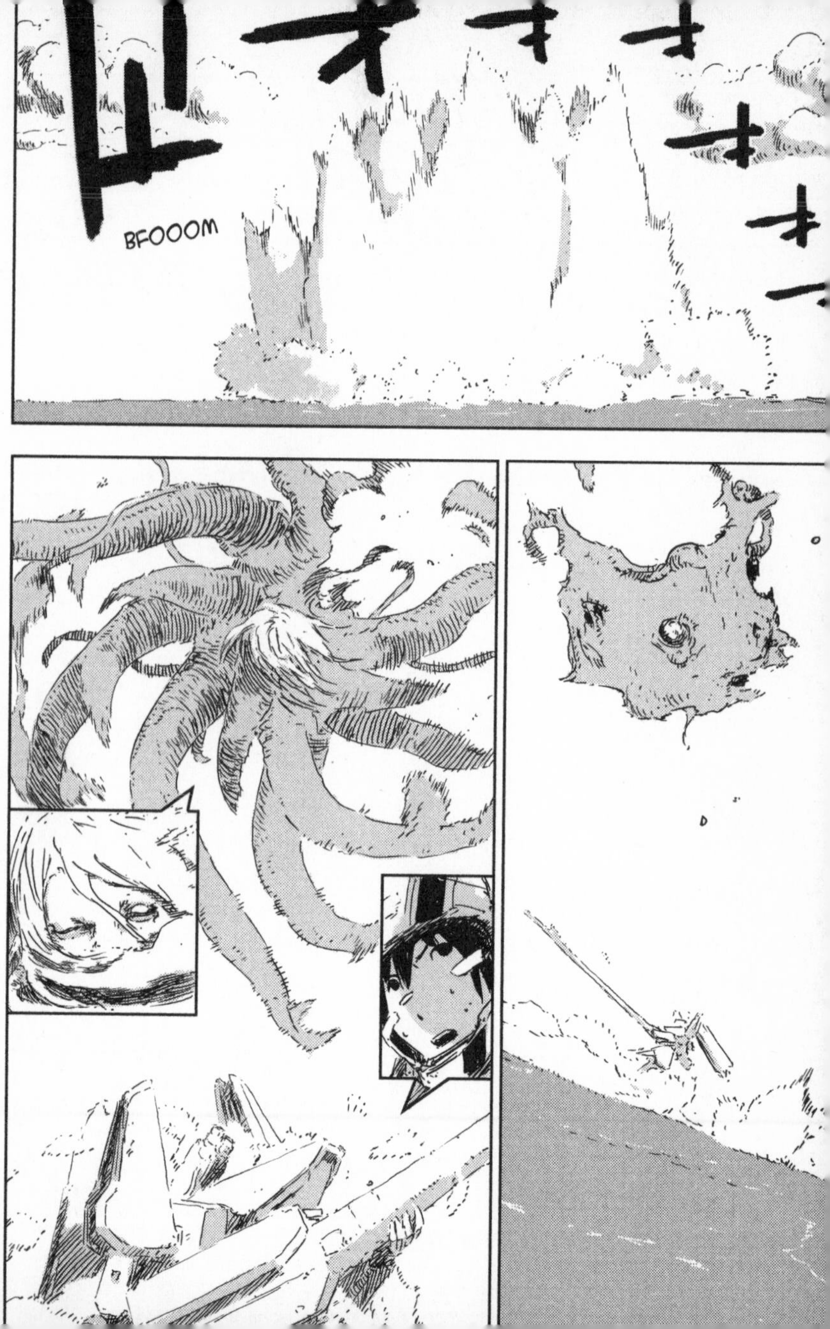
ドオォォォ
BFOOOM

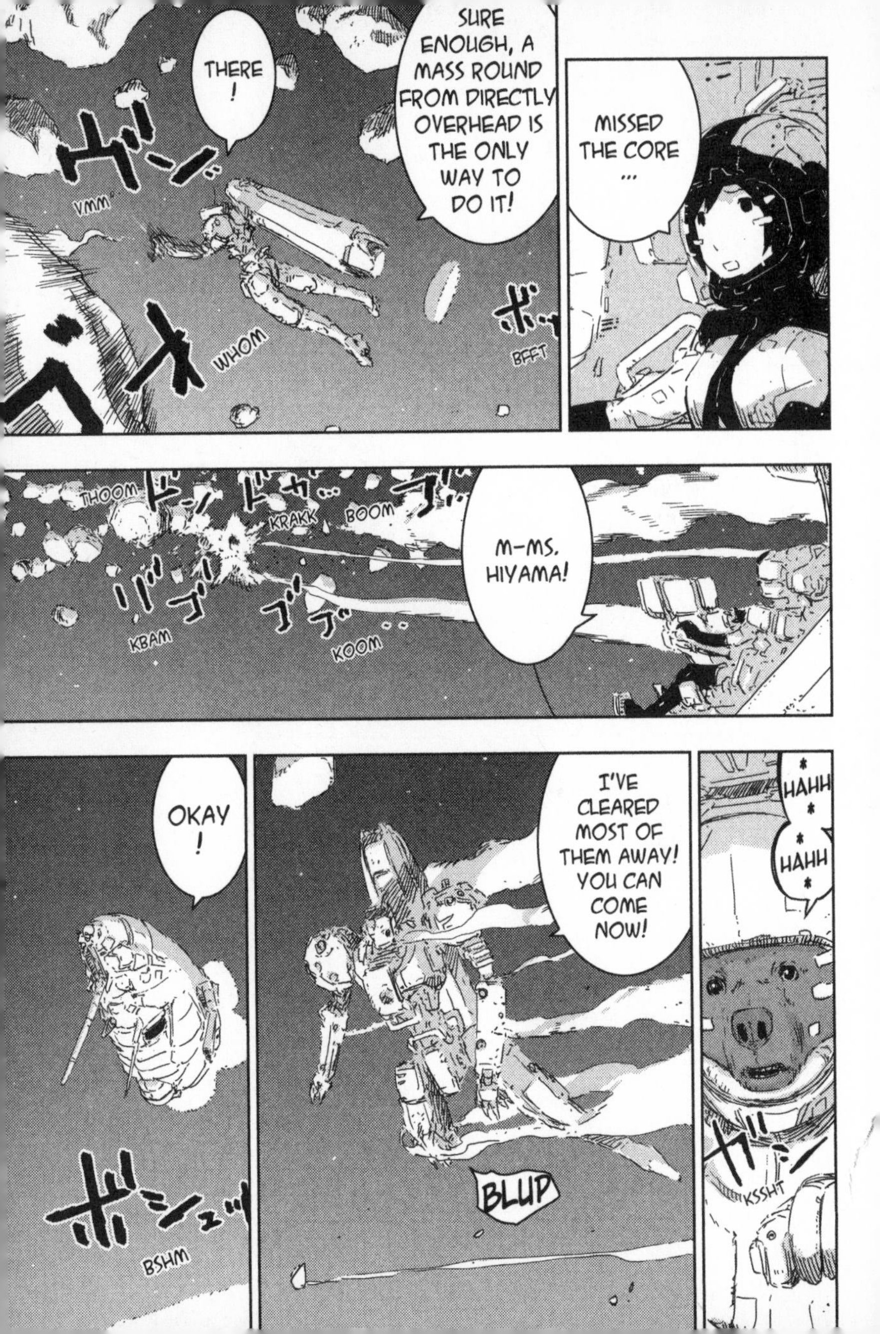
MISSED THE CORE ...
SURE ENOUGH, A MASS ROUND FROM DIRECTLY OVERHEAD IS THE ONLY WAY TO DO IT!
THERE!
VMM
WHOM
BFFT
M-MS. HIYAMA!
THOOM
KRAKK
BOOM
KBAM
KOOM
HAHH
HAHH
KSSHT
I'VE CLEARED MOST OF THEM AWAY! YOU CAN COME NOW!
BLUP
OKAY!
BSHM

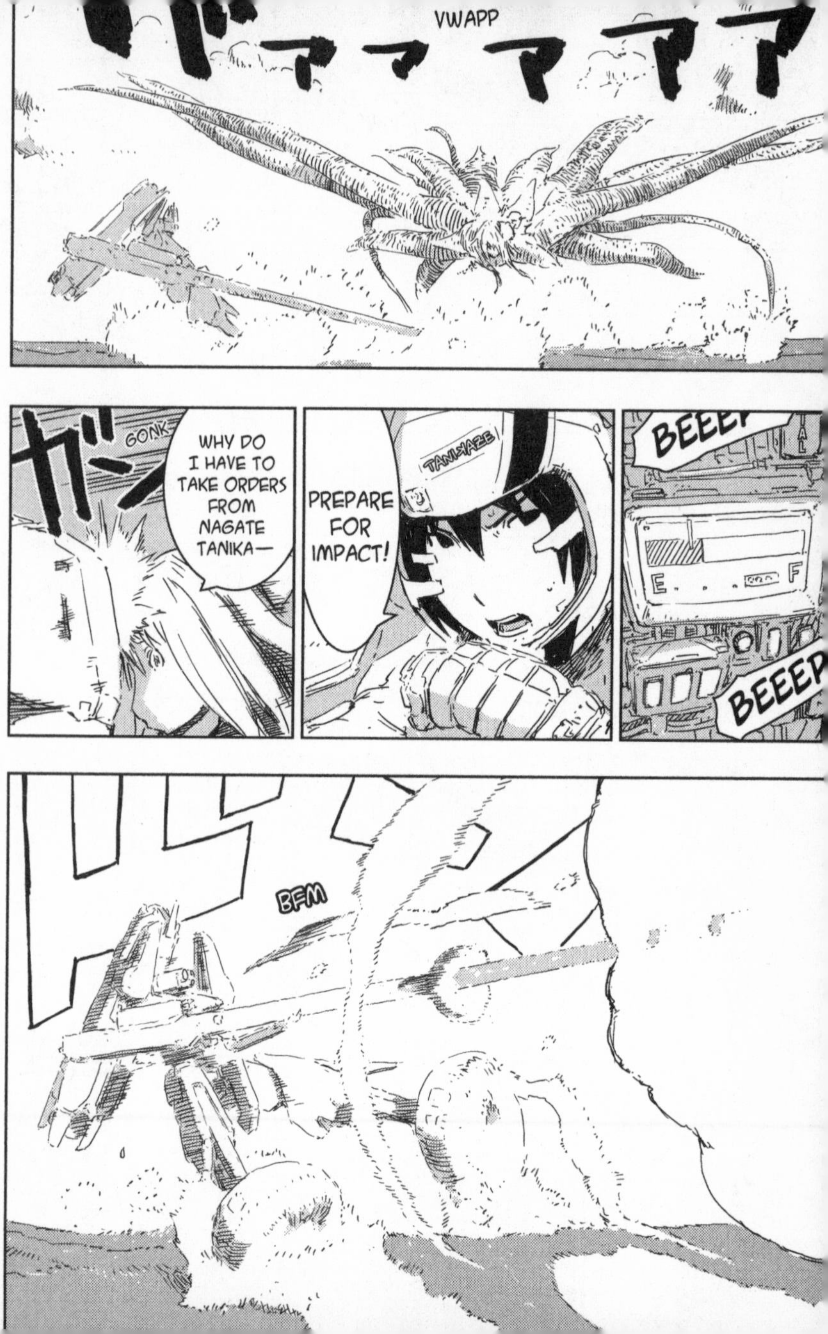
VWAPP
WHY DO I HAVE TO TAKE ORDERS FROM NAGATE TANIKA—
GONK
PREPARE FOR IMPACT!
TANIKAZE
BEEEP
BEEEP
BFM

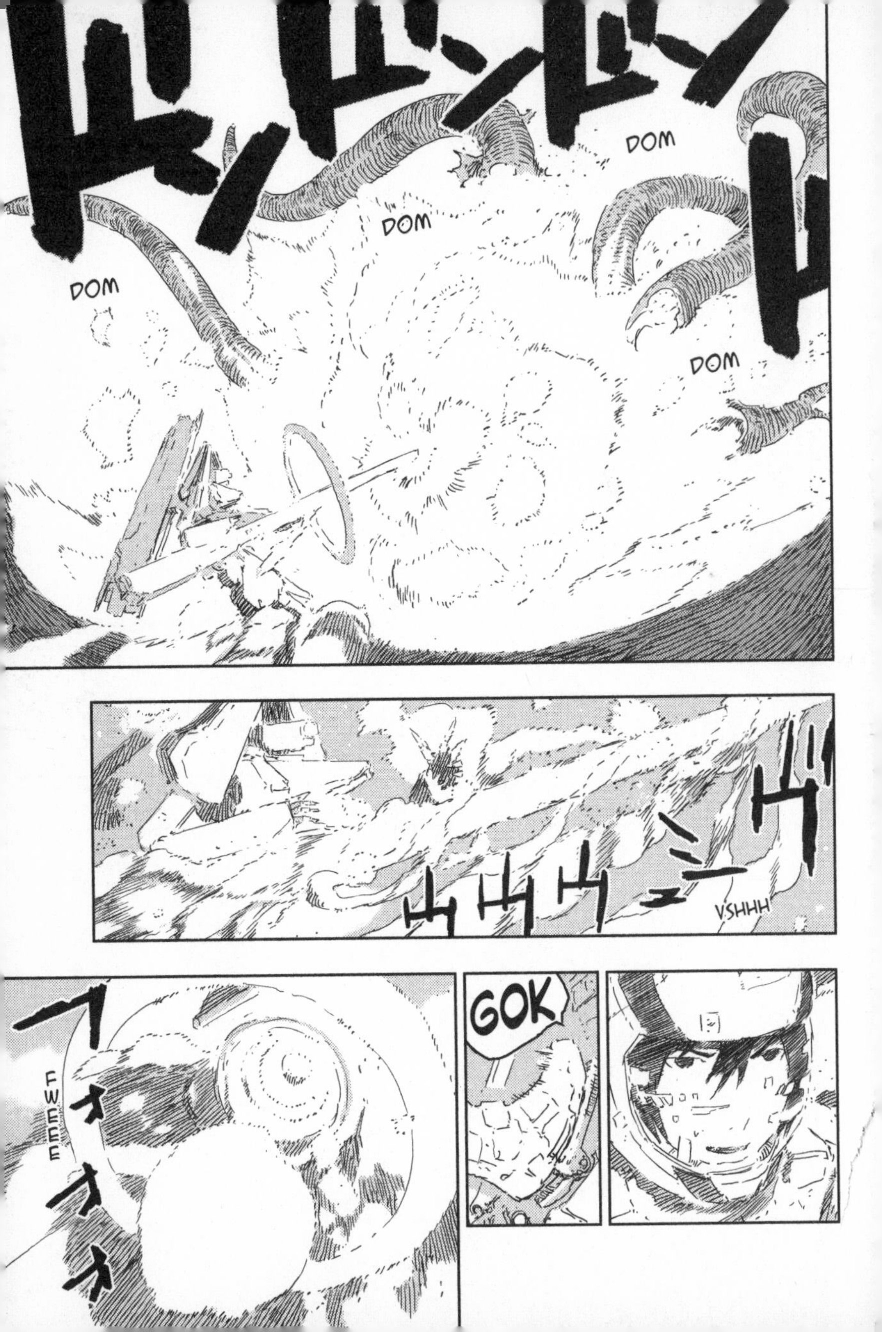
DOM
DOM
DOM
DOM
VSHHH
FWEEE
GOK

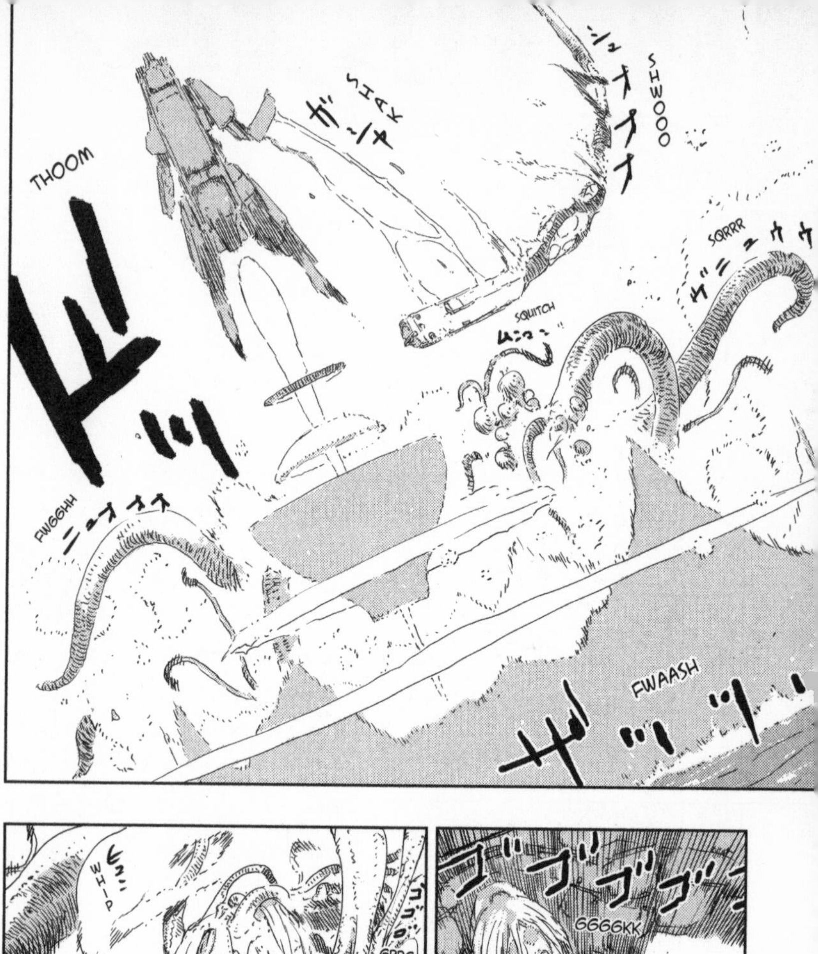
SHWOOO
SHAK
THOOM
SQRRR
SQUITCH
FWGGHH
FWAASH

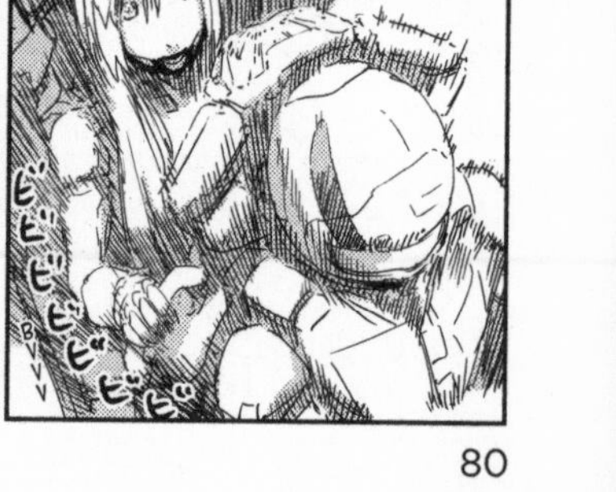
GGGGKK
BVVV

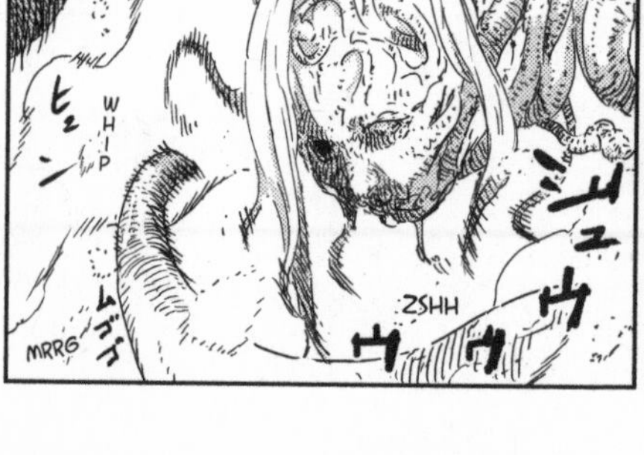
GRRG
WHIP
WHIP
ZSHH
MRRG

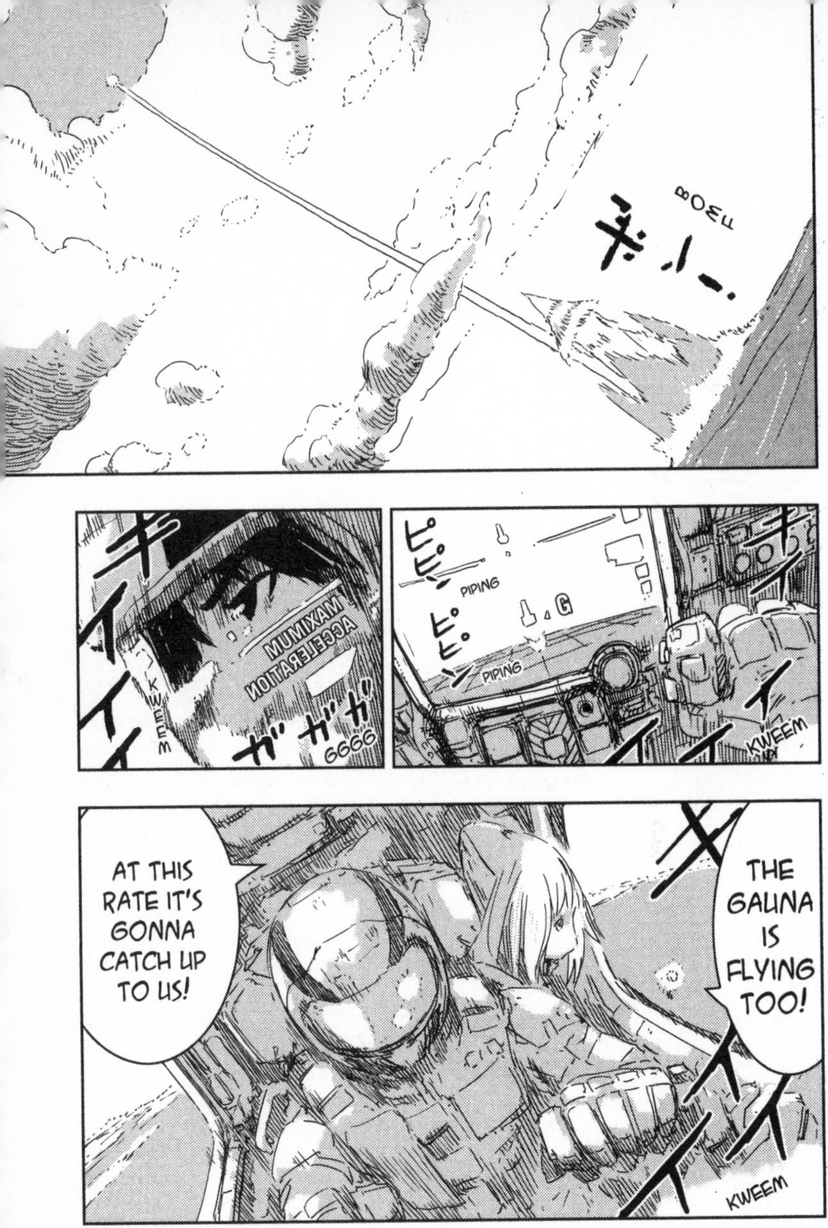
PIPING
PIPING
KWEEM
MAXIMUM ACCELERATION
KWEEM
GGGG
THE GAUNA IS FLYING TOO!
AT THIS RATE IT'S GONNA CATCH UP TO US!
KWEEM

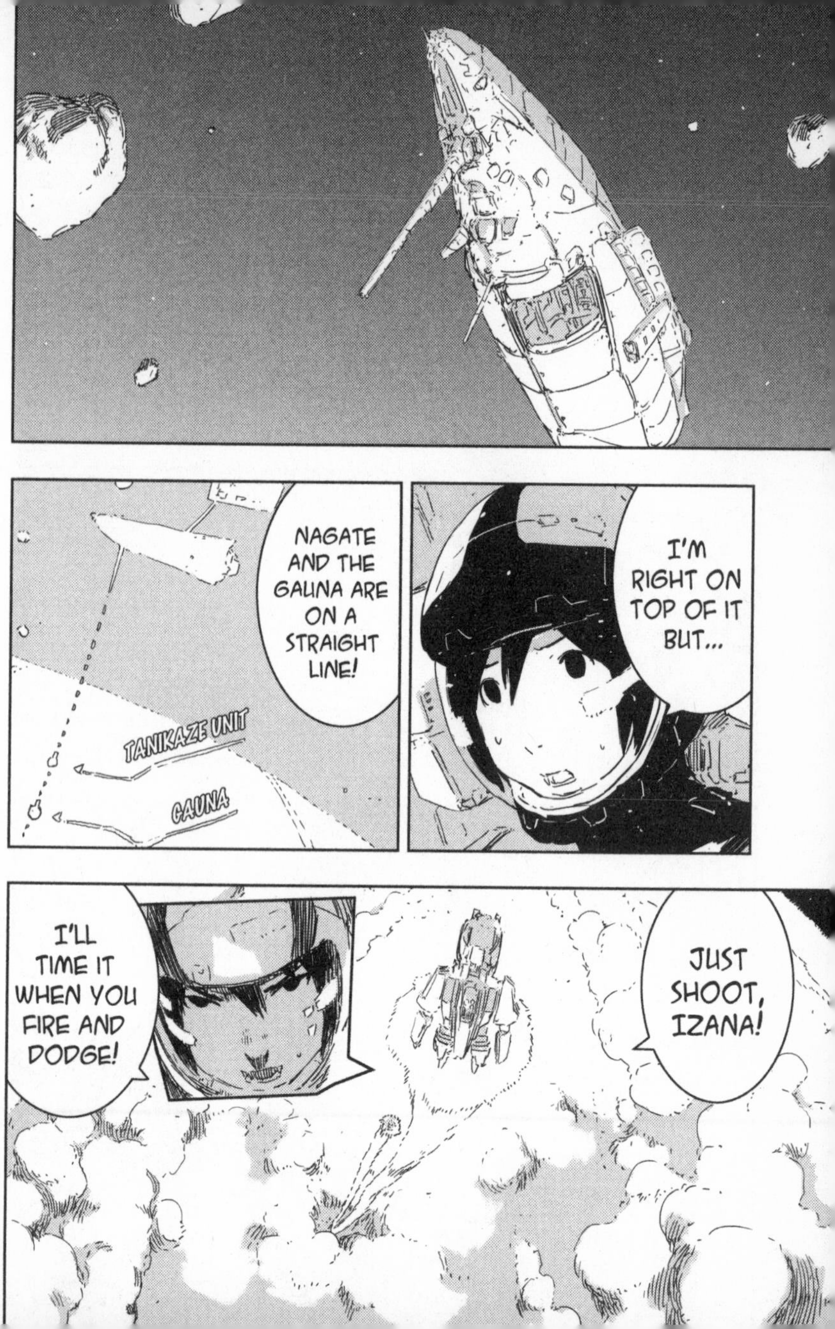
I'M RIGHT ON TOP OF IT BUT...
NAGATE AND THE GAUNA ARE ON A STRAIGHT LINE!
TANIKAZE UNIT
GAUNA
JUST SHOOT, IZANA!
I'LL TIME IT WHEN YOU FIRE AND DODGE!

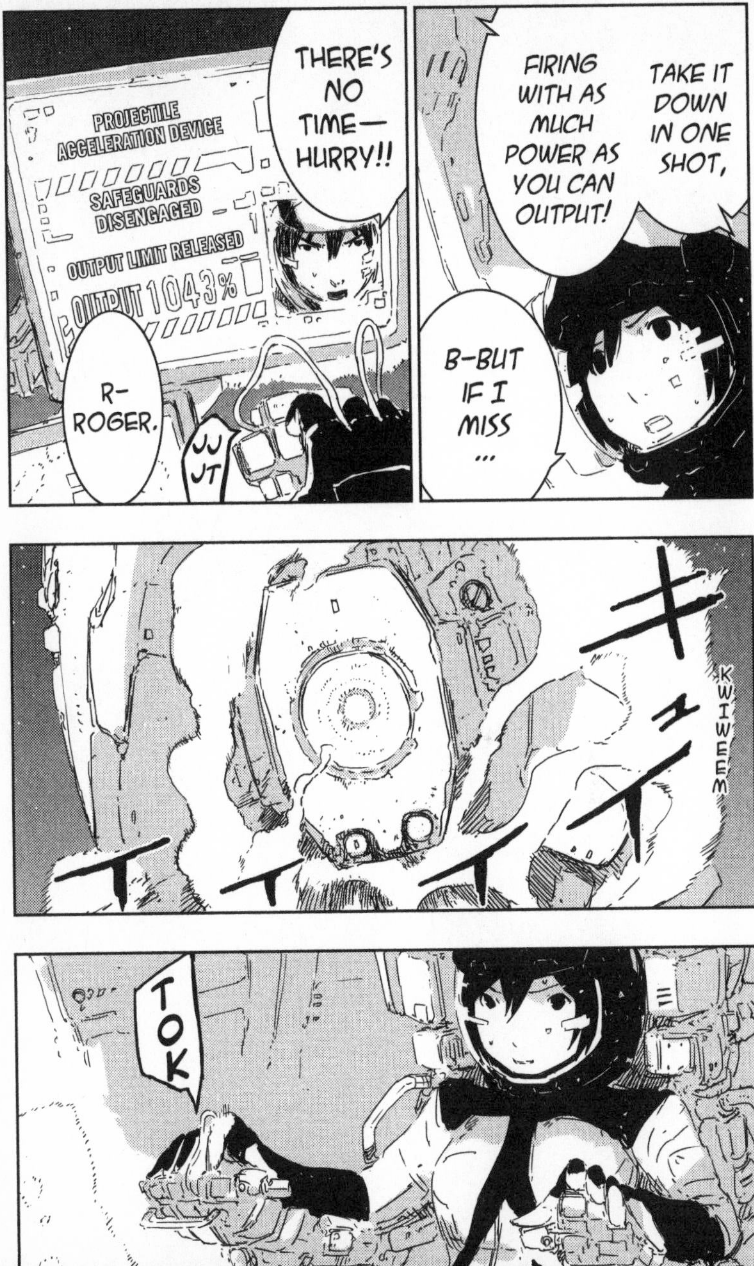
TAKE IT DOWN IN ONE SHOT,
FIRING WITH AS MUCH POWER AS YOU CAN OUTPUT!
B-BUT IF I MISS ...
THERE'S NO TIME— HURRY!!
PROJECTILE ACCELERATION DEVICE
SAFEGUARDS DISENGAGED
OUTPUT LIMIT RELEASED
OUTPUT 1043%
R-ROGER.
JUJUT
KWIWEEM
TOK

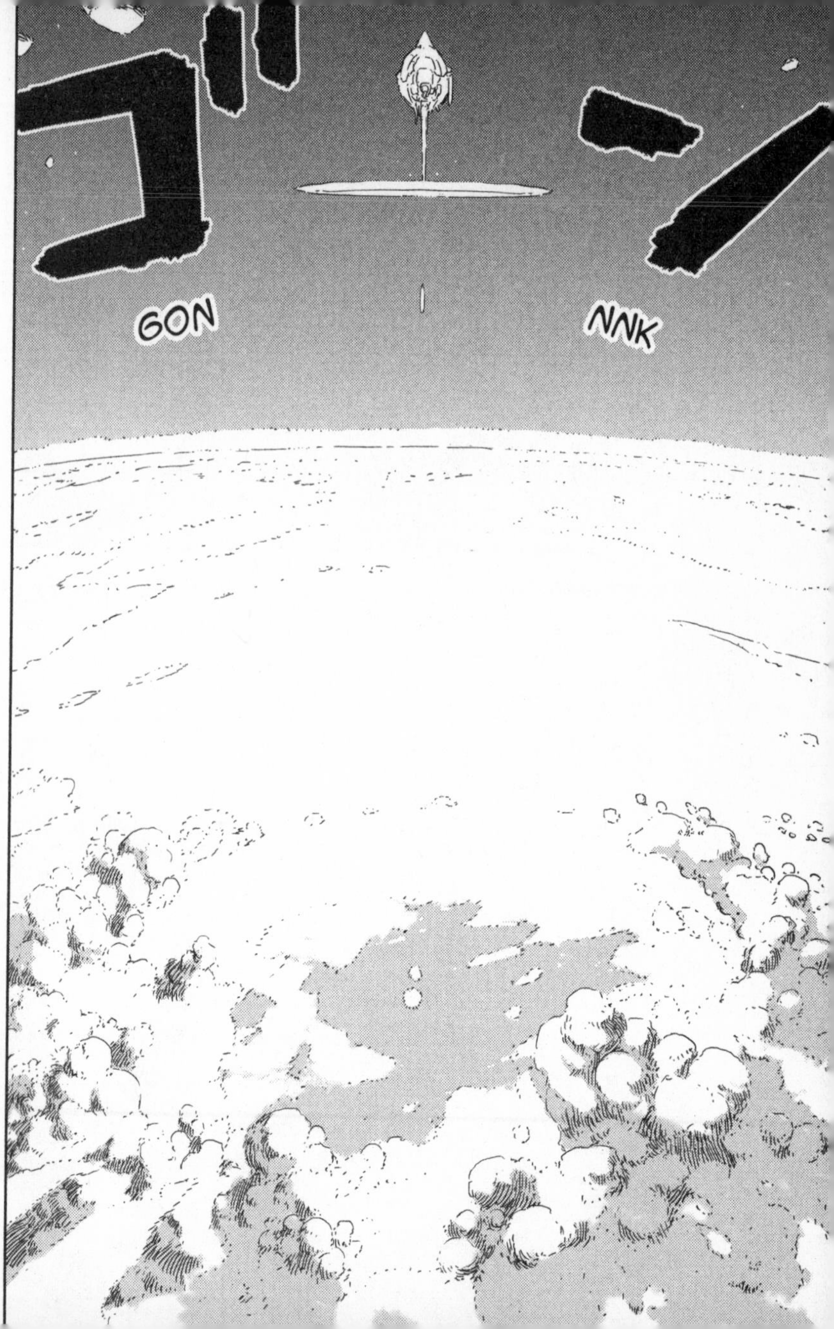
GON
NNK

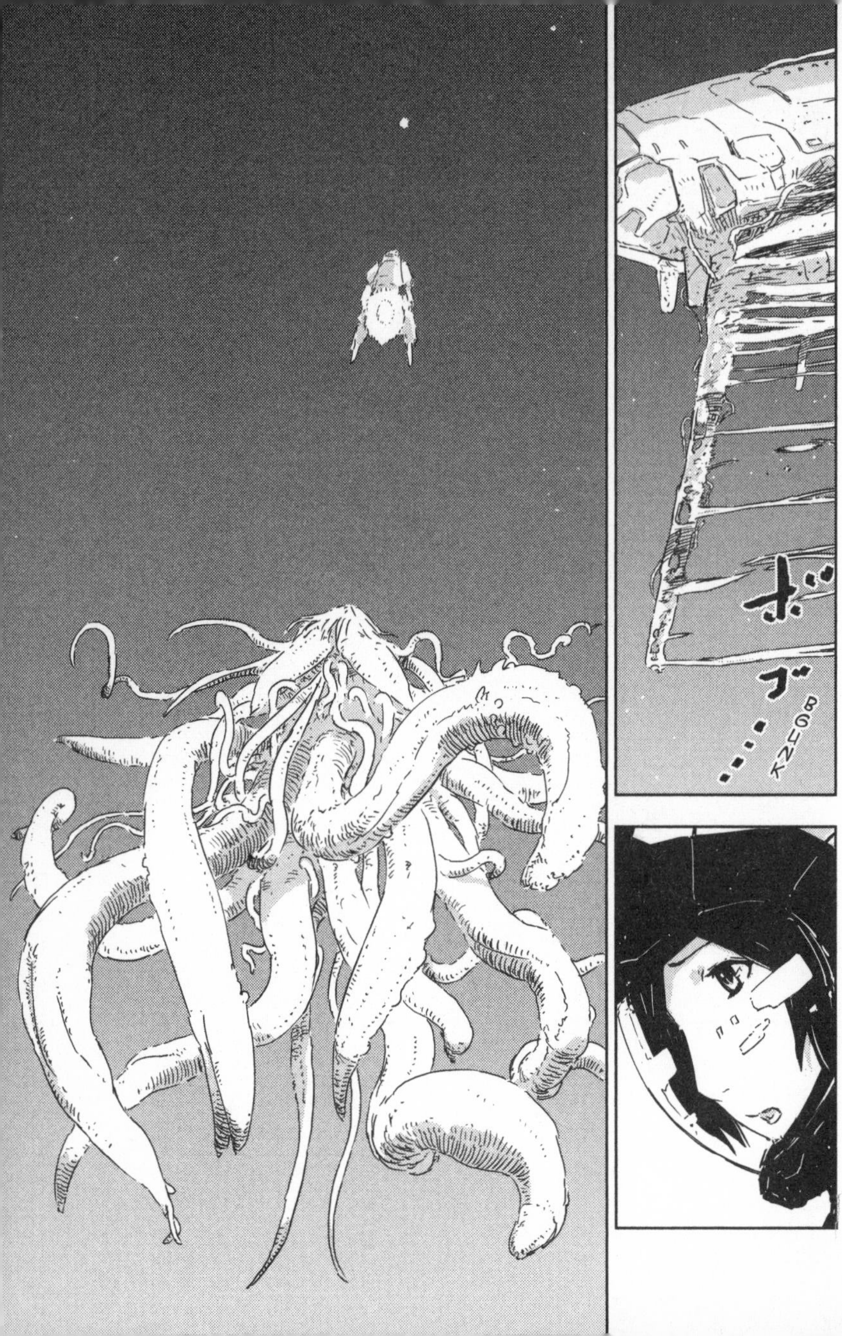
ボゴ……
BGUNK

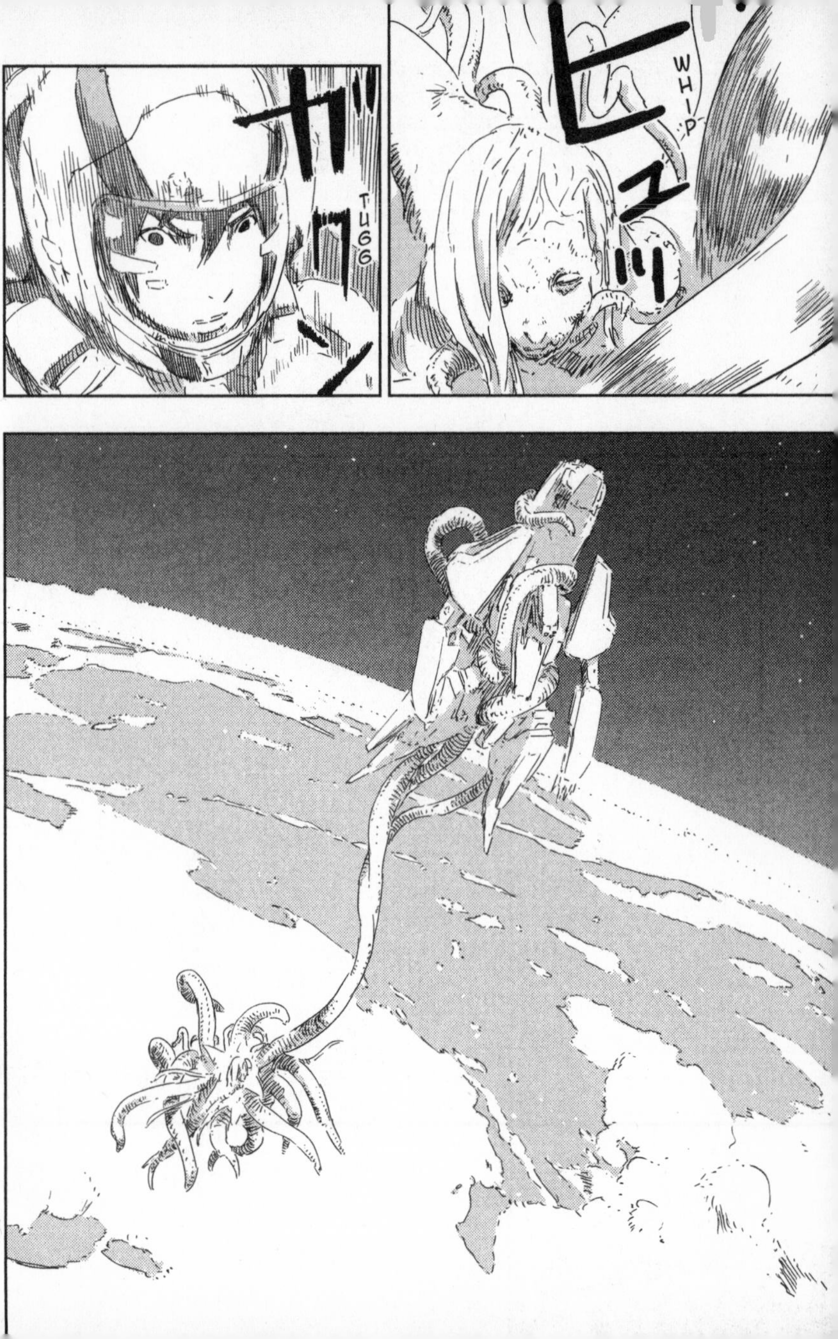
ヒュッ
WHIP
ガッ
TUGG

NA-
GATE.

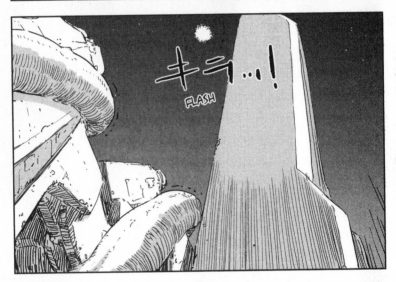

FLASH

PROPULSIVE FUEL FULL ACCESS

WILL I
MAKE
IT?

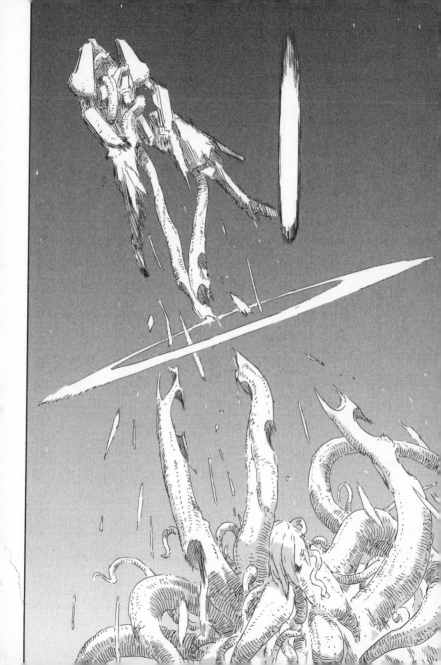

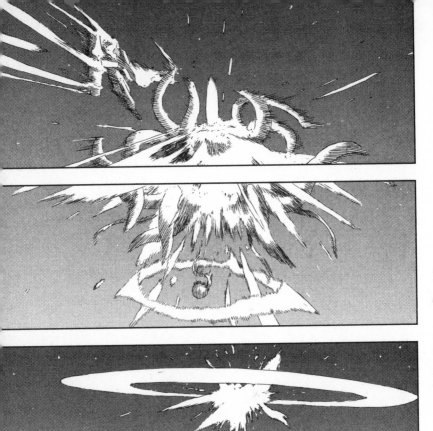

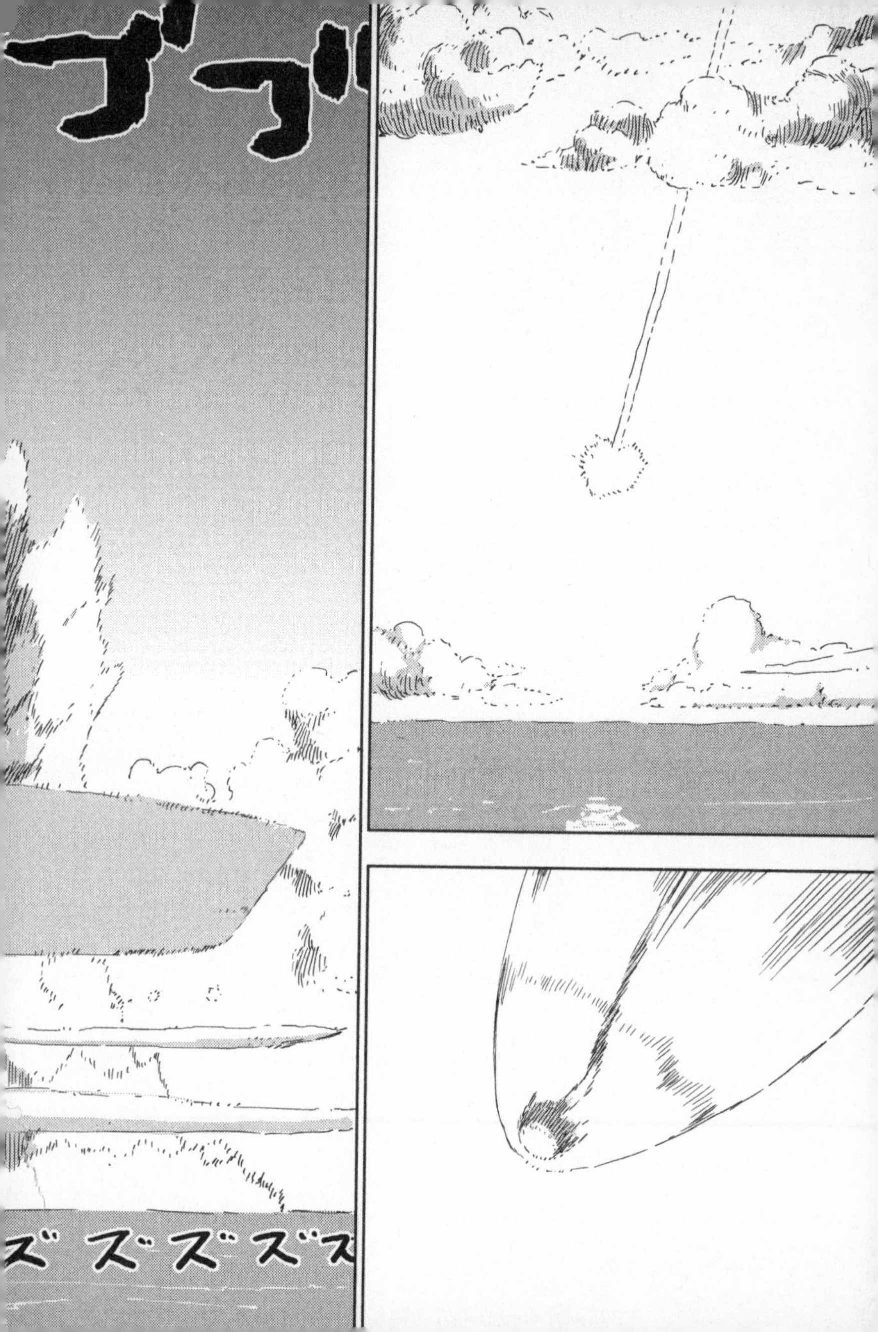
ゴゴ
ズズズズズ

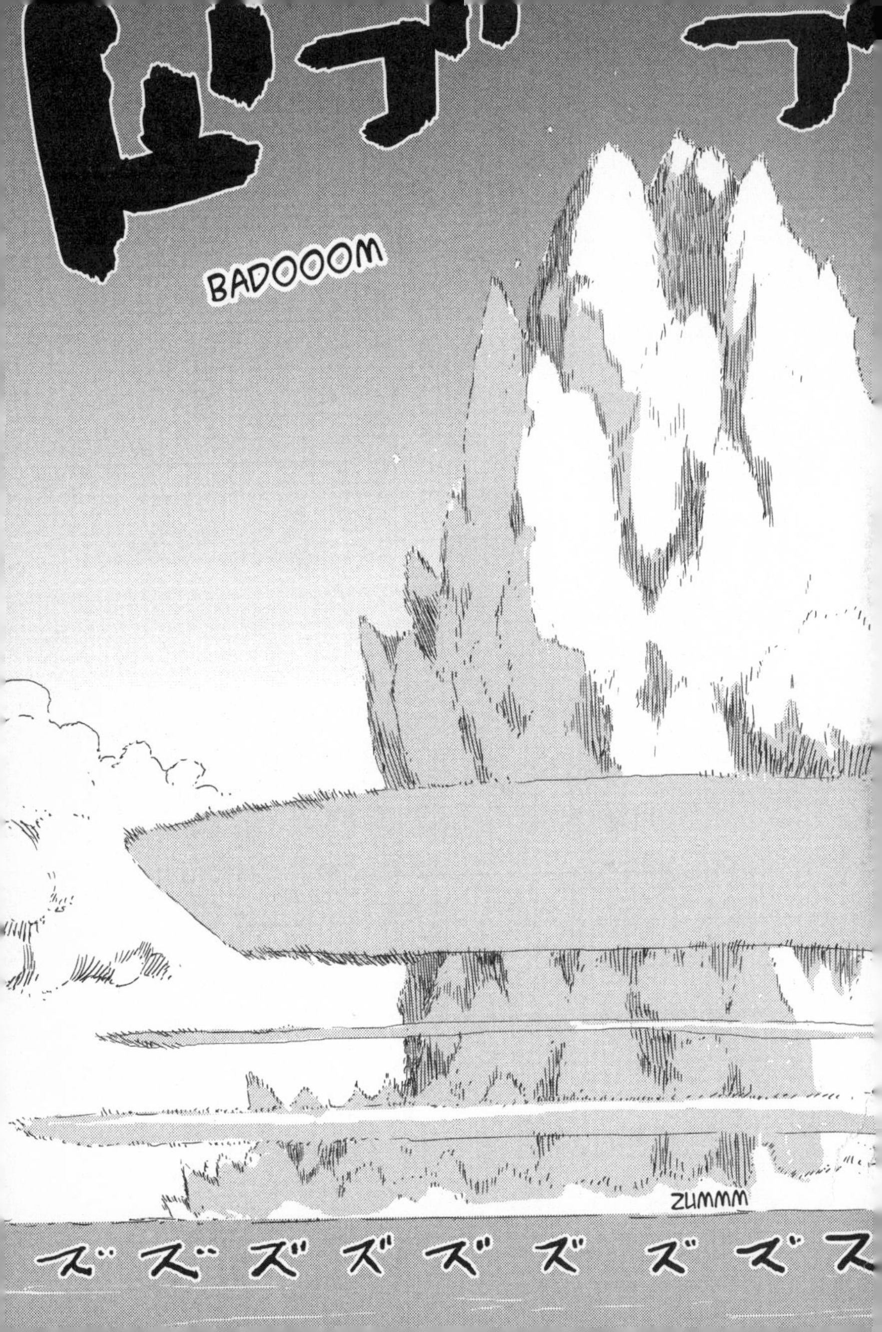
ドドドド
BADOOOM
ZUMMM
ズズズズズズズズズ

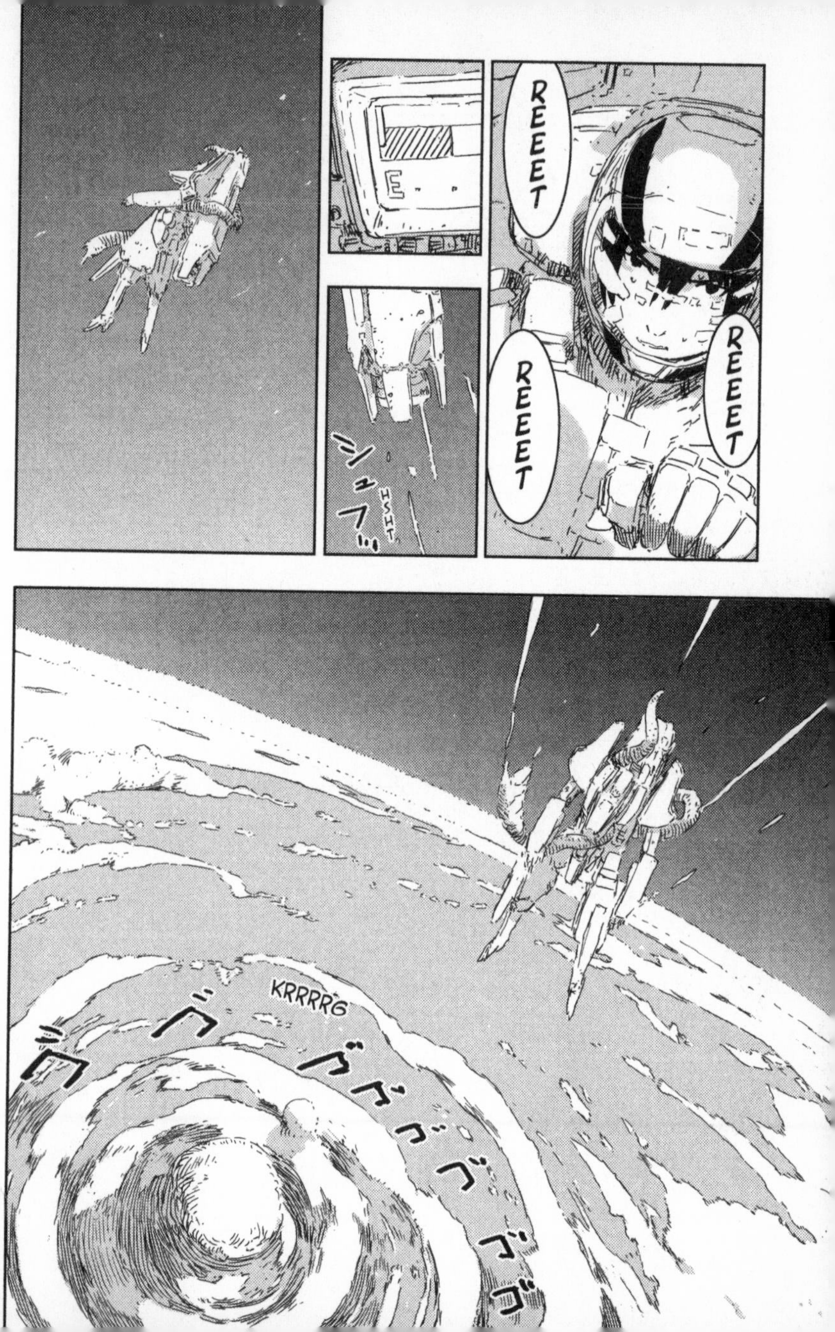

REEEET
REEEET
REEEET
HSHT
KRRRRG

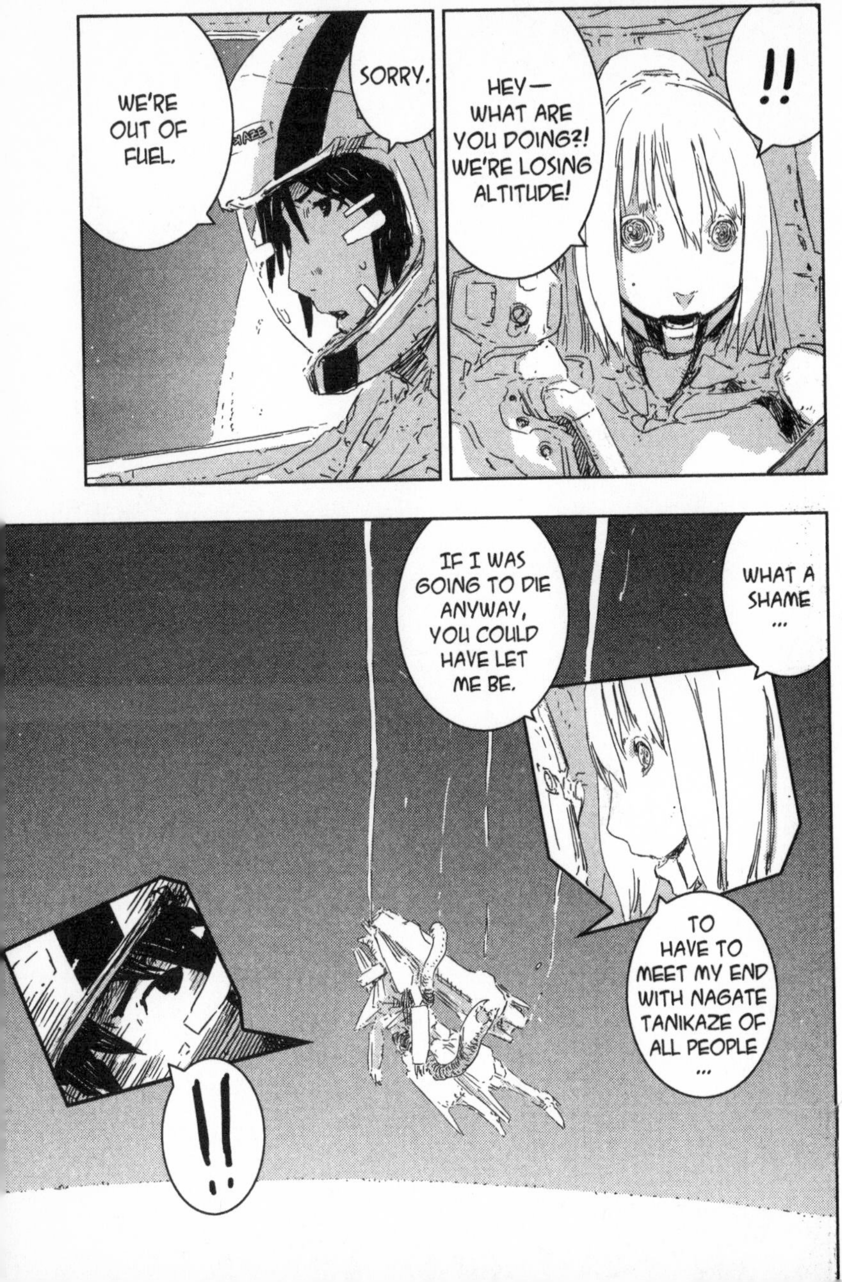
!!
HEY— WHAT ARE YOU DOING?! WE'RE LOSING ALTITUDE!
SORRY.
WE'RE OUT OF FUEL.
WHAT A SHAME ...
IF I WAS GOING TO DIE ANYWAY, YOU COULD HAVE LET ME BE.
TO HAVE TO MEET MY END WITH NAGATE TANIKAZE OF ALL PEOPLE ...
!!

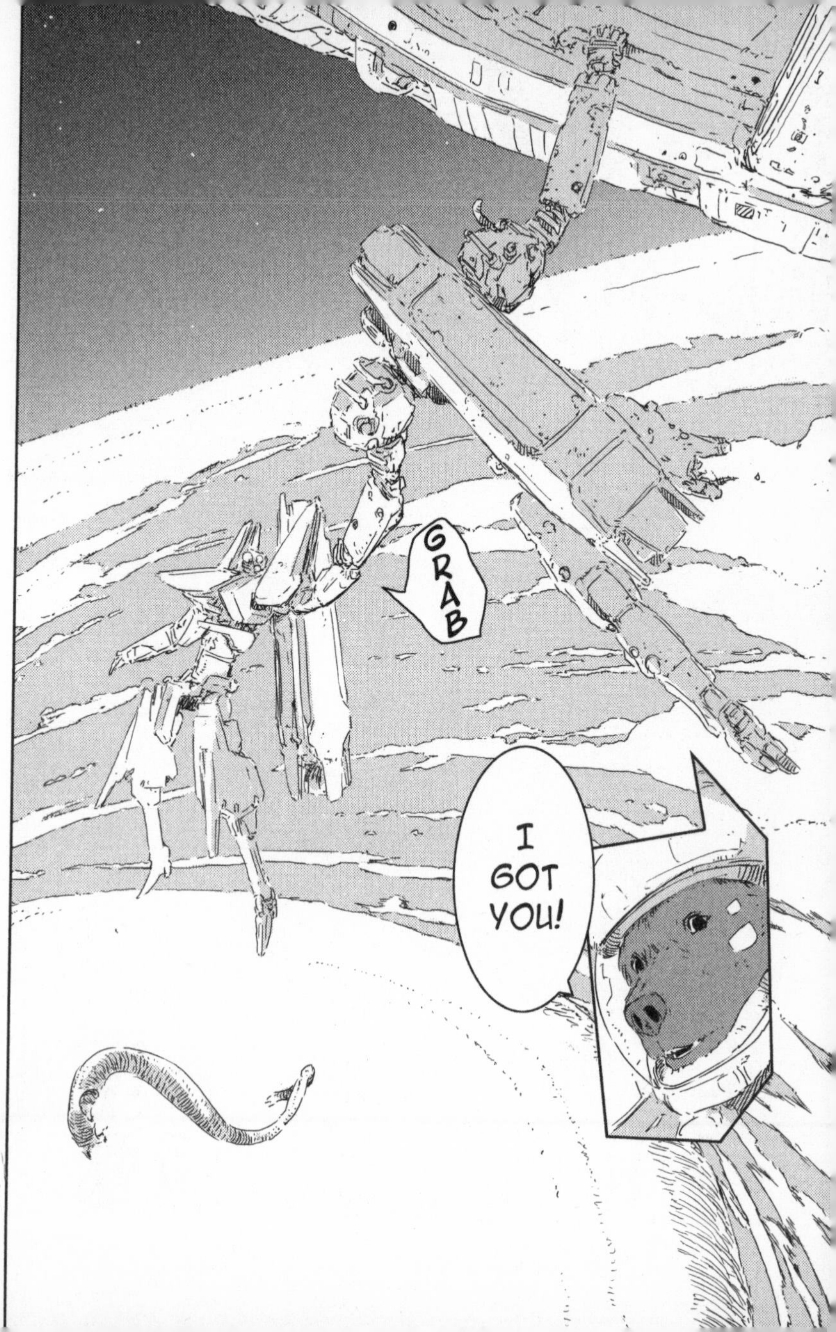
GRAB
I GOT YOU!

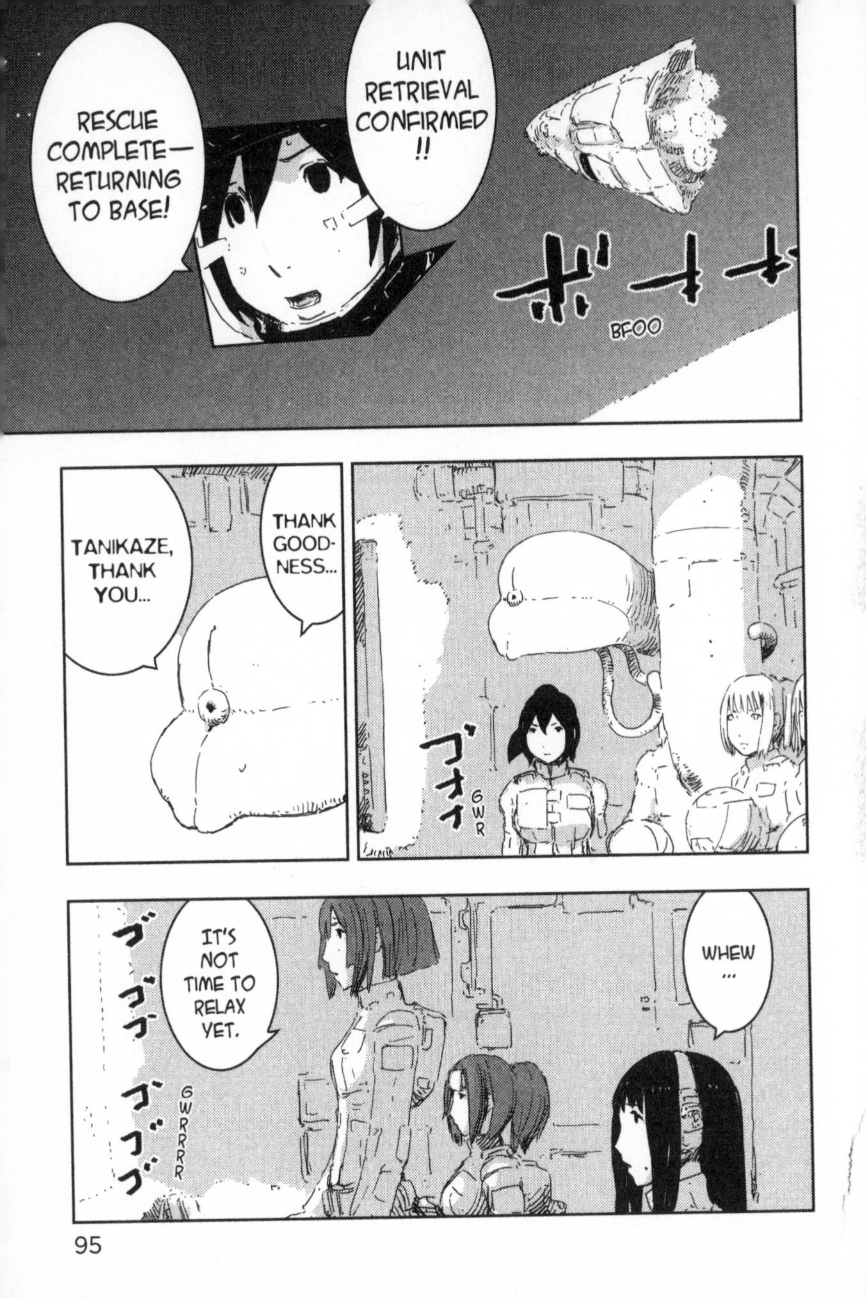
UNIT RETRIEVAL CONFIRMED !!
RESCUE COMPLETE—RETURNING TO BASE!
BFOO
GWR
THANK GOODNESS...
TANIKAZE, THANK YOU...
WHEW ...
IT'S NOT TIME TO RELAX YET.
GWRRRR

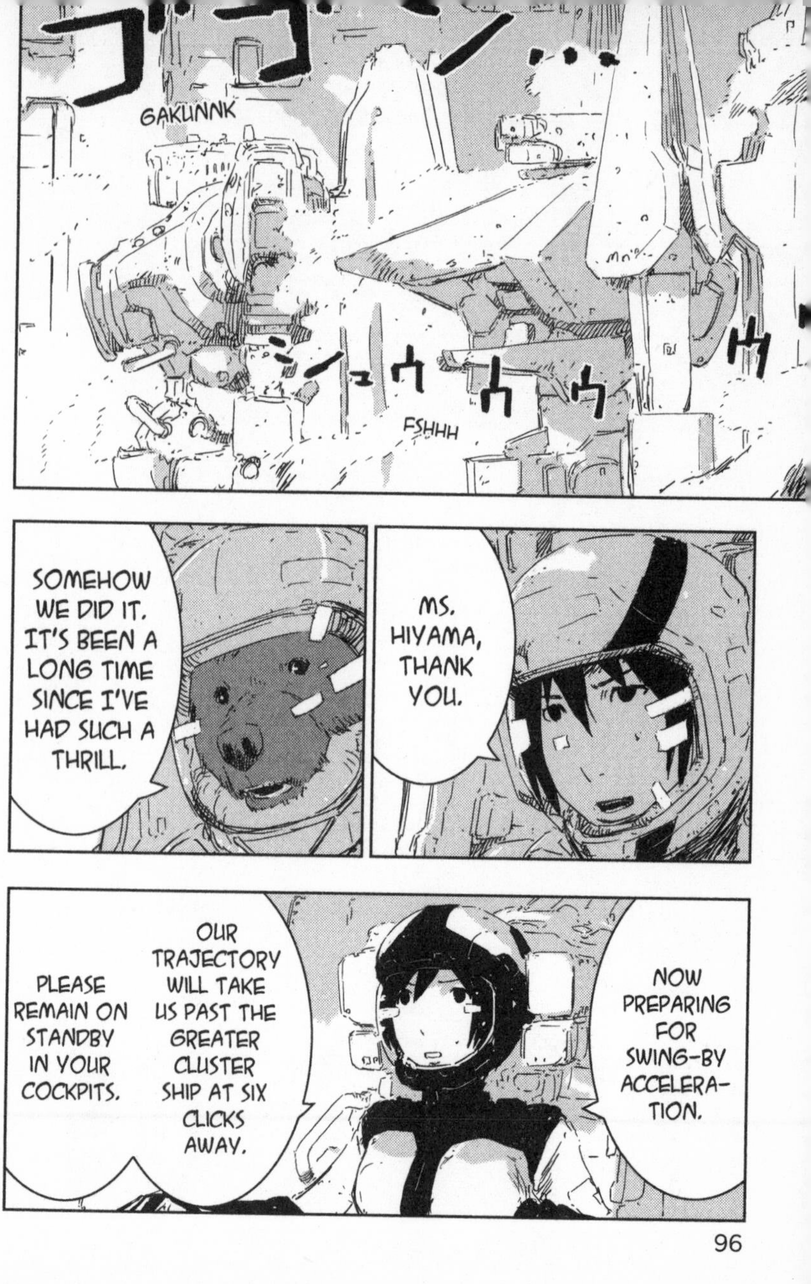
GAKUNNK
FSHHH
MS. HIYAMA, THANK YOU.
SOMEHOW WE DID IT. IT'S BEEN A LONG TIME SINCE I'VE HAD SUCH A THRILL.
NOW PREPARING FOR SWING-BY ACCELERA-TION.
OUR TRAJECTORY WILL TAKE US PAST THE GREATER CLUSTER SHIP AT SIX CLICKS AWAY.
PLEASE REMAIN ON STANDBY IN YOUR COCKPITS.

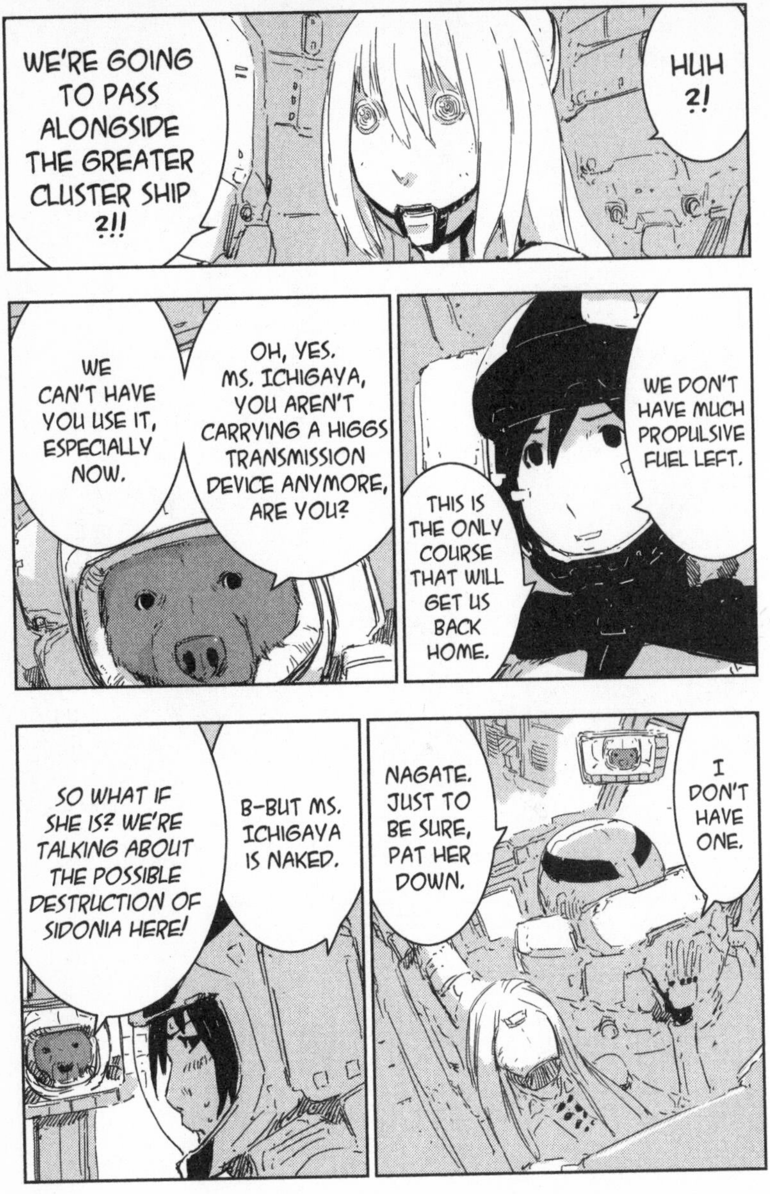
HUH ?!
WE'RE GOING TO PASS ALONGSIDE THE GREATER CLUSTER SHIP ?!!
WE DON'T HAVE MUCH PROPULSIVE FUEL LEFT.
THIS IS THE ONLY COURSE THAT WILL GET US BACK HOME.
OH, YES. MS. ICHIGAYA, YOU AREN'T CARRYING A HIGGS TRANSMISSION DEVICE ANYMORE, ARE YOU?
WE CAN'T HAVE YOU USE IT, ESPECIALLY NOW.
I DON'T HAVE ONE.
NAGATE. JUST TO BE SURE, PAT HER DOWN.
B-BUT MS. ICHIGAYA IS NAKED.
SO WHAT IF SHE IS? WE'RE TALKING ABOUT THE POSSIBLE DESTRUCTION OF SIDONIA HERE!

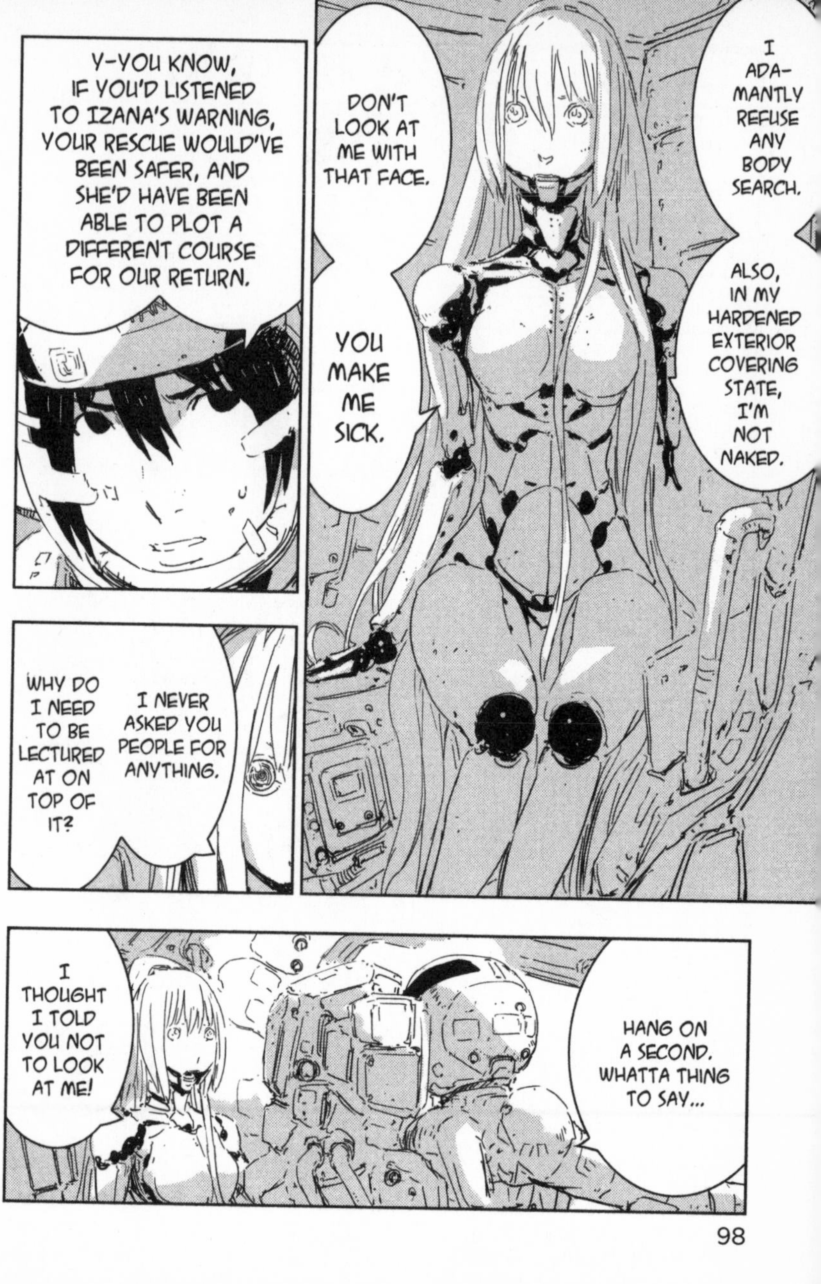
I ADAMANTLY REFUSE ANY BODY SEARCH.
ALSO, IN MY HARDENED EXTERIOR COVERING STATE, I'M NOT NAKED.
DON'T LOOK AT ME WITH THAT FACE.
YOU MAKE ME SICK.
Y-YOU KNOW, IF YOU'D LISTENED TO IZANA'S WARNING, YOUR RESCUE WOULD'VE BEEN SAFER, AND SHE'D HAVE BEEN ABLE TO PLOT A DIFFERENT COURSE FOR OUR RETURN.
I NEVER ASKED YOU PEOPLE FOR ANYTHING.
WHY DO I NEED TO BE LECTURED AT ON TOP OF IT?
HANG ON A SECOND. WHATTA THING TO SAY...
I THOUGHT I TOLD YOU NOT TO LOOK AT ME!

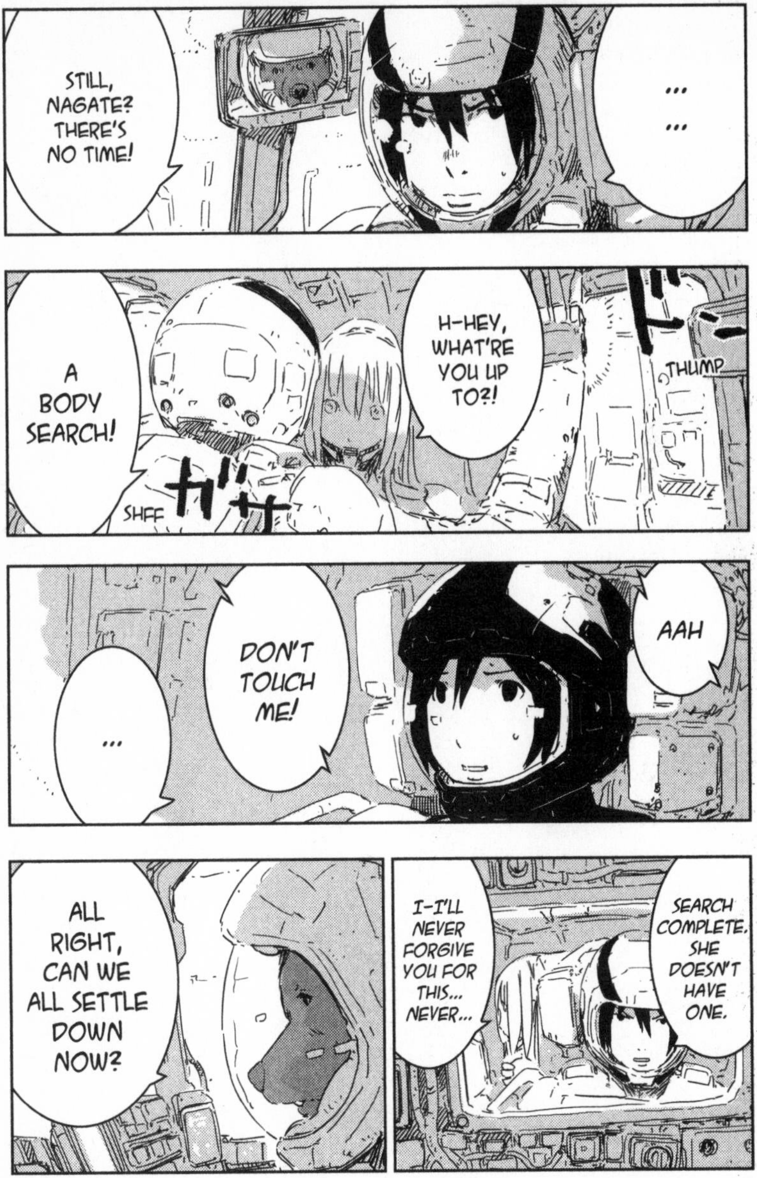
...
...
STILL, NAGATE? THERE'S NO TIME!
THUMP
H-HEY, WHAT'RE YOU UP TO?!
A BODY SEARCH!
SHFF
AAH
DON'T TOUCH ME!
...
SEARCH COMPLETE. SHE DOESN'T HAVE ONE.
I-I'LL NEVER FORGIVE YOU FOR THIS... NEVER...
ALL RIGHT, CAN WE ALL SETTLE DOWN NOW?

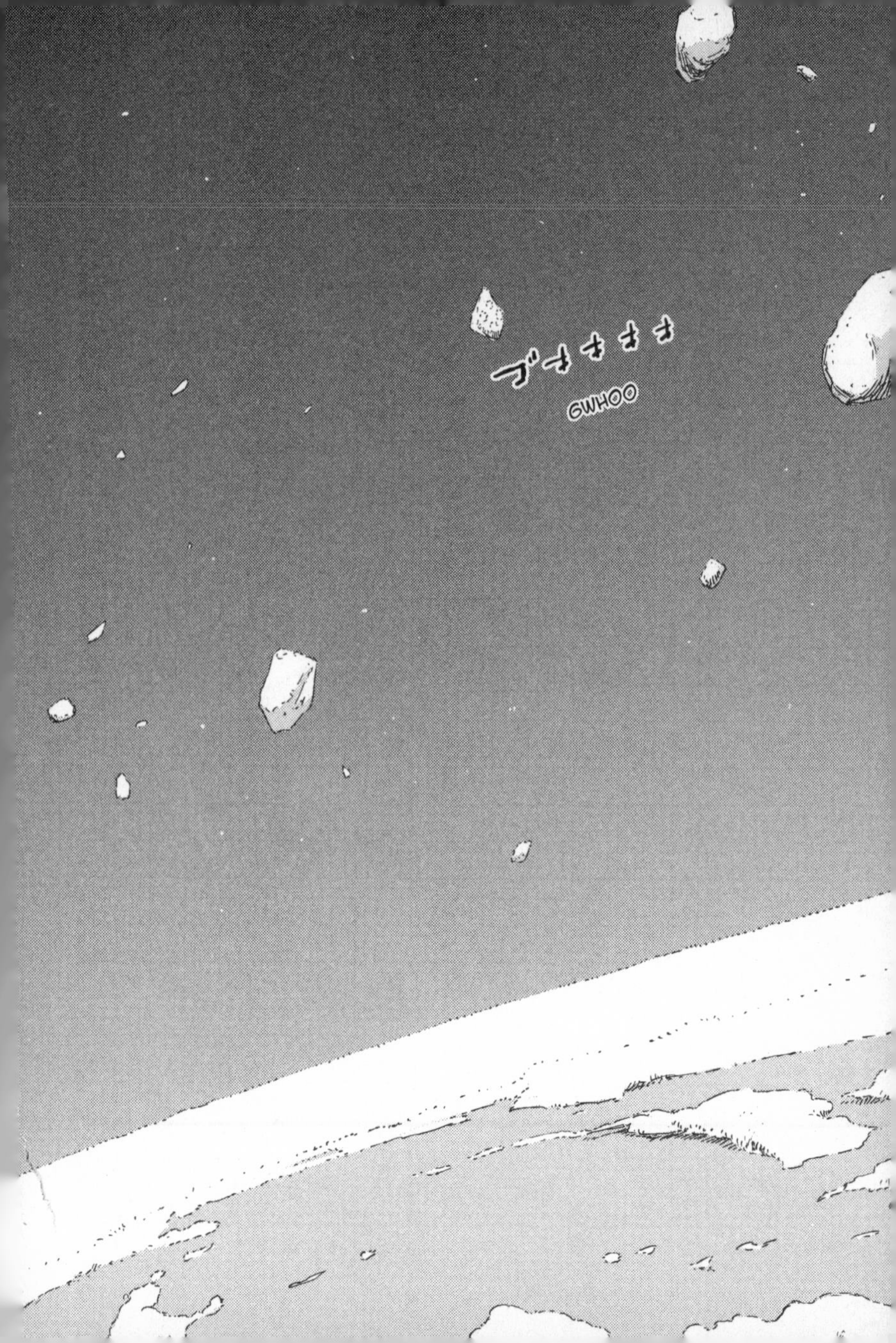
ゴォォォォ
GWHOO

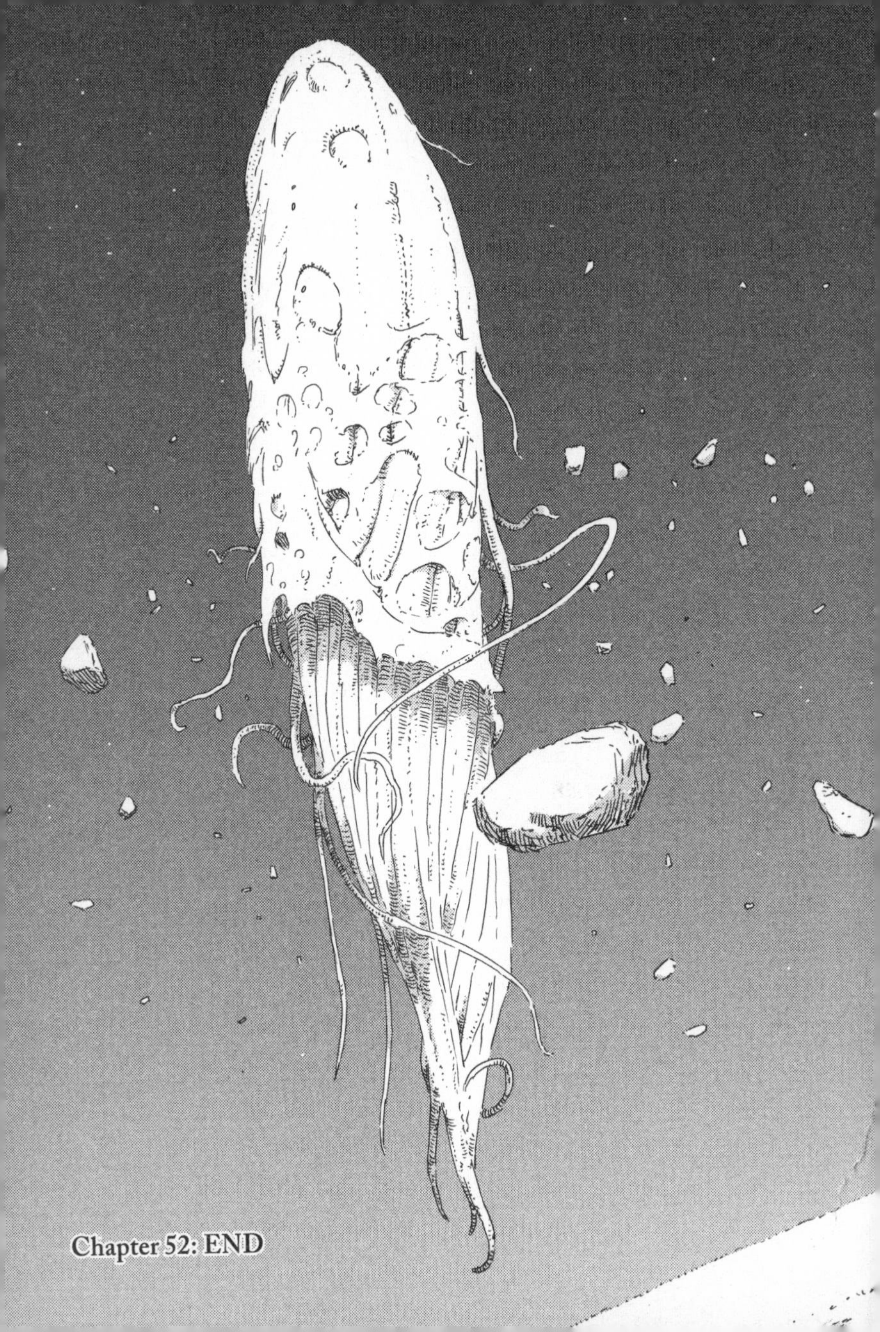
Chapter 52: END

シドニアの騎士

KNIGHTS OF SIDONIA

Chapter 53: The Greater Cluster Ship's Presence

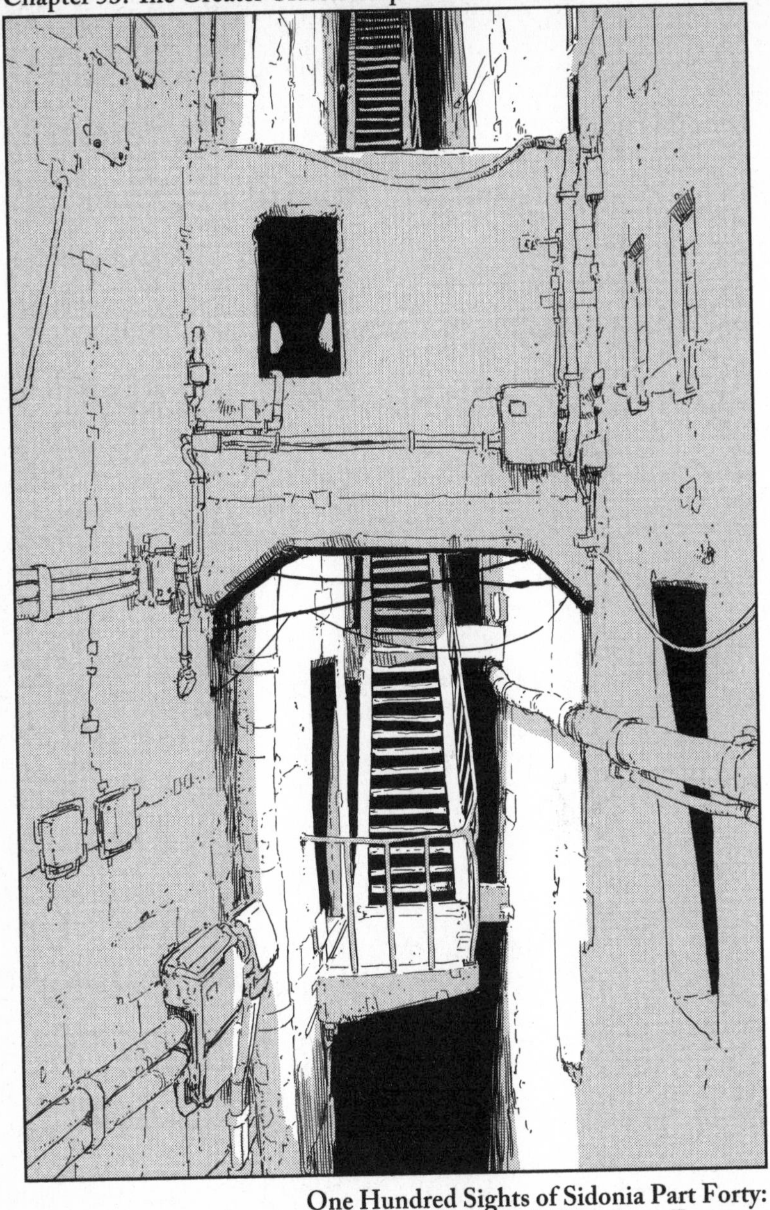

One Hundred Sights of Sidonia Part Forty:
Crew Hall No. 8 Rear Entrance

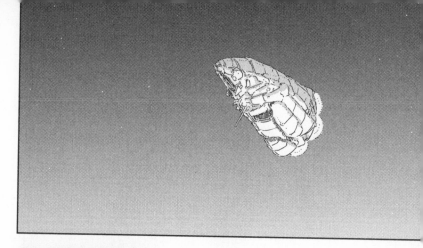

ズズ・・
WHZZ

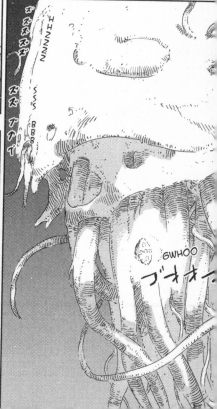

ゴズズギズズアァイ
HHZZZZ
BBB

GWHOO
ブォオー

THE
UMBRELLA'S
OPENING...

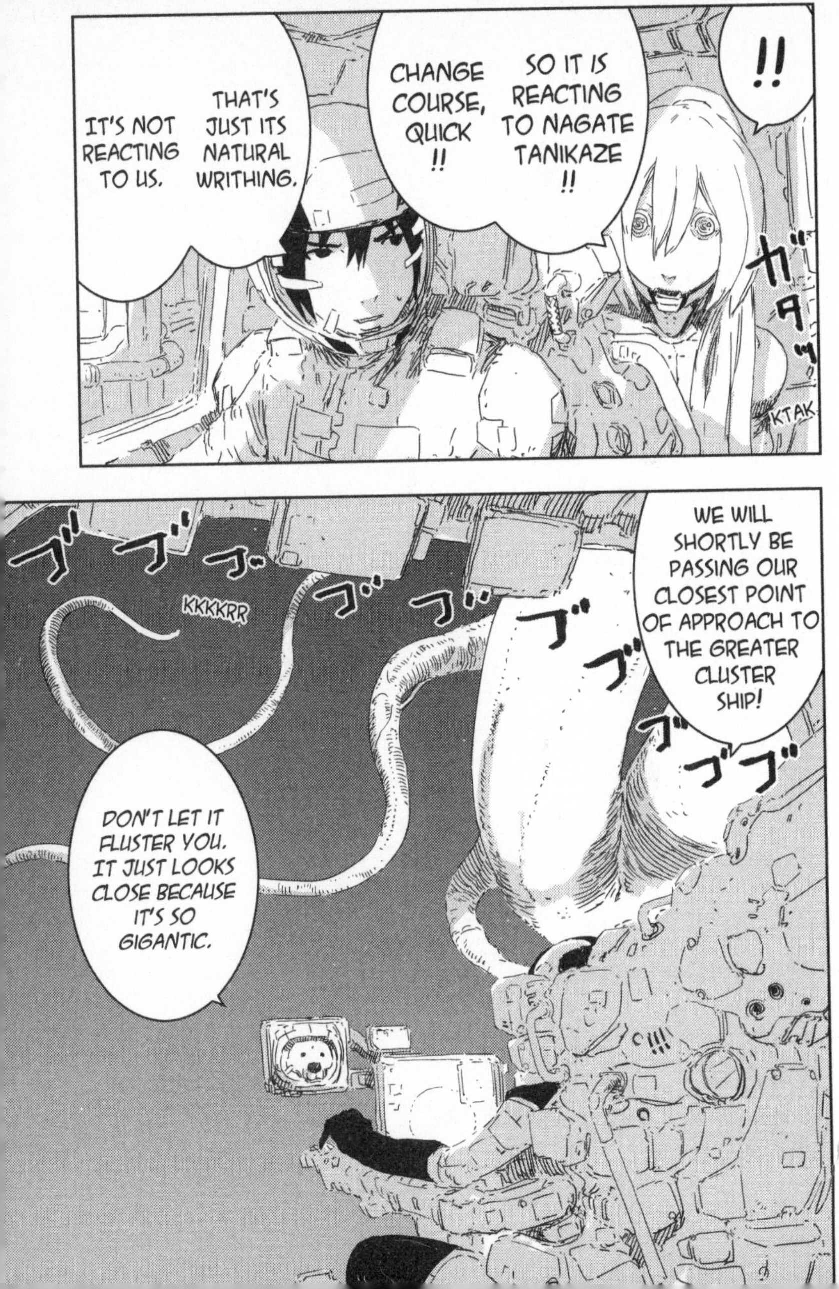
!!
SO IT IS REACTING TO NAGATE TANIKAZE !!
CHANGE COURSE, QUICK !!
THAT'S JUST ITS NATURAL WRITHING.
IT'S NOT REACTING TO US.
ガタッ
KTAK
WE WILL SHORTLY BE PASSING OUR CLOSEST POINT OF APPROACH TO THE GREATER CLUSTER SHIP!
KKKKRR
DON'T LET IT FLUSTER YOU. IT JUST LOOKS CLOSE BECAUSE IT'S SO GIGANTIC.
!!!

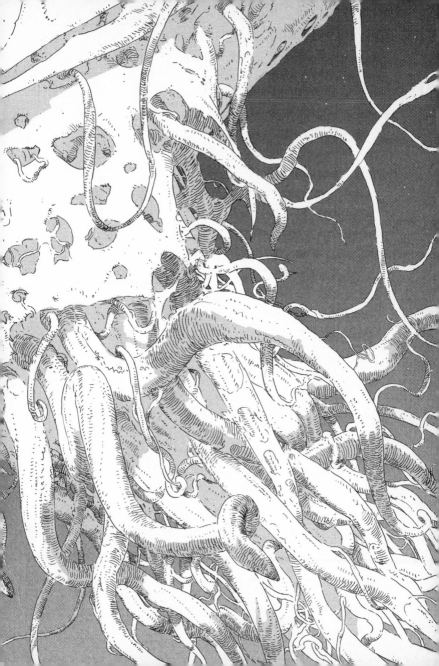

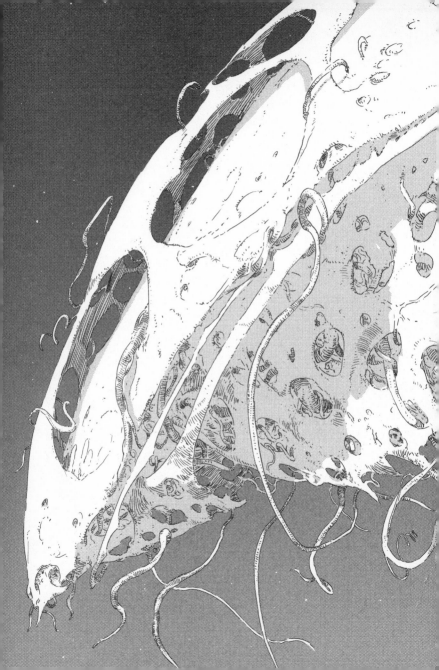

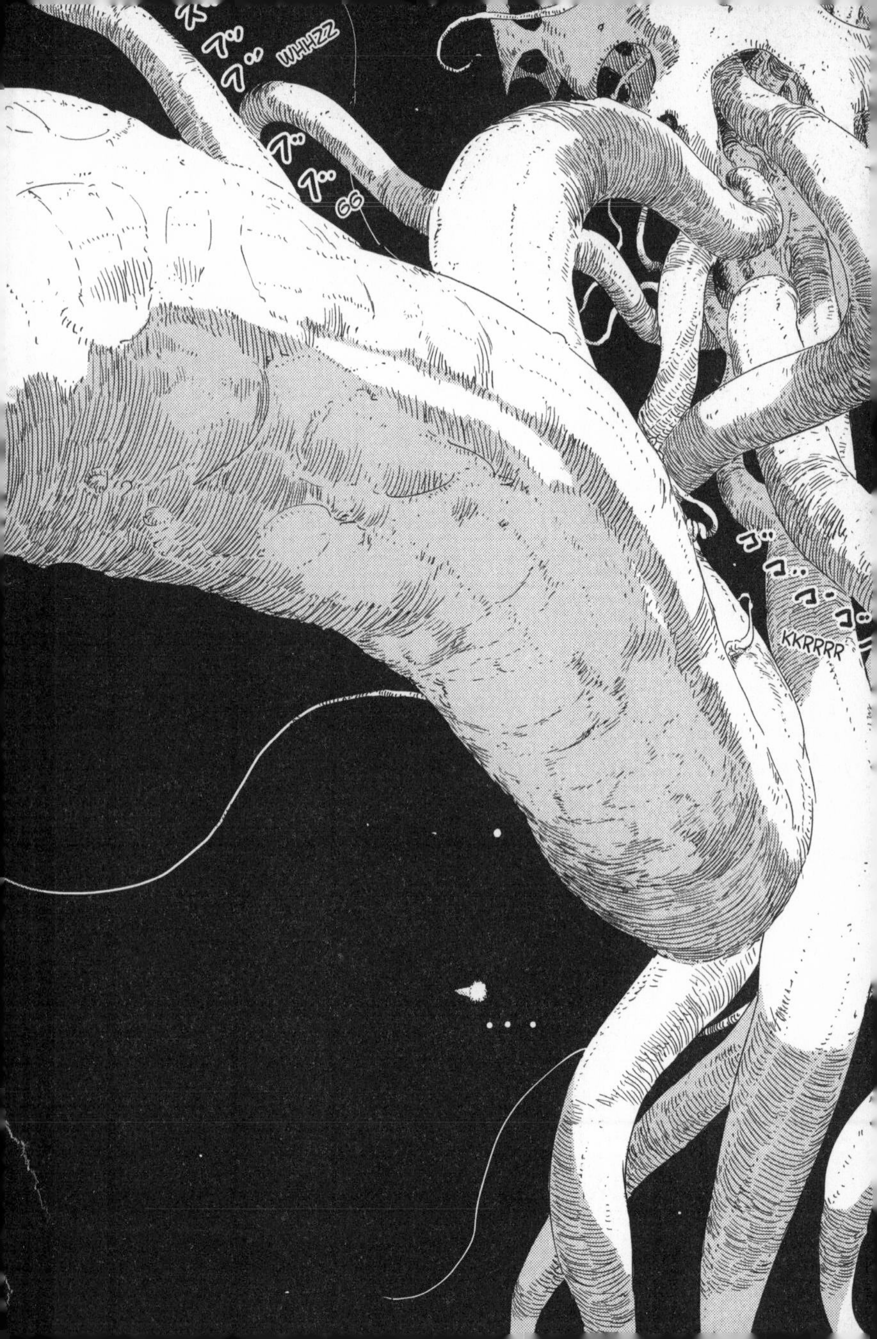
WHZZ
KKRRRR

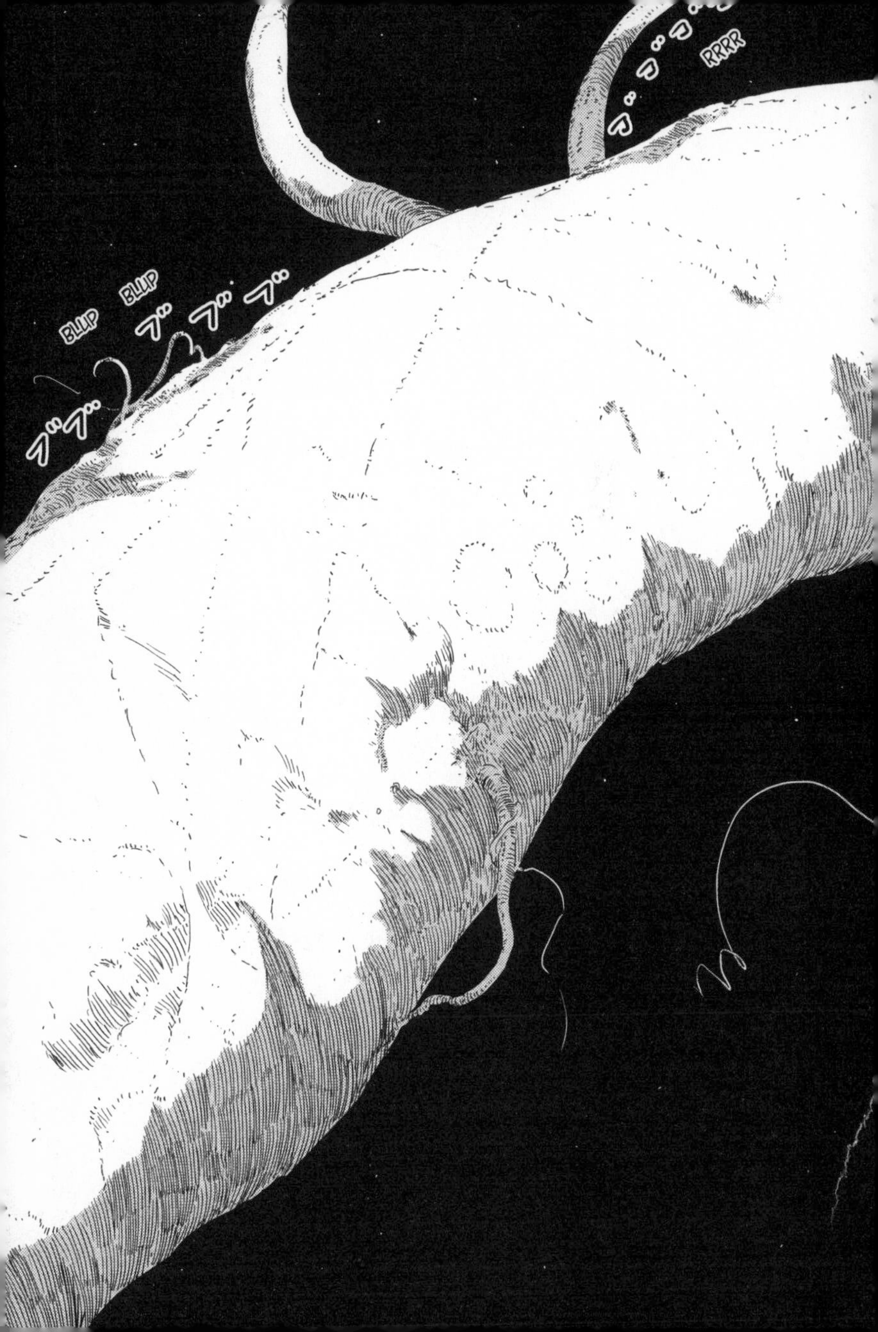
ブ゛ブ゛ブ゛ブ゛
RRRR
ブブブブ
BLIP BLIP

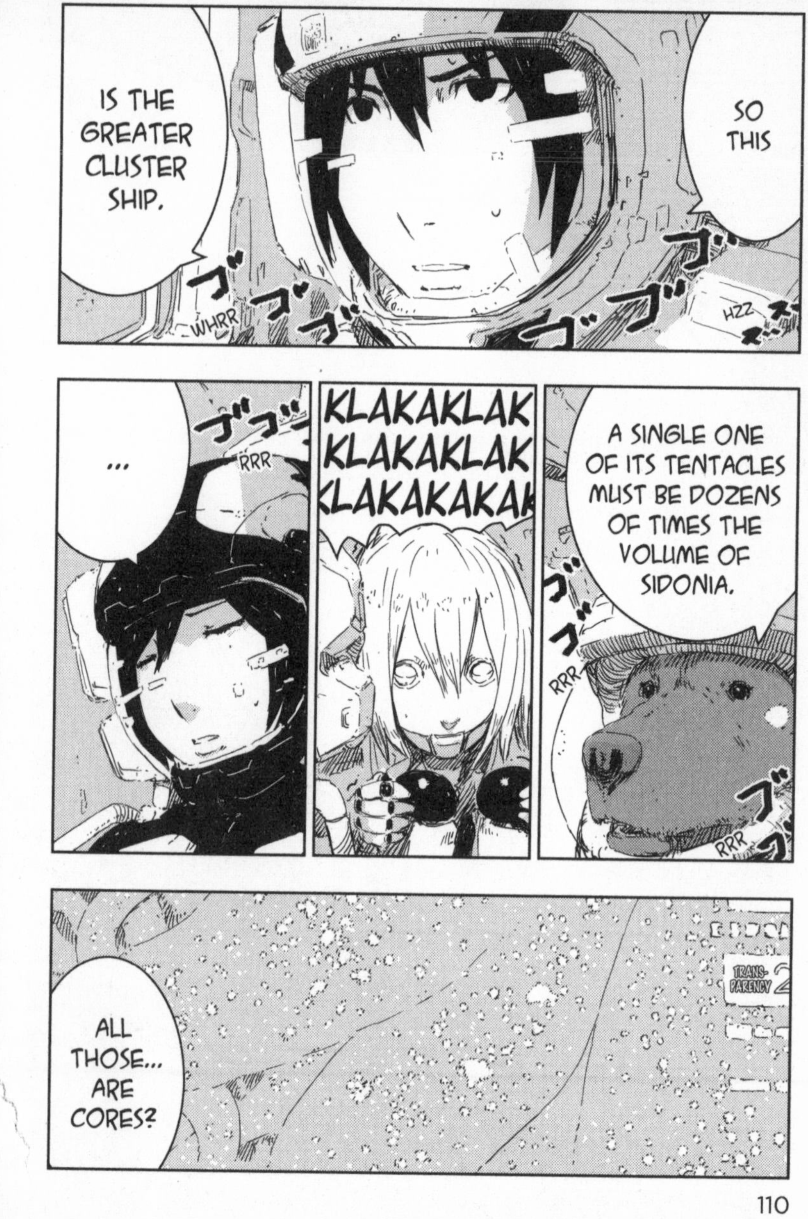
SO THIS
IS THE GREATER CLUSTER SHIP.
WHRR
HZZ
A SINGLE ONE OF ITS TENTACLES MUST BE DOZENS OF TIMES THE VOLUME OF SIDONIA.
RRR
RRR
KLAKAKLAK KLAKAKLAK KLAKAKAKAK
...
RRR
TRANS-PARENCY 2
ALL THOSE... ARE CORES?

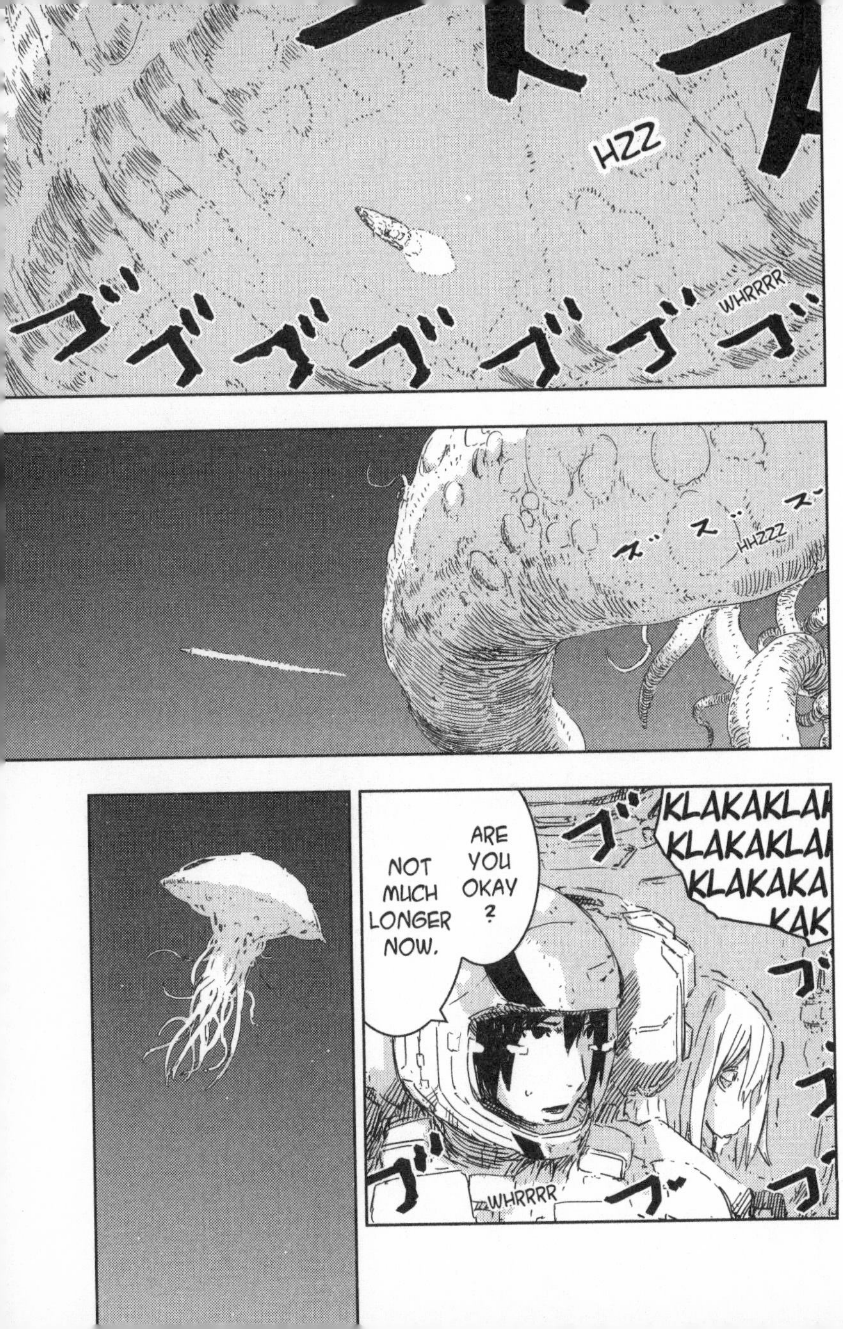
HZZ
WHRRRR
HHZZZ
KLAKAKLA
KLAKAKLA
KLAKAKA
KAK
ARE YOU OKAY?
NOT MUCH LONGER NOW.
WHRRRR

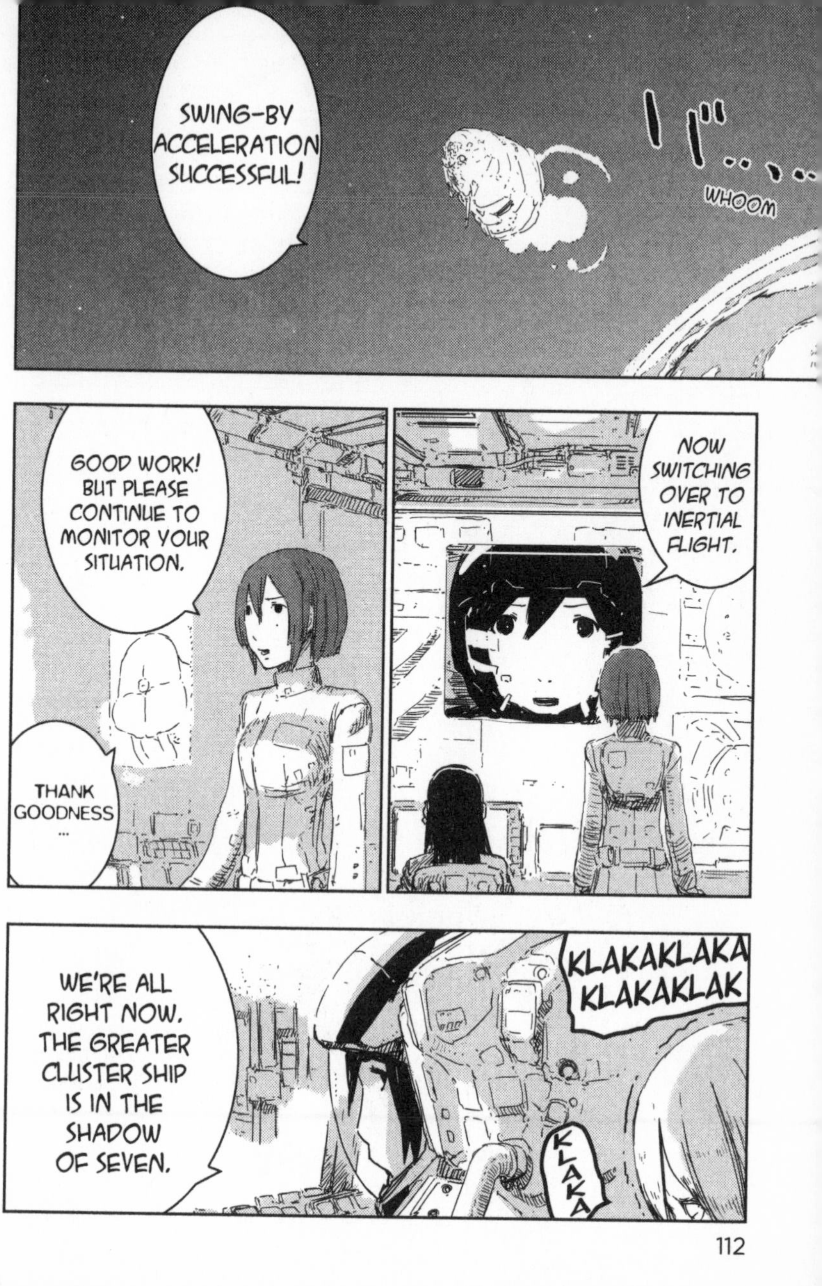
WHOOM
SWING-BY ACCELERATION SUCCESSFUL!
NOW SWITCHING OVER TO INERTIAL FLIGHT.
GOOD WORK! BUT PLEASE CONTINUE TO MONITOR YOUR SITUATION.
THANK GOODNESS …
KLAKAKLAKA KLAKAKLAK
WE'RE ALL RIGHT NOW. THE GREATER CLUSTER SHIP IS IN THE SHADOW OF SEVEN.
KLAKA

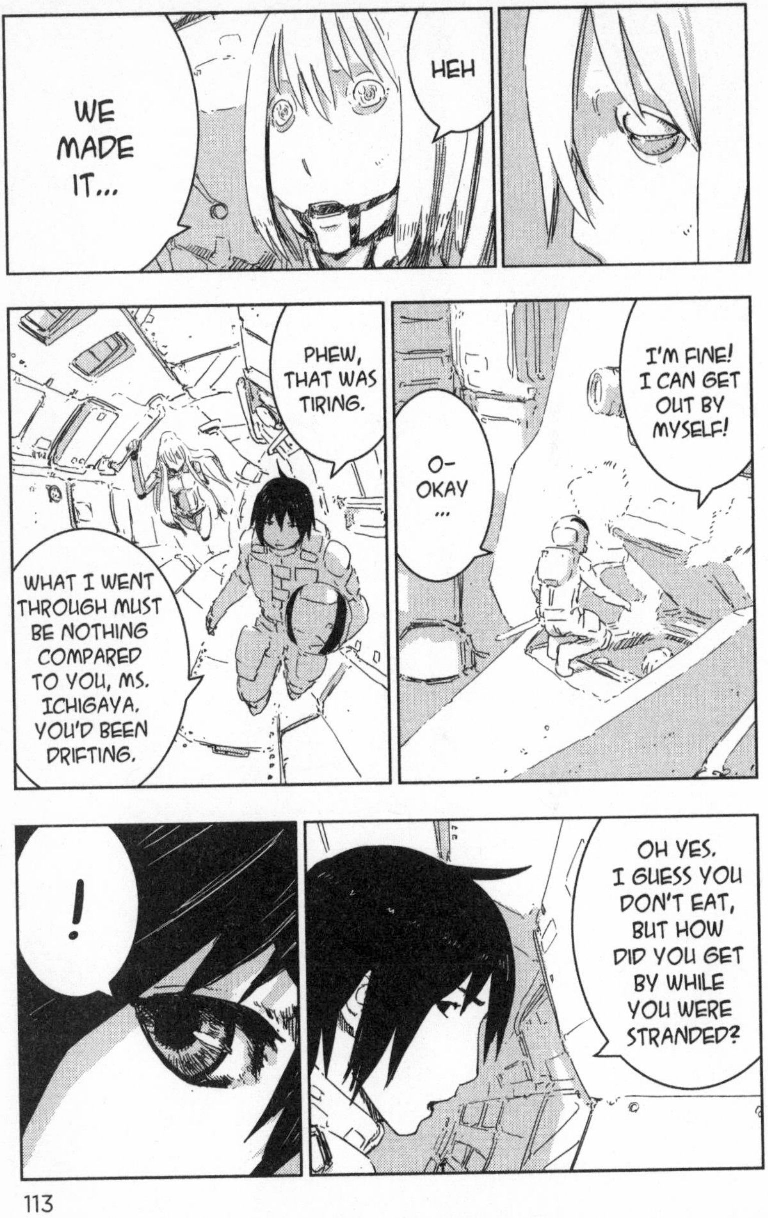

HEH
WE MADE IT...
I'M FINE! I CAN GET OUT BY MYSELF!
O-OKAY...
PHEW, THAT WAS TIRING.
WHAT I WENT THROUGH MUST BE NOTHING COMPARED TO YOU, MS. ICHIGAYA. YOU'D BEEN DRIFTING.
OH YES. I GUESS YOU DON'T EAT, BUT HOW DID YOU GET BY WHILE YOU WERE STRANDED?
!

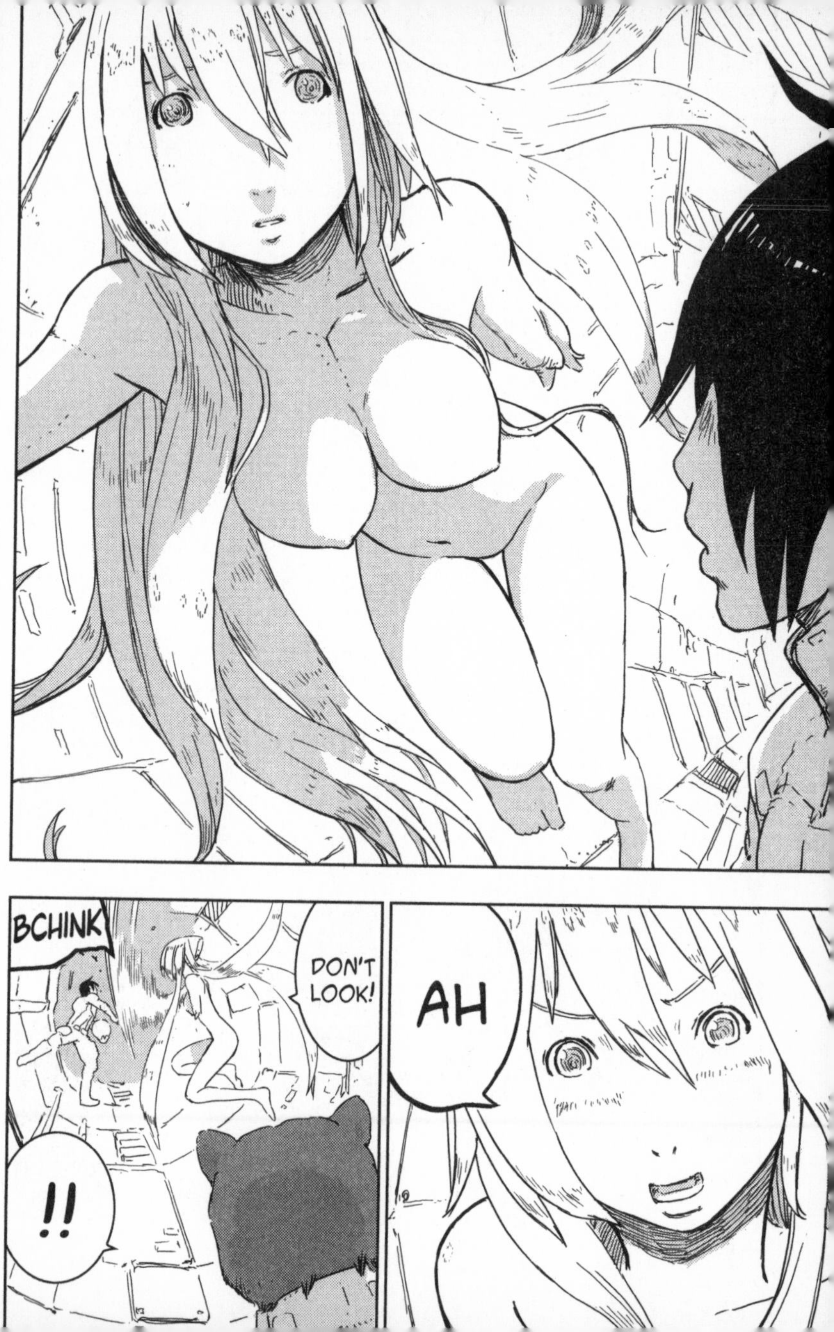
AH
BCHINK
DON'T LOOK!
!!

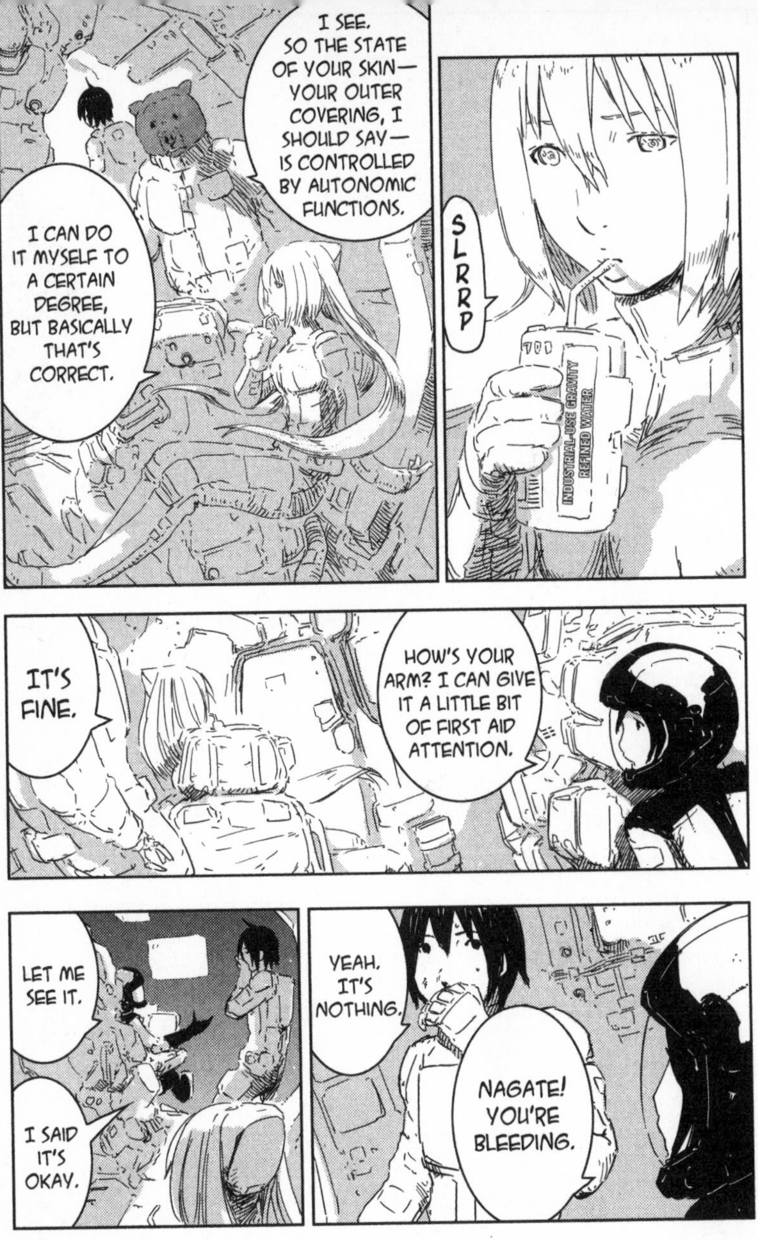
SLRRP
INDUSTRIAL-USE GRAVITY
REFINED WATER
I SEE. SO THE STATE OF YOUR SKIN— YOUR OUTER COVERING, I SHOULD SAY— IS CONTROLLED BY AUTONOMIC FUNCTIONS.
I CAN DO IT MYSELF TO A CERTAIN DEGREE, BUT BASICALLY THAT'S CORRECT.
HOW'S YOUR ARM? I CAN GIVE IT A LITTLE BIT OF FIRST AID ATTENTION.
IT'S FINE.
NAGATE! YOU'RE BLEEDING.
YEAH, IT'S NOTHING.
LET ME SEE IT.
I SAID IT'S OKAY.

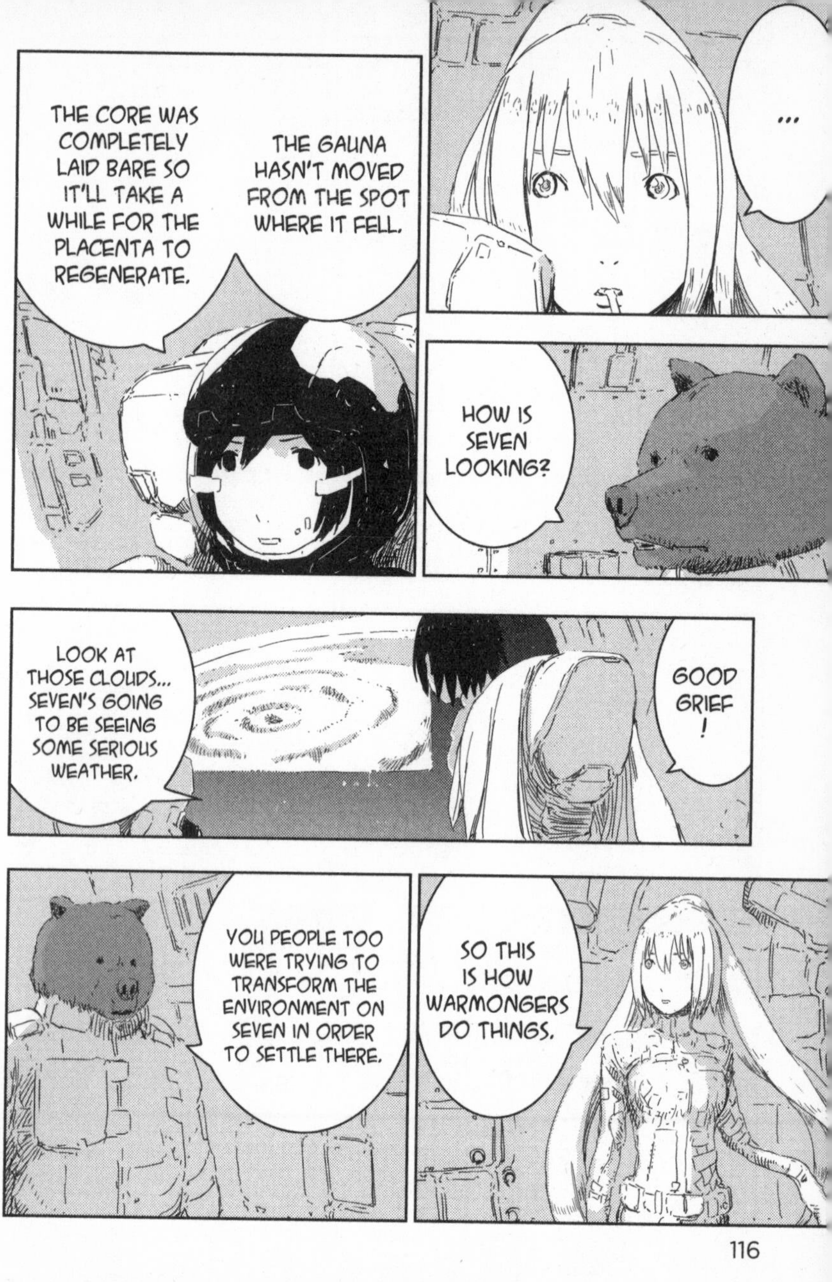
...
HOW IS SEVEN LOOKING?
THE GAUNA HASN'T MOVED FROM THE SPOT WHERE IT FELL.
THE CORE WAS COMPLETELY LAID BARE SO IT'LL TAKE A WHILE FOR THE PLACENTA TO REGENERATE.
GOOD GRIEF!
LOOK AT THOSE CLOUDS... SEVEN'S GOING TO BE SEEING SOME SERIOUS WEATHER.
SO THIS IS HOW WARMONGERS DO THINGS.
YOU PEOPLE TOO WERE TRYING TO TRANSFORM THE ENVIRONMENT ON SEVEN IN ORDER TO SETTLE THERE.

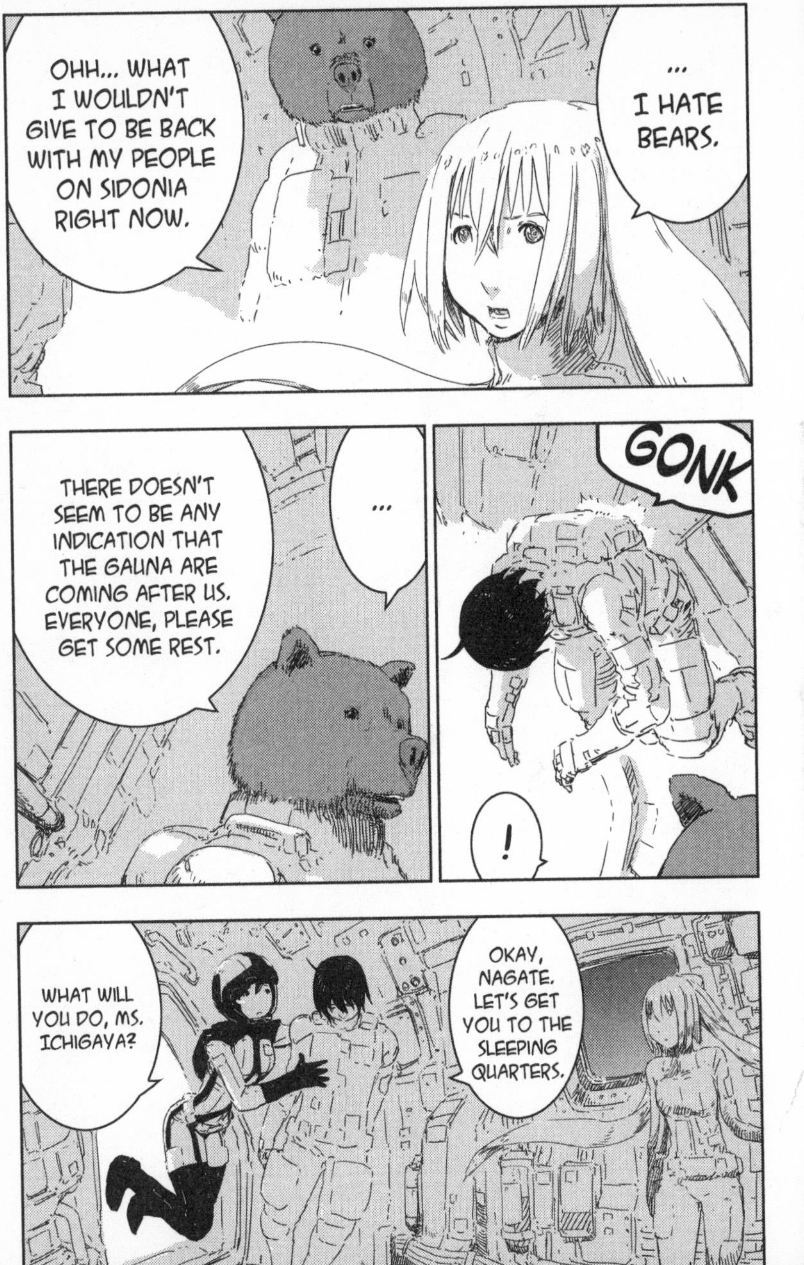

... I HATE BEARS.
OHH... WHAT I WOULDN'T GIVE TO BE BACK WITH MY PEOPLE ON SIDONIA RIGHT NOW.
GONK
!
...
THERE DOESN'T SEEM TO BE ANY INDICATION THAT THE GAUNA ARE COMING AFTER US. EVERYONE, PLEASE GET SOME REST.
OKAY, NAGATE. LET'S GET YOU TO THE SLEEPING QUARTERS.
WHAT WILL YOU DO, MS. ICHIGAYA?

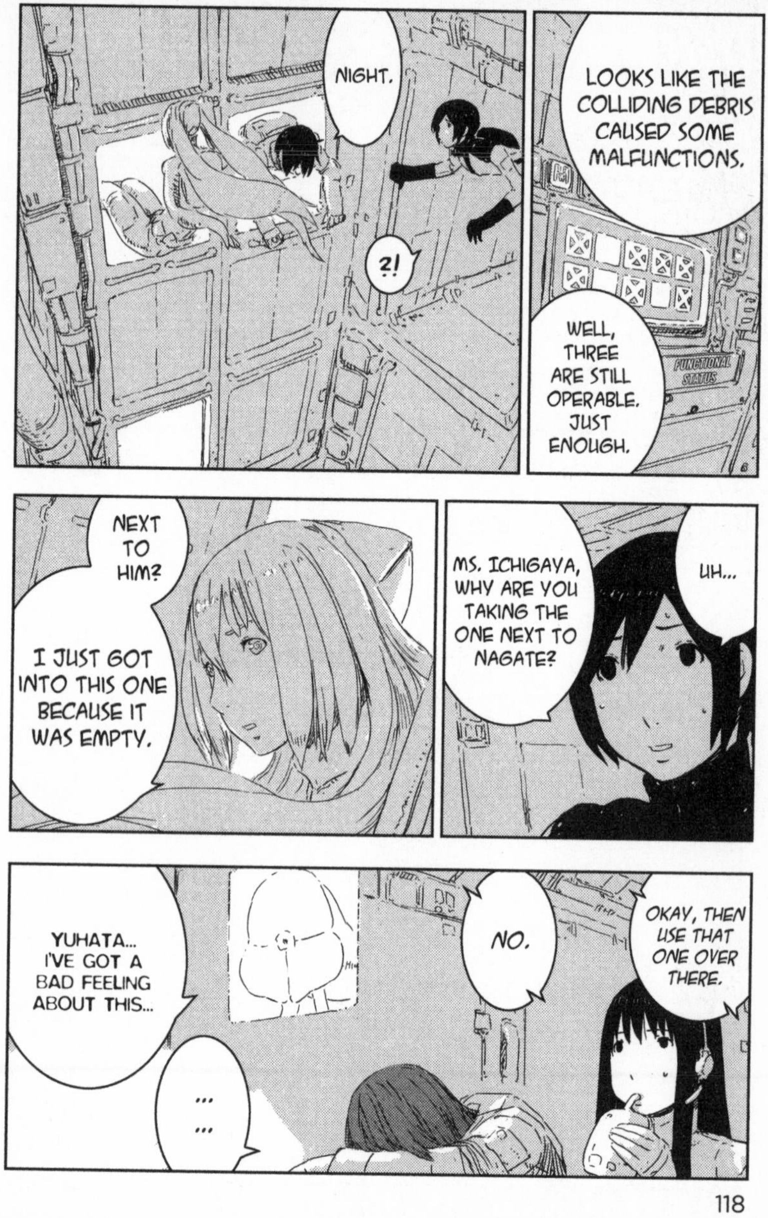
LOOKS LIKE THE COLLIDING DEBRIS CAUSED SOME MALFUNCTIONS.
FUNCTIONAL STATUS
WELL, THREE ARE STILL OPERABLE. JUST ENOUGH.
NIGHT.
?!
UH...
MS. ICHIGAYA, WHY ARE YOU TAKING THE ONE NEXT TO NAGATE?
NEXT TO HIM?
I JUST GOT INTO THIS ONE BECAUSE IT WAS EMPTY.
OKAY, THEN USE THAT ONE OVER THERE.
NO.
YUHATA... I'VE GOT A BAD FEELING ABOUT THIS...
... ...

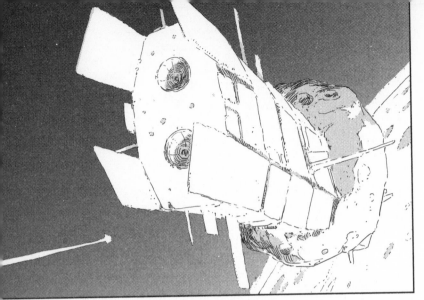

WEL-
COME
BACK!

ブナ----ッ
GWUMM

SCOOT

119

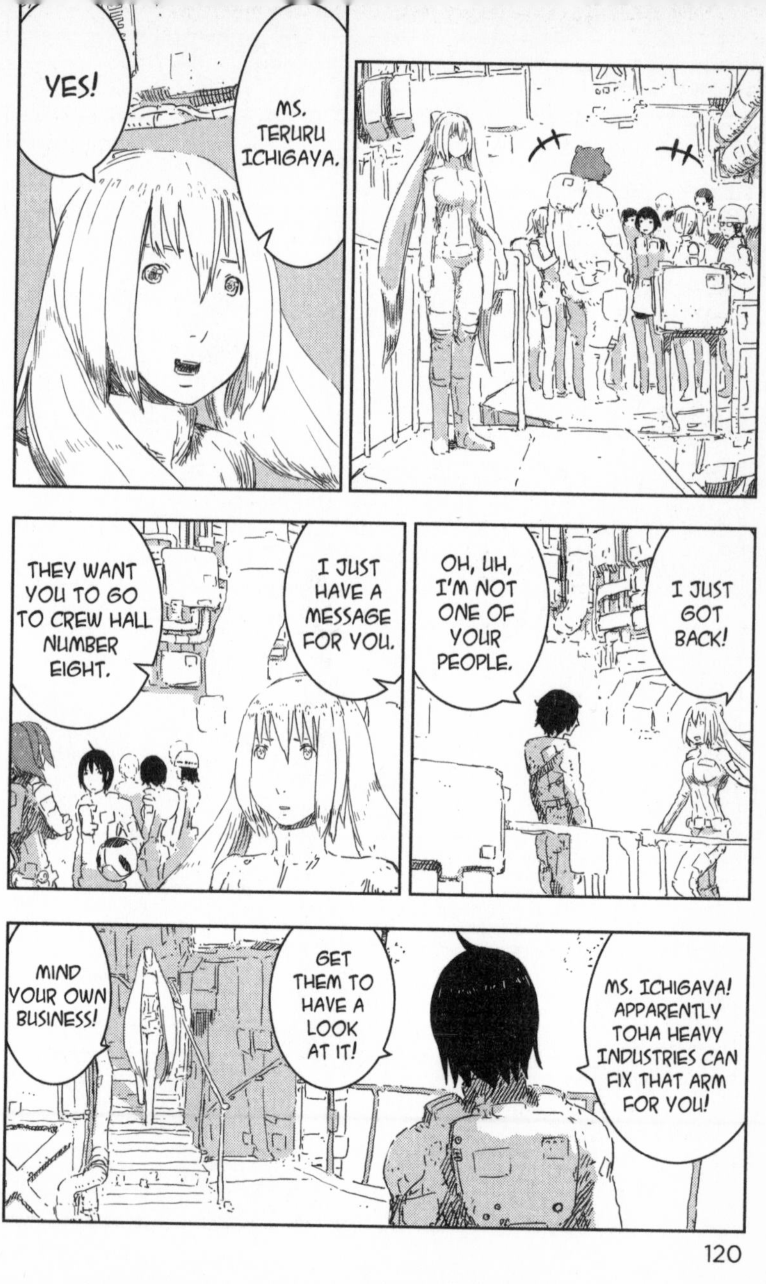
MS. TERURU ICHIGAYA.
YES!
I JUST GOT BACK!
OH, UH, I'M NOT ONE OF YOUR PEOPLE.
I JUST HAVE A MESSAGE FOR YOU.
THEY WANT YOU TO GO TO CREW HALL NUMBER EIGHT.
MS. ICHIGAYA! APPARENTLY TOHA HEAVY INDUSTRIES CAN FIX THAT ARM FOR YOU!
GET THEM TO HAVE A LOOK AT IT!
MIND YOUR OWN BUSINESS!

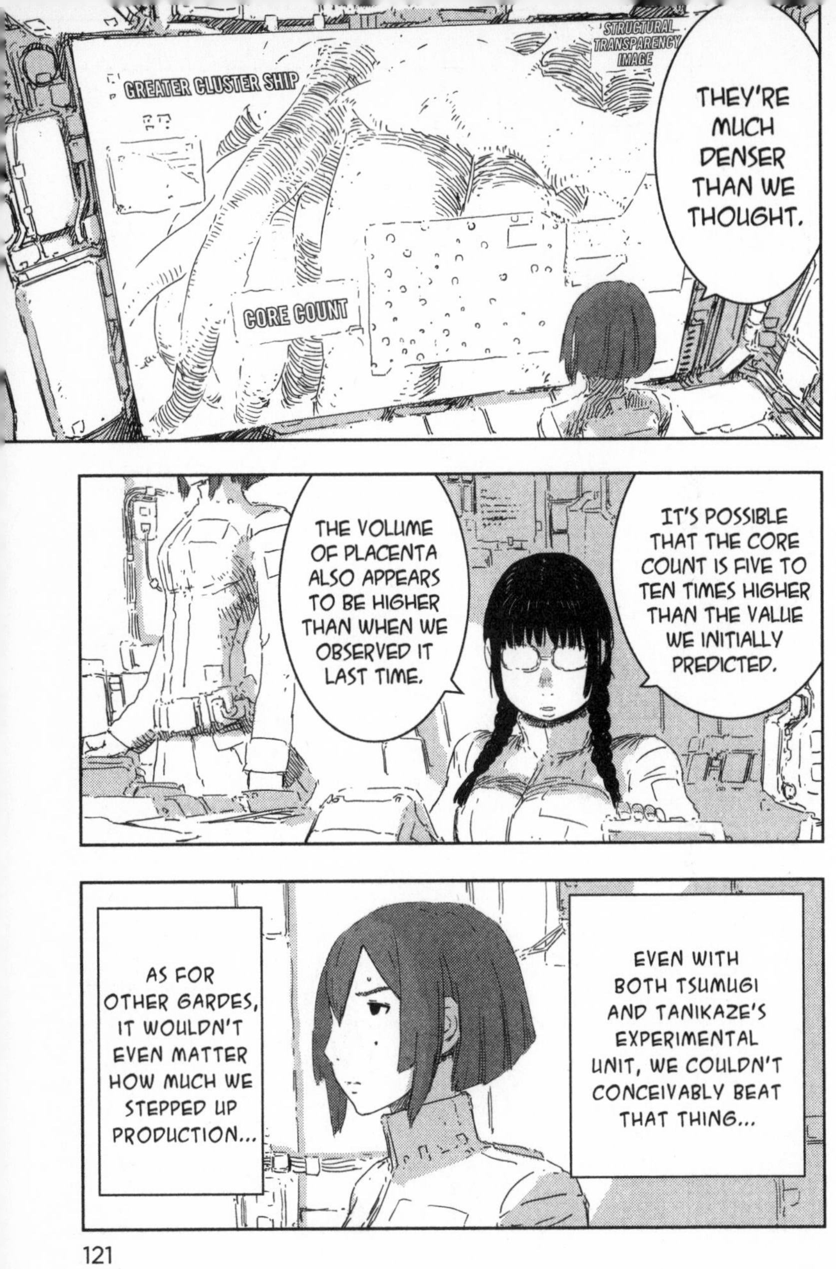
GREATER CLUSTER SHIP
STRUCTURAL TRANSPARENCY IMAGE
CORE COUNT
THEY'RE MUCH DENSER THAN WE THOUGHT.
IT'S POSSIBLE THAT THE CORE COUNT IS FIVE TO TEN TIMES HIGHER THAN THE VALUE WE INITIALLY PREDICTED.
THE VOLUME OF PLACENTA ALSO APPEARS TO BE HIGHER THAN WHEN WE OBSERVED IT LAST TIME.
EVEN WITH BOTH TSUMUGI AND TANIKAZE'S EXPERIMENTAL UNIT, WE COULDN'T CONCEIVABLY BEAT THAT THING...
AS FOR OTHER GARDES, IT WOULDN'T EVEN MATTER HOW MUCH WE STEPPED UP PRODUCTION...

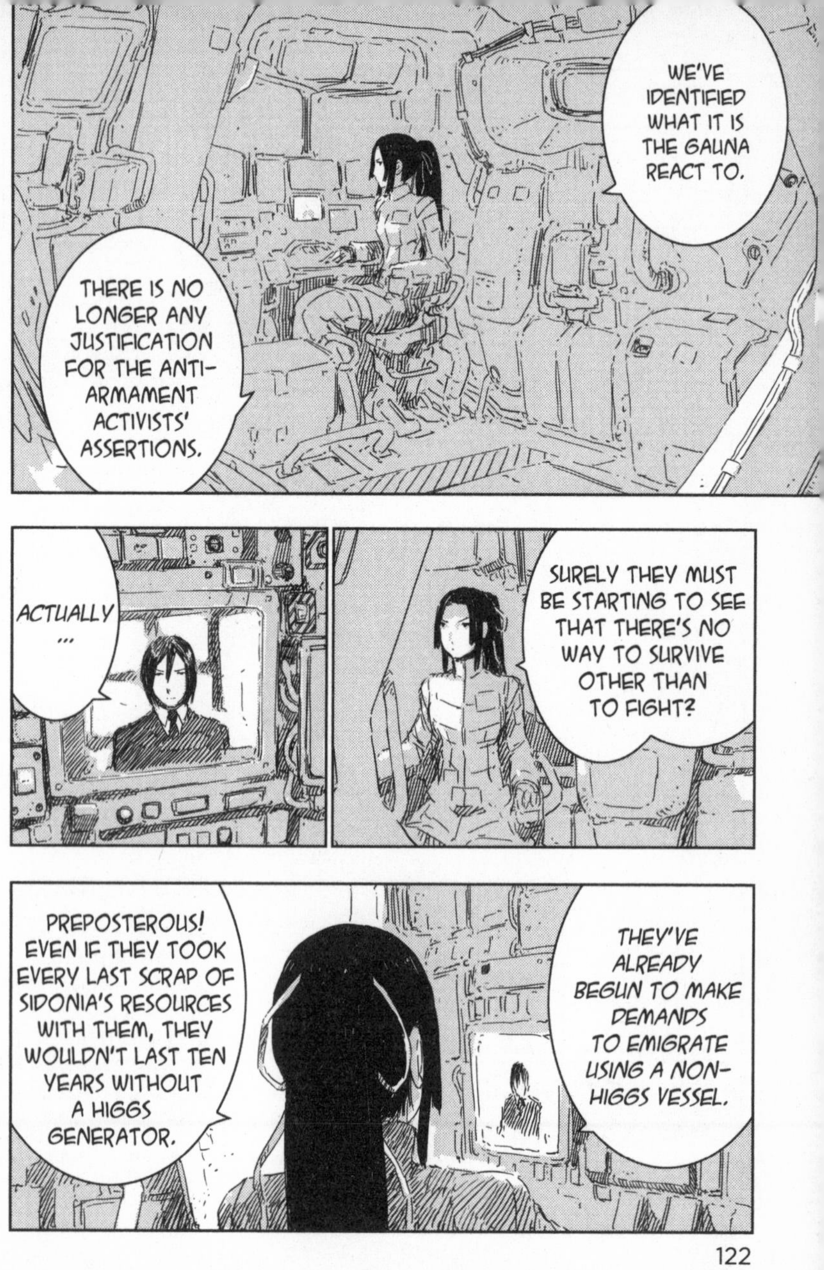
WE'VE IDENTIFIED WHAT IT IS THE GAUNA REACT TO.
THERE IS NO LONGER ANY JUSTIFICATION FOR THE ANTI-ARMAMENT ACTIVISTS' ASSERTIONS.
SURELY THEY MUST BE STARTING TO SEE THAT THERE'S NO WAY TO SURVIVE OTHER THAN TO FIGHT?
ACTUALLY ...
THEY'VE ALREADY BEGUN TO MAKE DEMANDS TO EMIGRATE USING A NON-HIGGS VESSEL.
PREPOSTEROUS! EVEN IF THEY TOOK EVERY LAST SCRAP OF SIDONIA'S RESOURCES WITH THEM, THEY WOULDN'T LAST TEN YEARS WITHOUT A HIGGS GENERATOR.

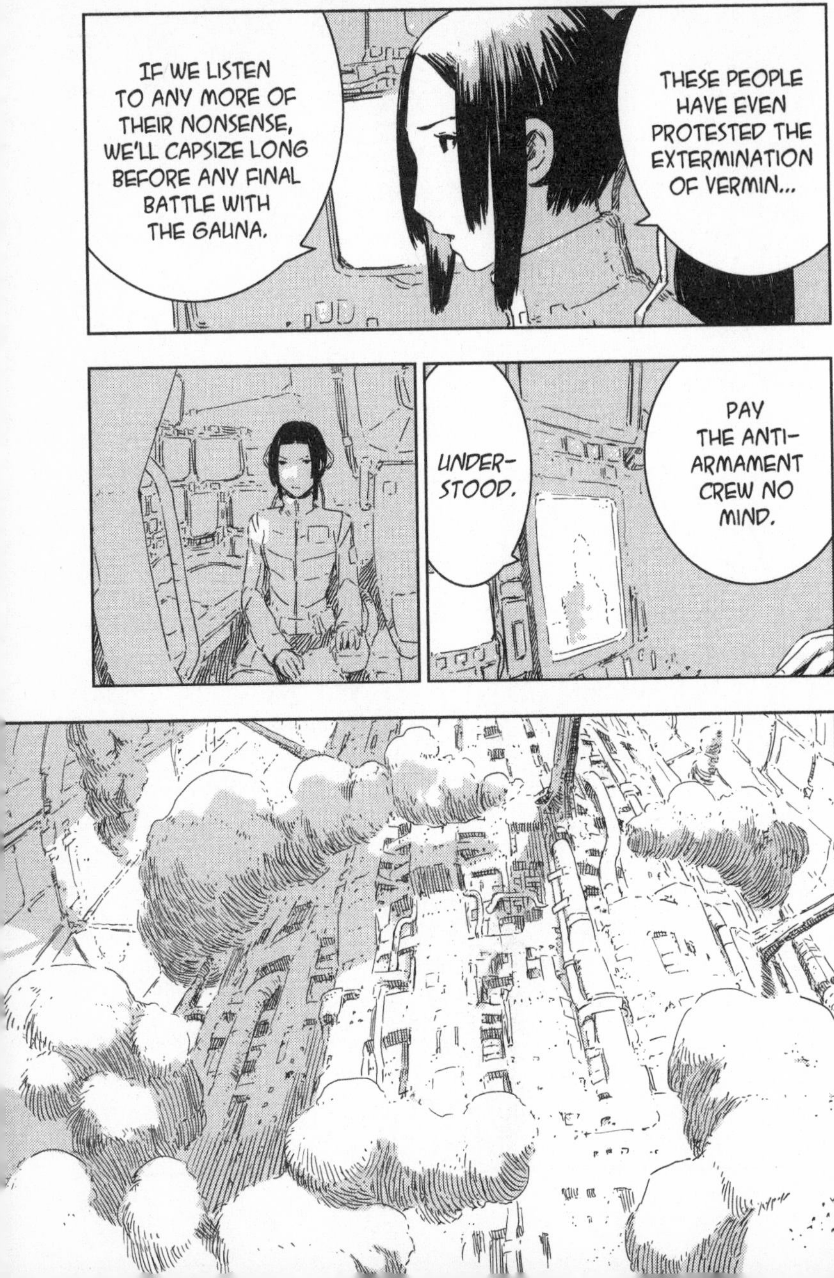
THESE PEOPLE HAVE EVEN PROTESTED THE EXTERMINATION OF VERMIN...
IF WE LISTEN TO ANY MORE OF THEIR NONSENSE, WE'LL CAPSIZE LONG BEFORE ANY FINAL BATTLE WITH THE GAUNA.
PAY THE ANTI-ARMAMENT CREW NO MIND.
UNDER-STOOD.

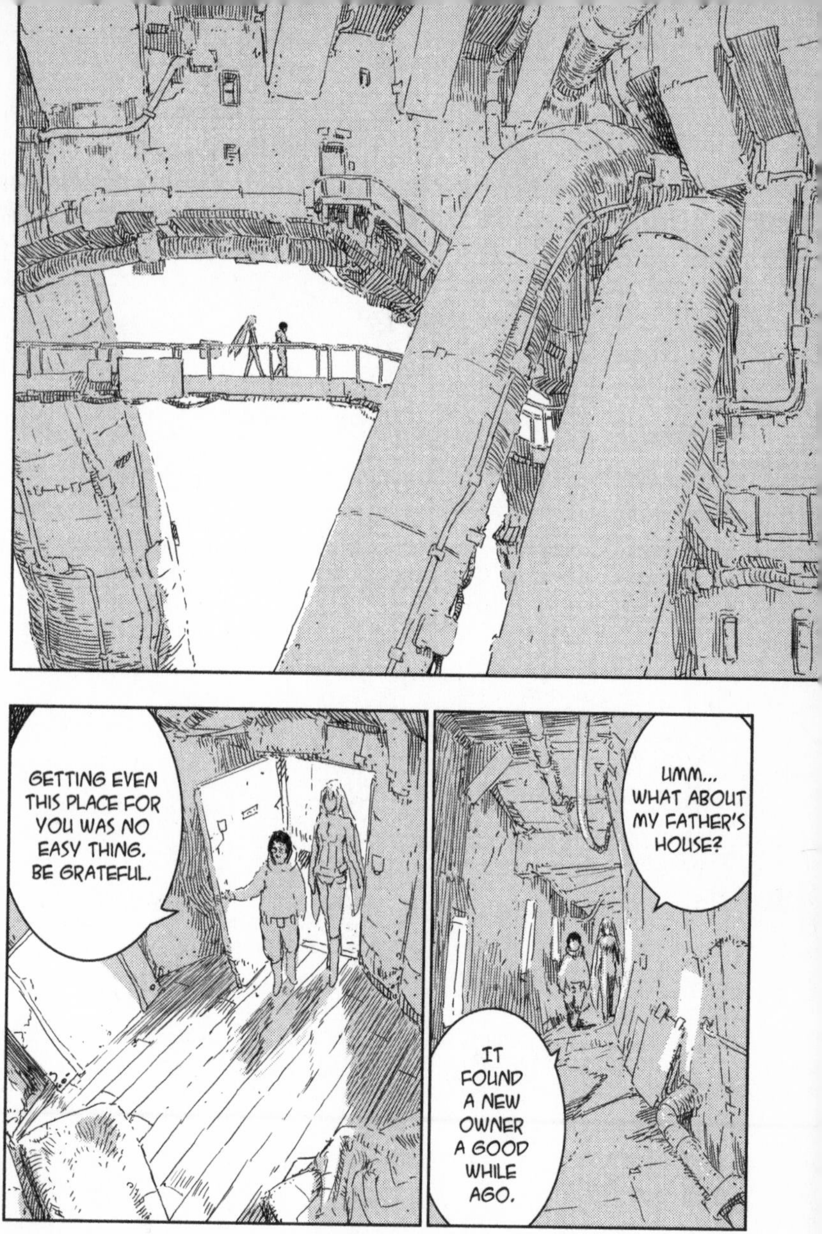
UMM... WHAT ABOUT MY FATHER'S HOUSE?
IT FOUND A NEW OWNER A GOOD WHILE AGO.
GETTING EVEN THIS PLACE FOR YOU WAS NO EASY THING. BE GRATEFUL.

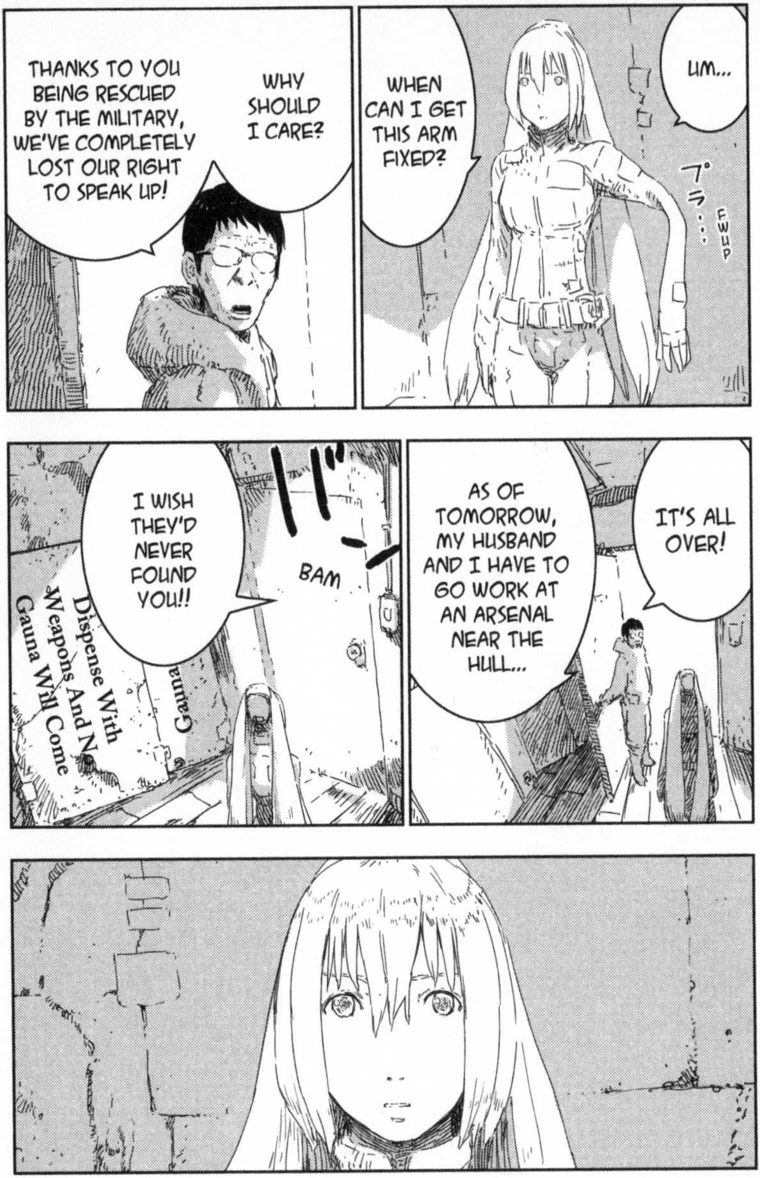
UM...
WHEN CAN I GET THIS ARM FIXED?
プラ...
FWUP
WHY SHOULD I CARE?
THANKS TO YOU BEING RESCUED BY THE MILITARY, WE'VE COMPLETELY LOST OUR RIGHT TO SPEAK UP!
IT'S ALL OVER!
AS OF TOMORROW, MY HUSBAND AND I HAVE TO GO WORK AT AN ARSENAL NEAR THE HULL...
BAM
I WISH THEY'D NEVER FOUND YOU!!
Dispense With Weapons And N
Gauna Will Come
Gauna

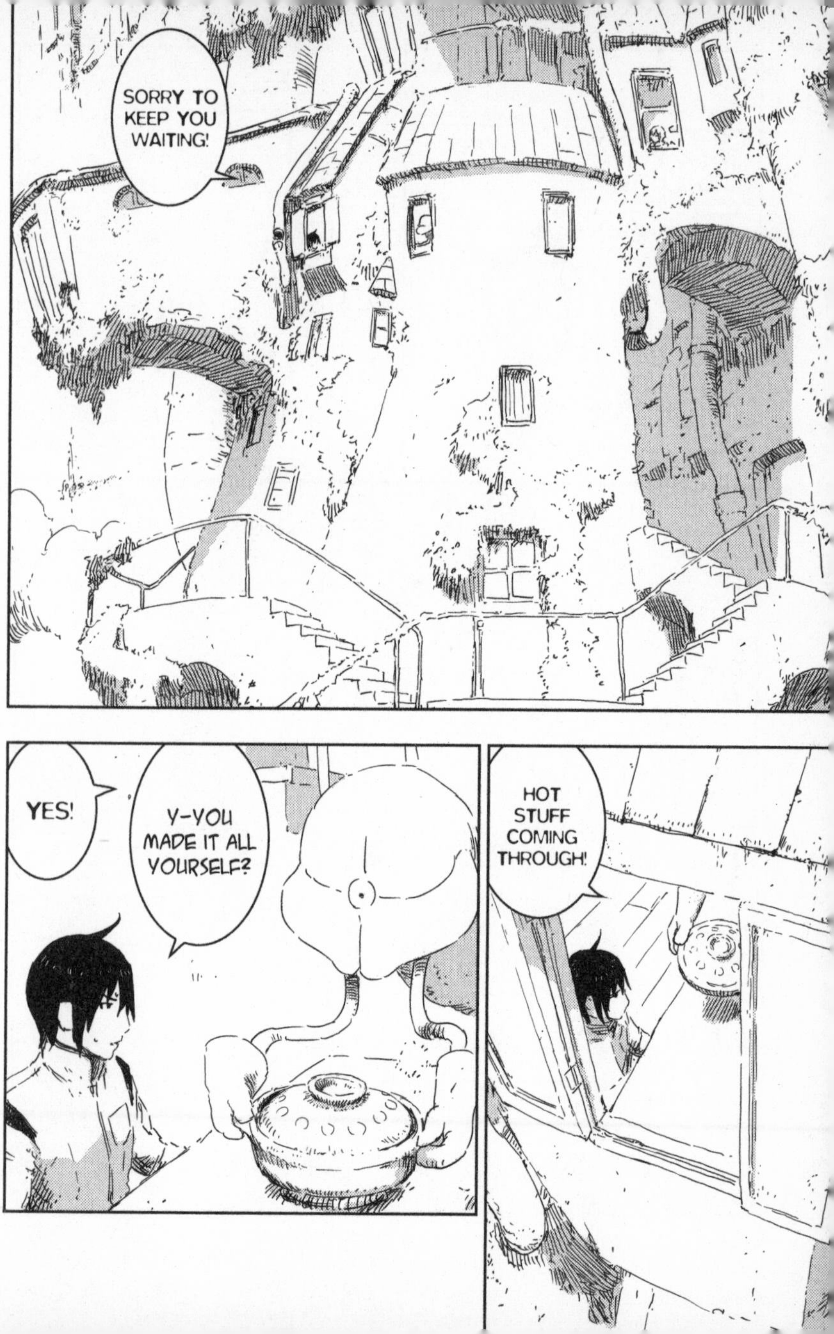
SORRY TO KEEP YOU WAITING!
HOT STUFF COMING THROUGH!
Y-YOU MADE IT ALL YOURSELF?
YES!

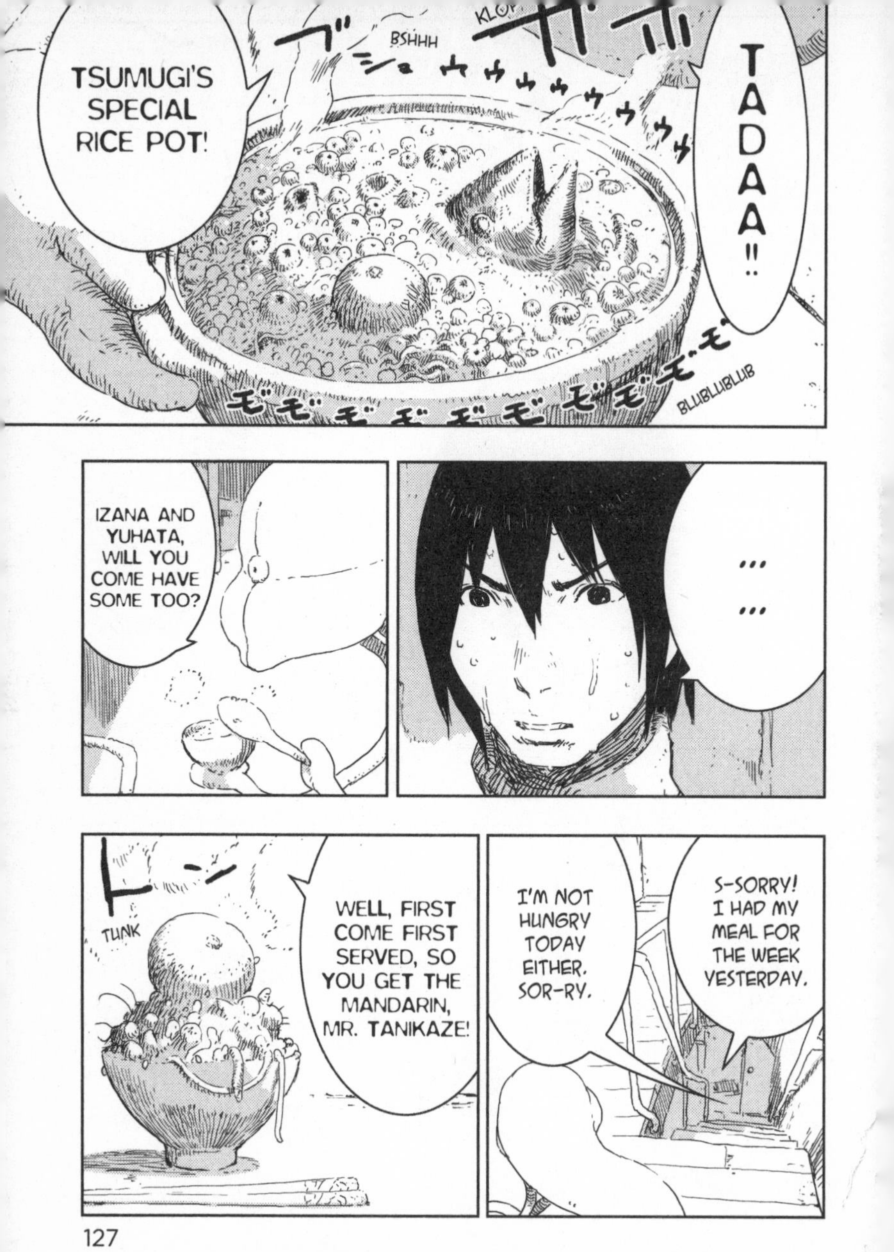
KLOP
BSHHH
TADAA!!
TSUMUGI'S SPECIAL RICE POT!
BLUBLUBLUB
……
IZANA AND YUHATA, WILL YOU COME HAVE SOME TOO?
S-SORRY! I HAD MY MEAL FOR THE WEEK YESTERDAY.
I'M NOT HUNGRY TODAY EITHER. SOR-RY.
TUNK
WELL, FIRST COME FIRST SERVED, SO YOU GET THE MANDARIN, MR. TANIKAZE!

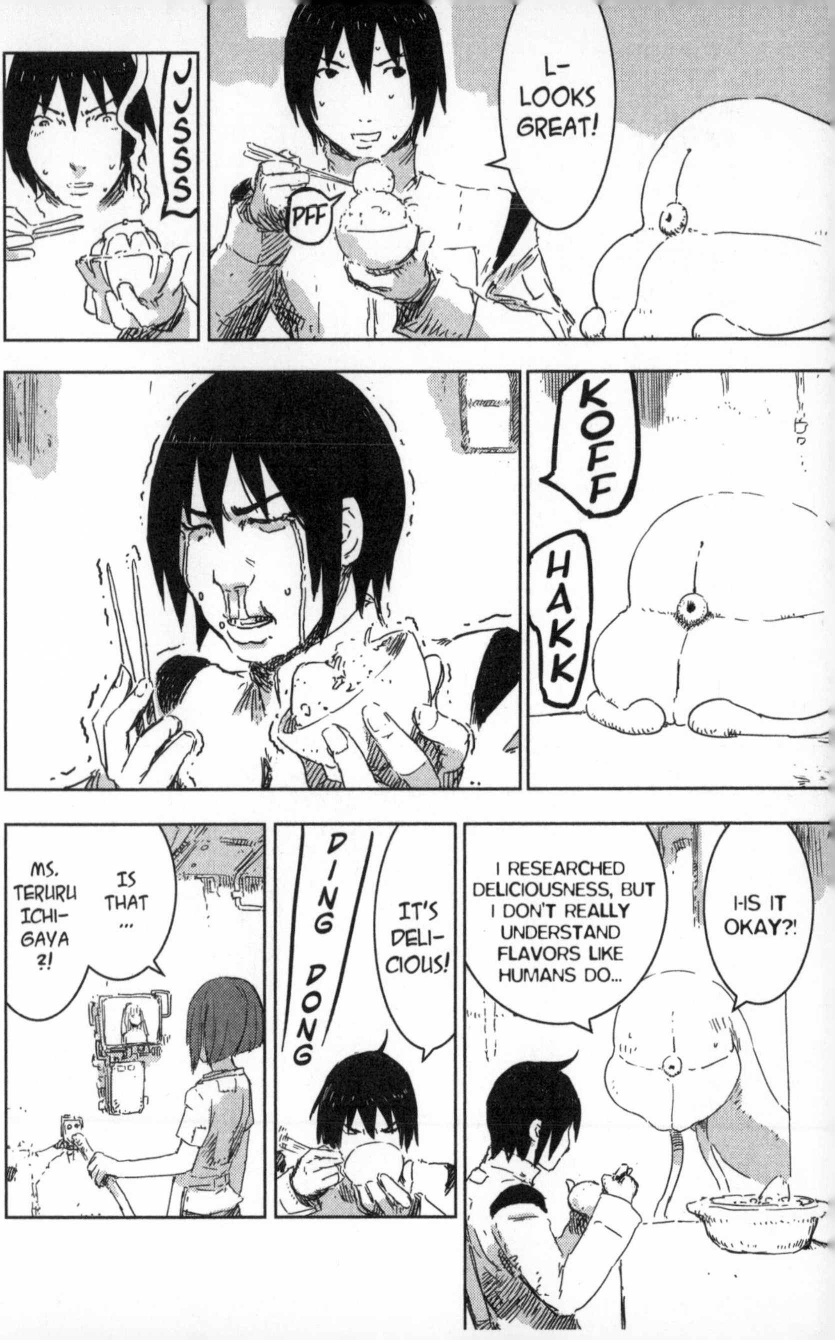
L-
LOOKS
GREAT!
PFF
JUSSS
KOFF
HAKK
I-IS IT OKAY?!
I RESEARCHED DELICIOUSNESS, BUT I DON'T REALLY UNDERSTAND FLAVORS LIKE HUMANS DO...
IT'S DELI-CIOUS!
DING DONG
IS THAT ...
MS. TERURU ICHI-GAYA ?!

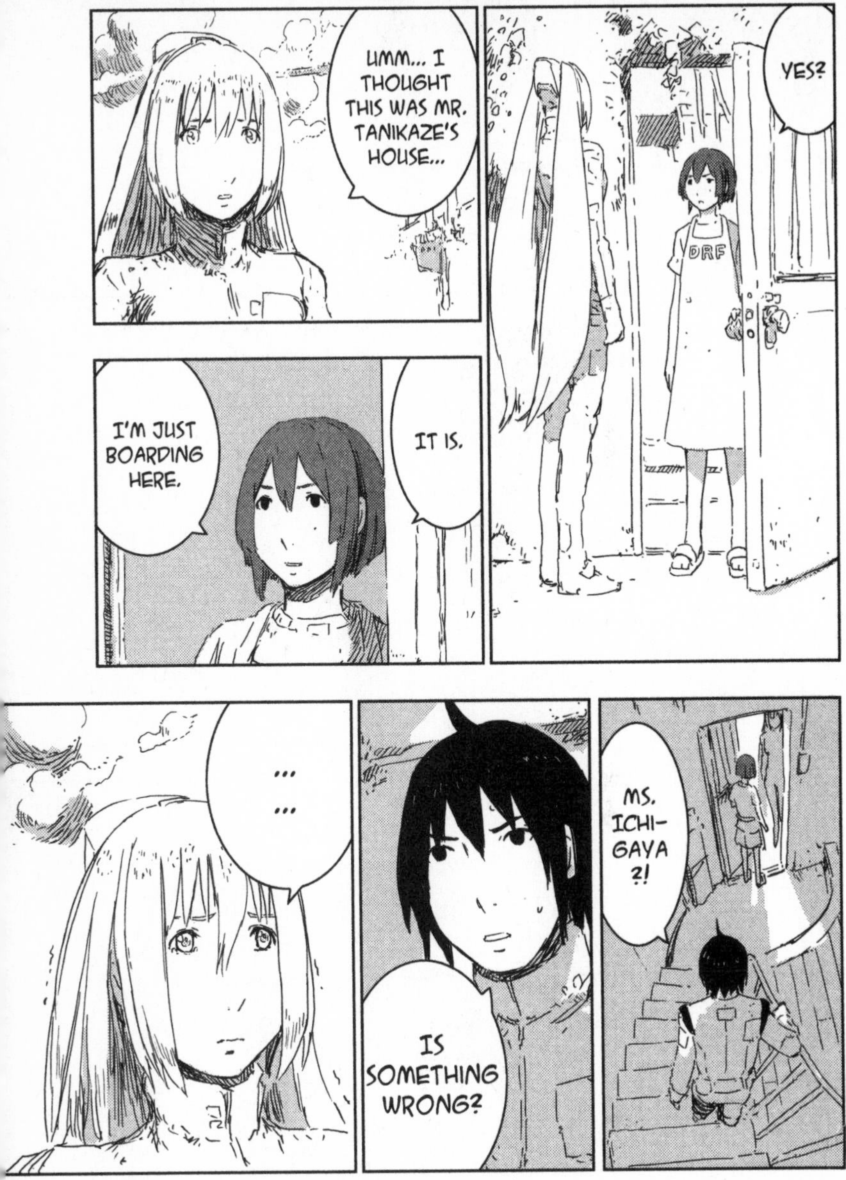
YES?
UMM... I THOUGHT THIS WAS MR. TANIKAZE'S HOUSE...
IT IS.
I'M JUST BOARDING HERE.
MS. ICHIGAYA?!
IS SOMETHING WRONG?
...
...

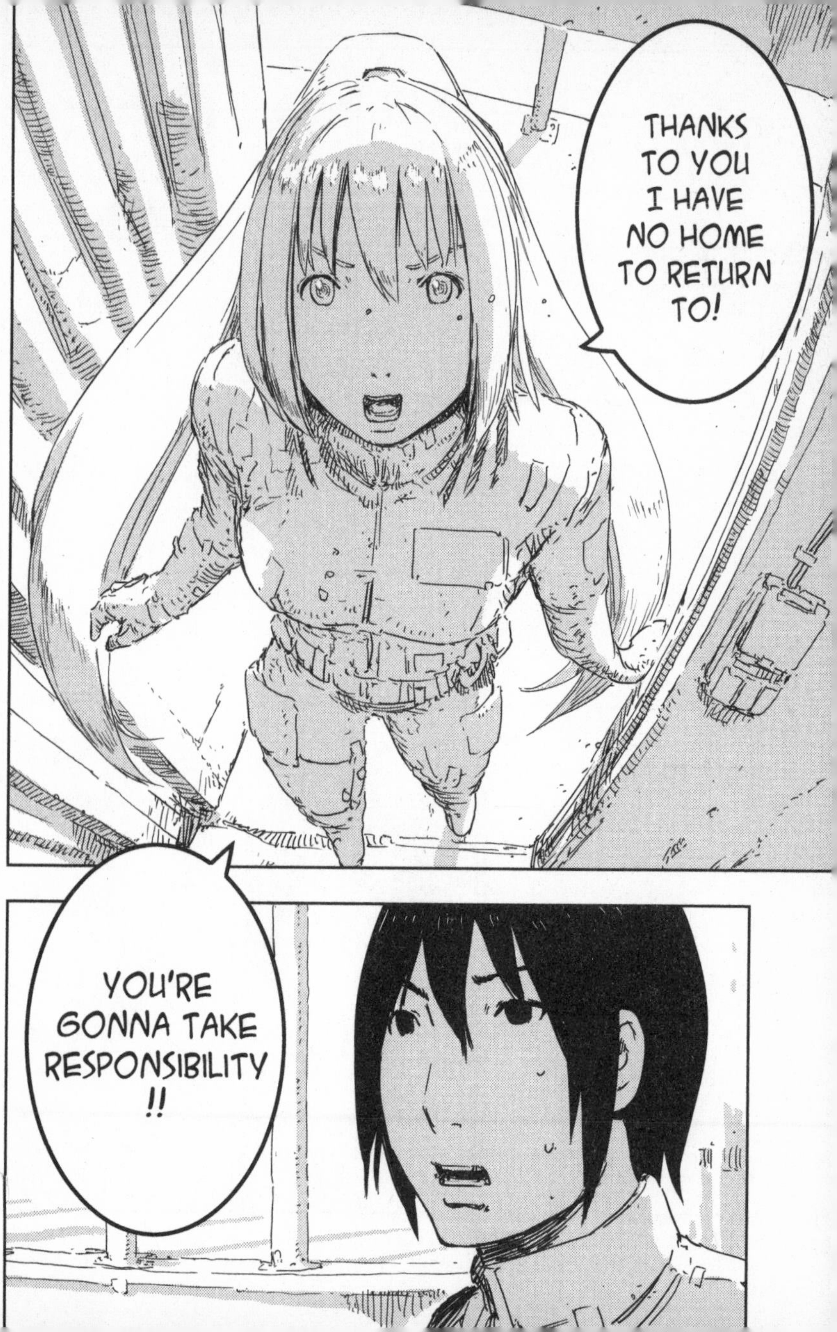
THANKS TO YOU I HAVE NO HOME TO RETURN TO!
YOU'RE GONNA TAKE RESPONSIBILITY !!

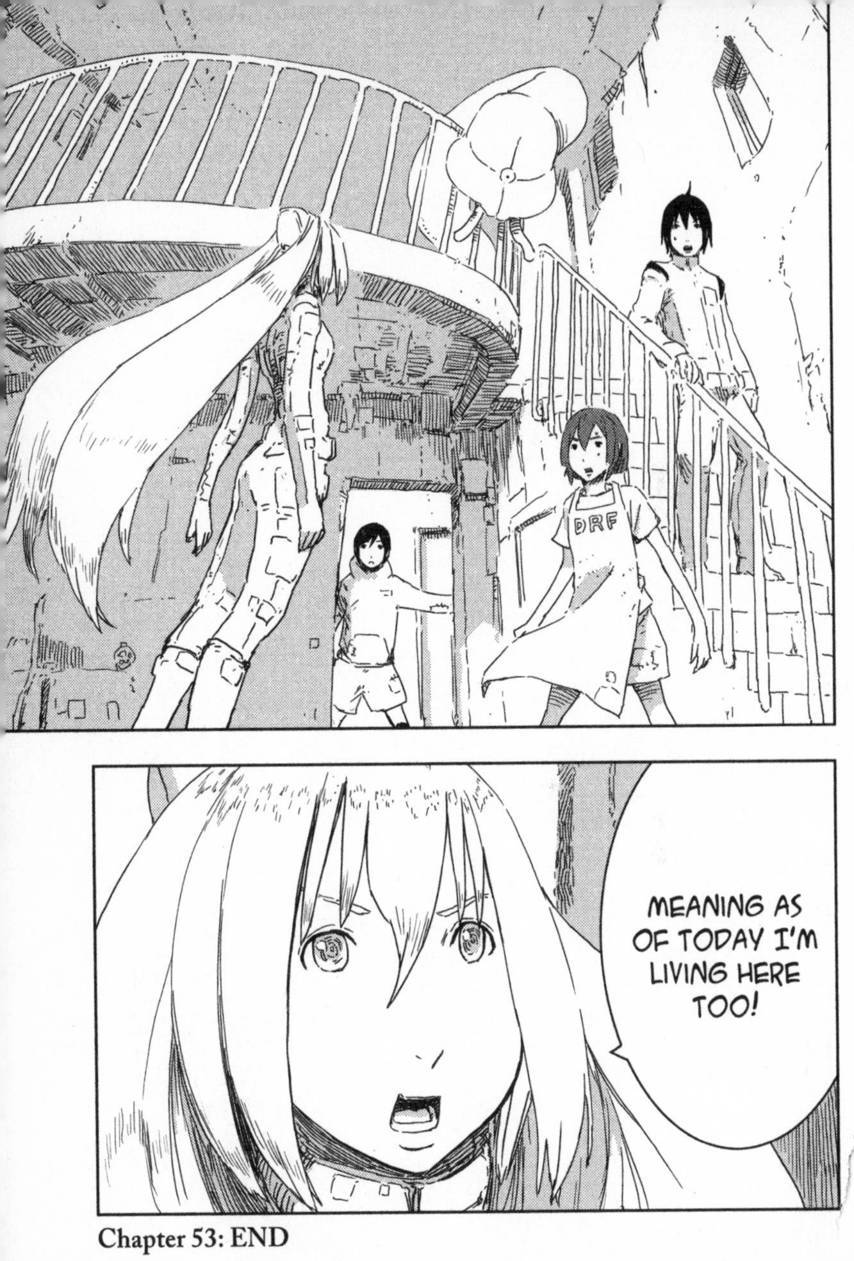
DRF
MEANING AS OF TODAY I'M LIVING HERE TOO!

Chapter 53: END

シドニアの騎士

KNIGHTS OF SIDONIA

Chapter 54: Teruru Ichigaya's Conversion

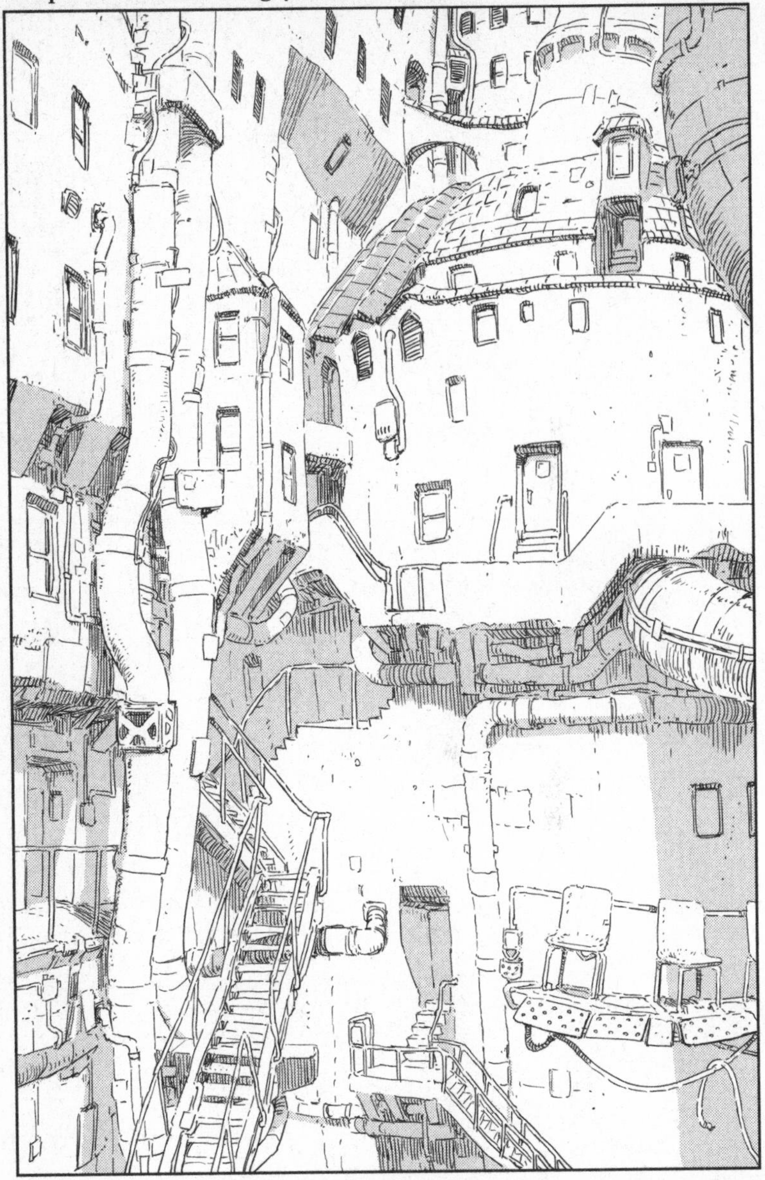

One Hundred Sights of Sidonia Part Forty-One:
Honoka Sisters Residence and Environs

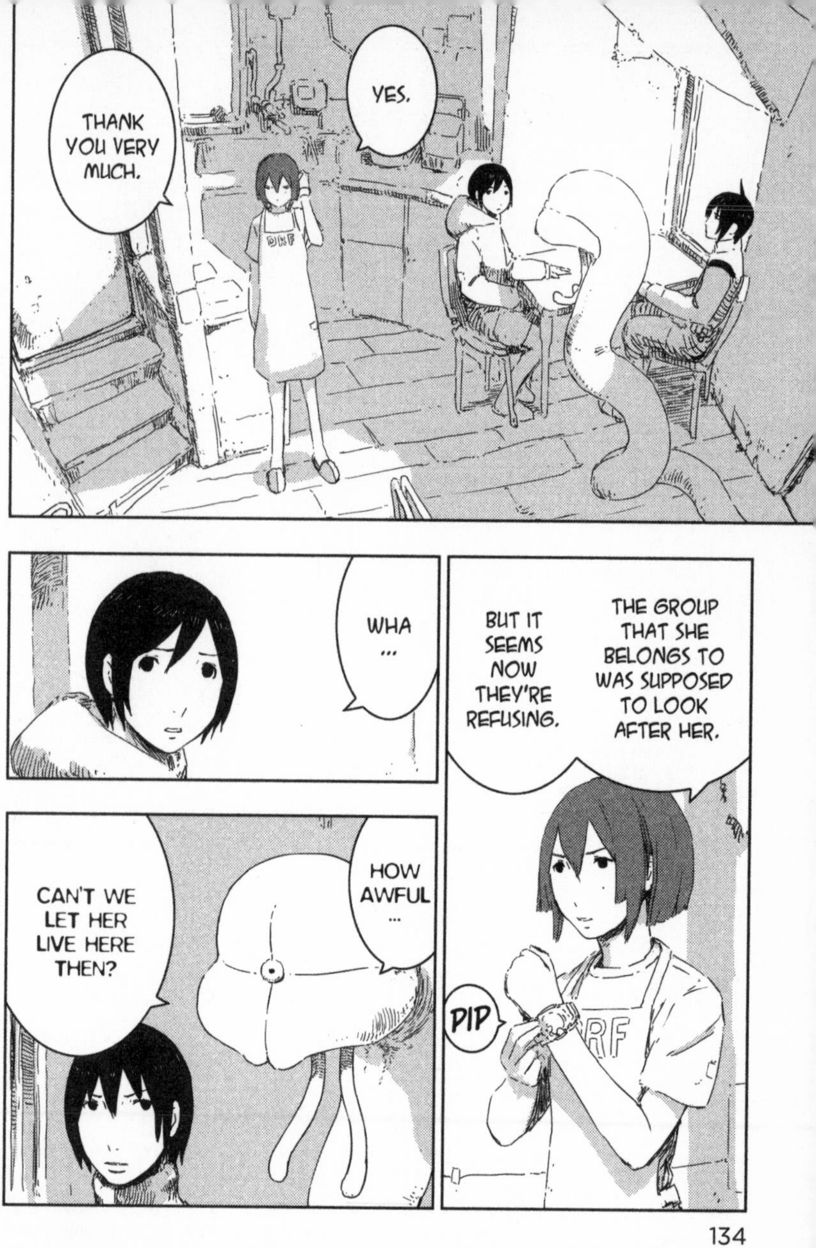
YES.
THANK YOU VERY MUCH.
THE GROUP THAT SHE BELONGS TO WAS SUPPOSED TO LOOK AFTER HER.
BUT IT SEEMS NOW THEY'RE REFUSING.
PIP
WHA ...
HOW AWFUL ...
CAN'T WE LET HER LIVE HERE THEN?

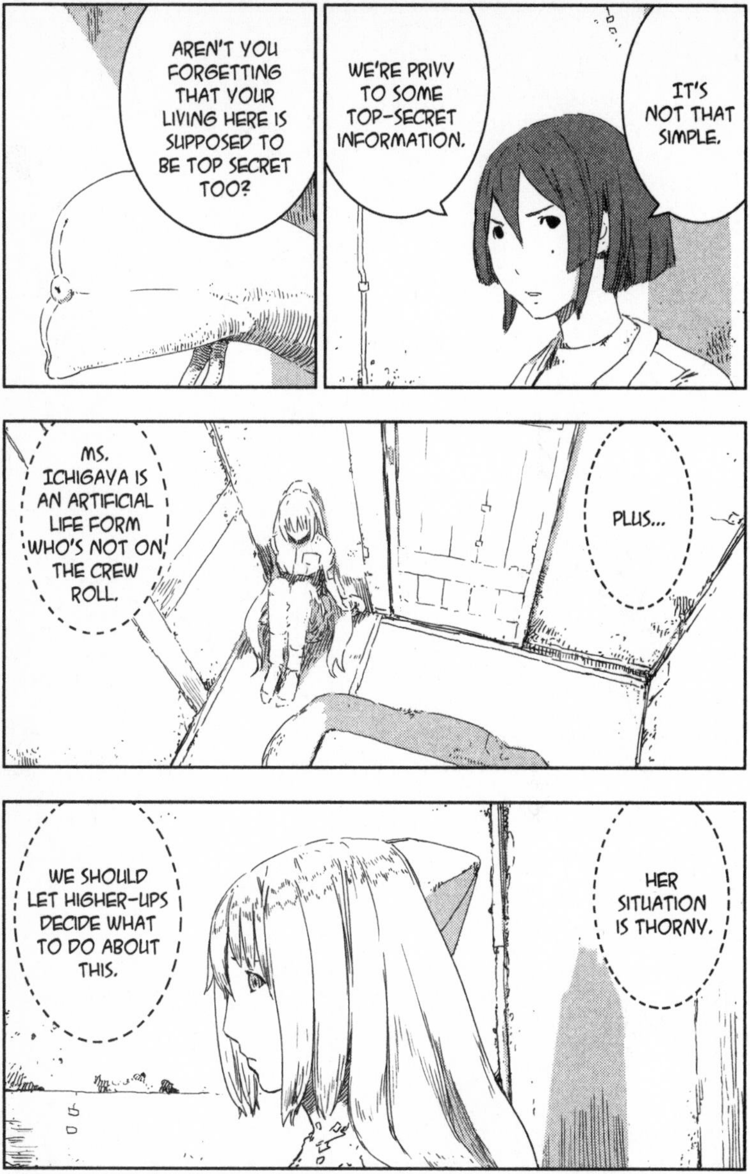
IT'S NOT THAT SIMPLE.
WE'RE PRIVY TO SOME TOP-SECRET INFORMATION.
AREN'T YOU FORGETTING THAT YOUR LIVING HERE IS SUPPOSED TO BE TOP SECRET TOO?
PLUS...
MS. ICHIGAYA IS AN ARTIFICIAL LIFE FORM WHO'S NOT ON THE CREW ROLL.
HER SITUATION IS THORNY.
WE SHOULD LET HIGHER-UPS DECIDE WHAT TO DO ABOUT THIS.

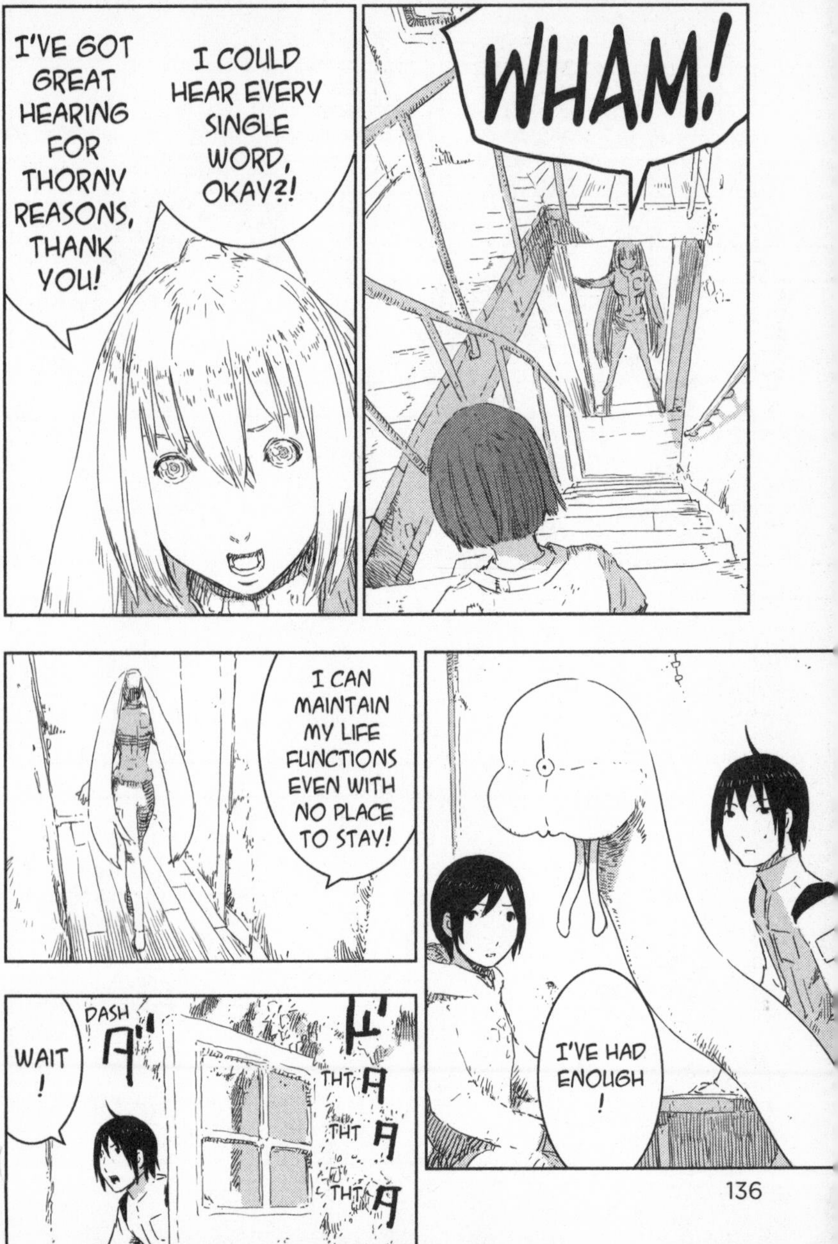
WHAM!
I COULD HEAR EVERY SINGLE WORD, OKAY?!
I'VE GOT GREAT HEARING FOR THORNY REASONS, THANK YOU!
I'VE HAD ENOUGH!
I CAN MAINTAIN MY LIFE FUNCTIONS EVEN WITH NO PLACE TO STAY!
DASH
THT THT THT
WAIT!

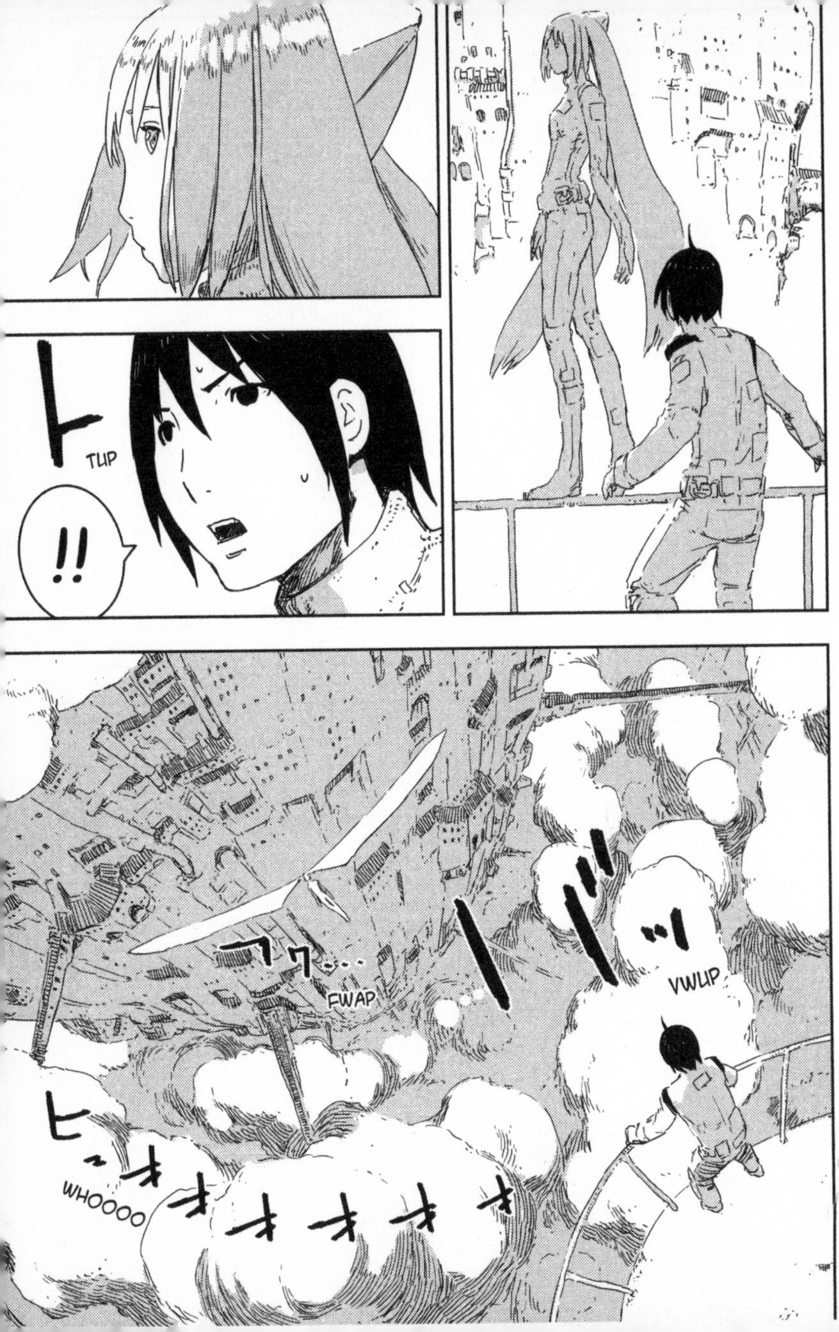

ト
TUP
!!
VWUP
FWAP
WHOOOO

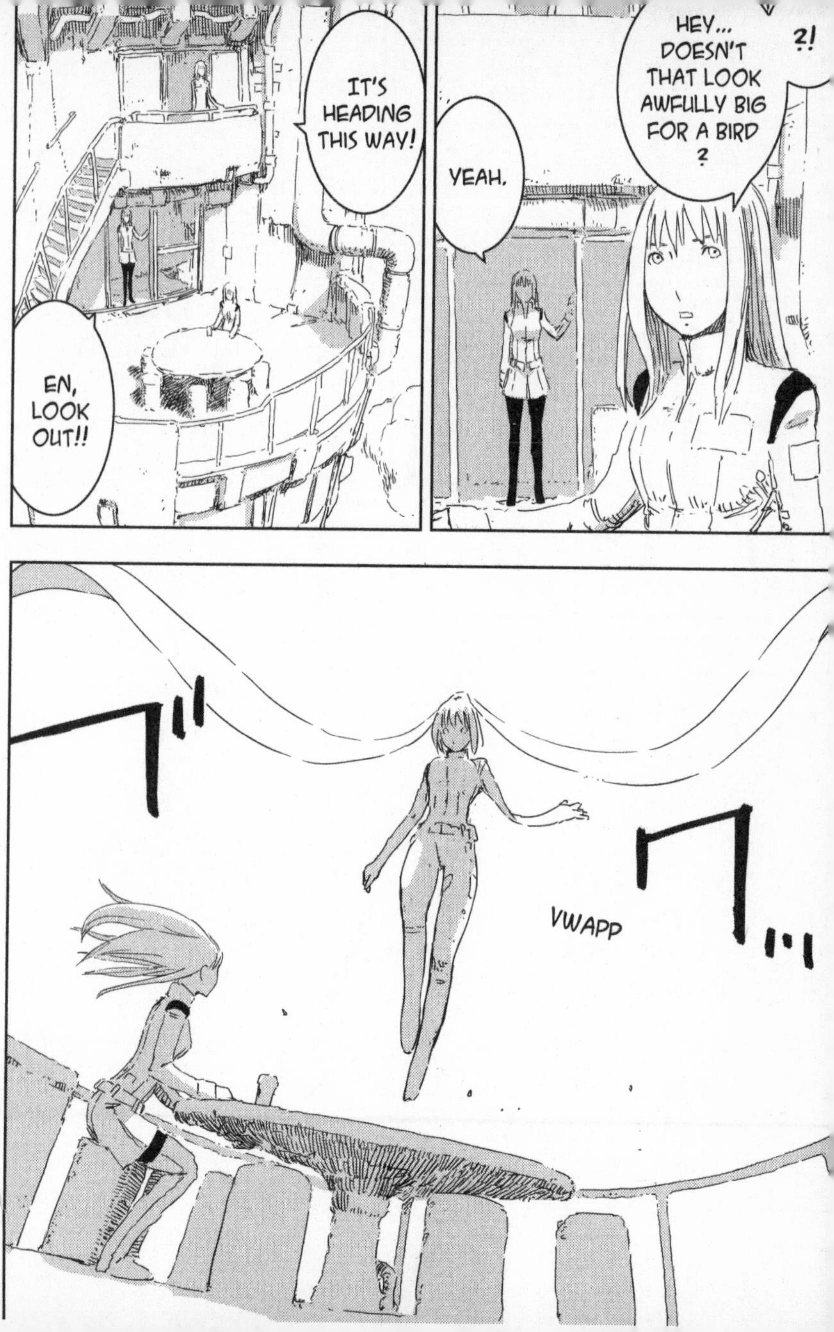
?!
HEY... DOESN'T THAT LOOK AWFULLY BIG FOR A BIRD?
YEAH.
IT'S HEADING THIS WAY!
EN, LOOK OUT!!
VWAPP

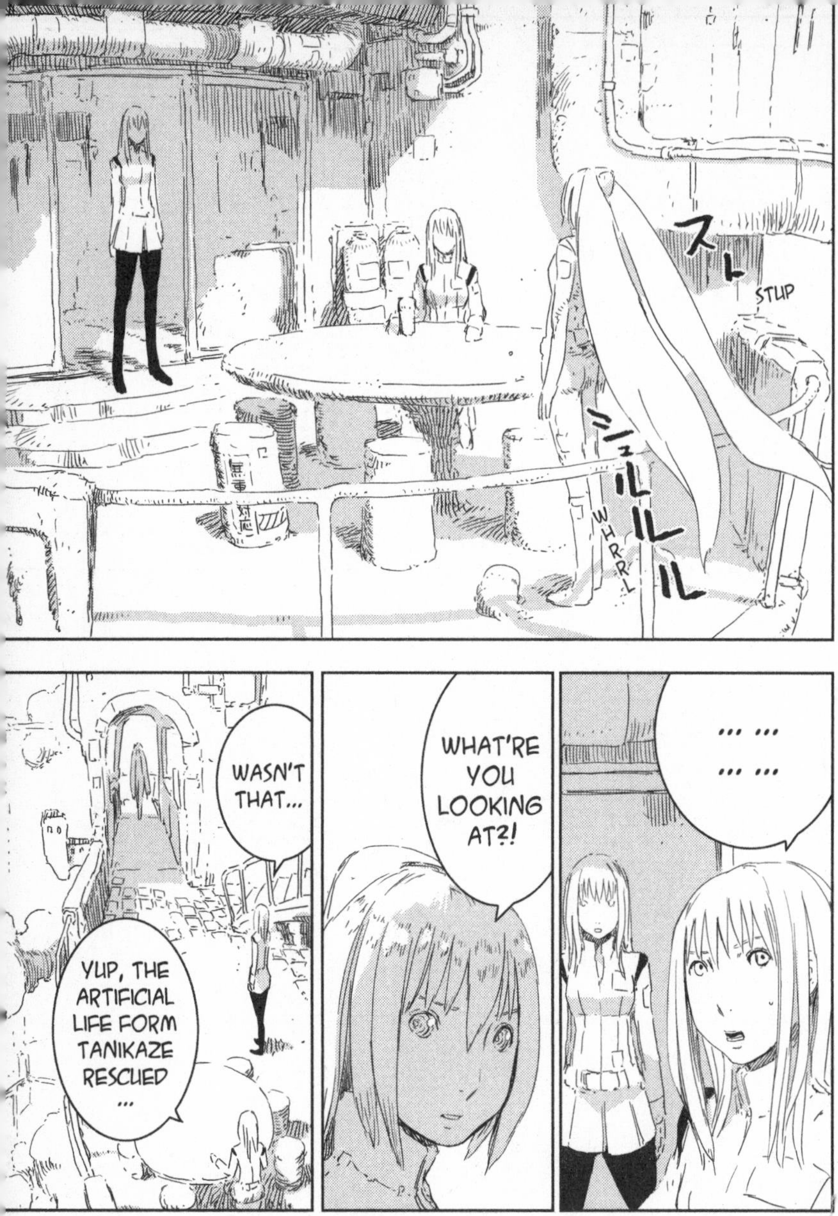
スト
STUP
シュルルル
WHRRL
... ...
... ...
WHAT'RE YOU LOOKING AT?!
WASN'T THAT...
YUP, THE ARTIFICIAL LIFE FORM TANIKAZE RESCUED ...

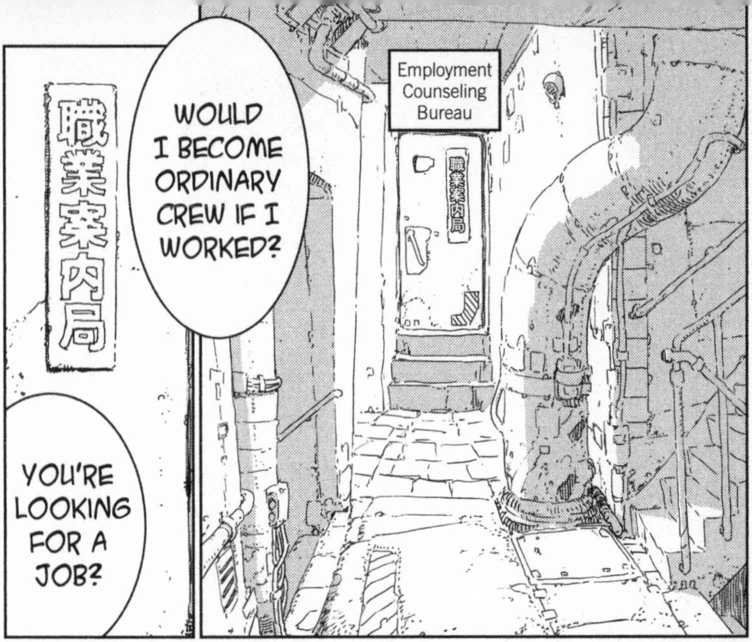
Employment Counseling Bureau
職業案内局
WOULD I BECOME ORDINARY CREW IF I WORKED?
職業案内局
YOU'RE LOOKING FOR A JOB?

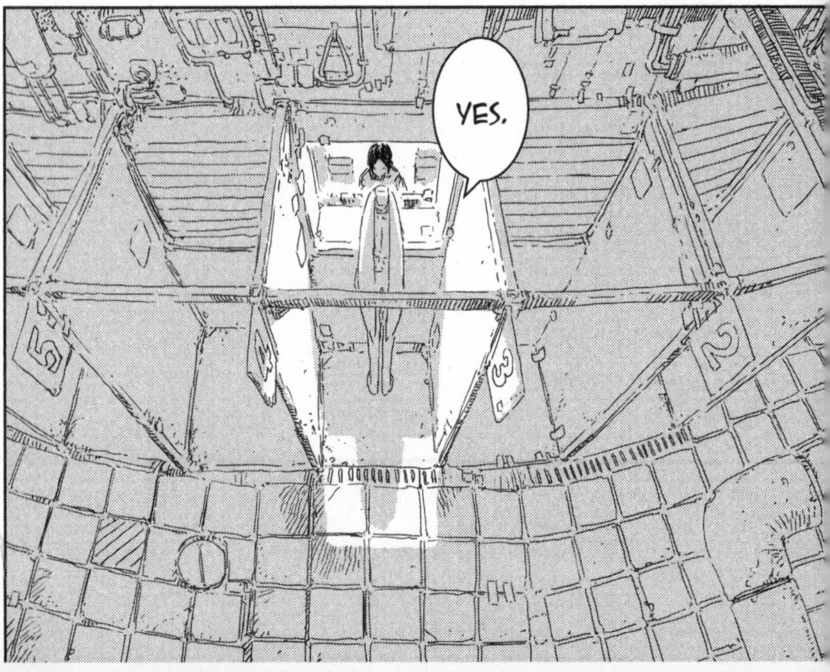
YES.

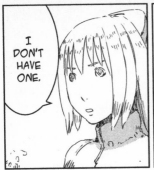

WE AREN'T READING A CREW ID CARD.
HAVE YOU FOR-GOTTEN IT?
I DON'T HAVE ONE.
THEN TELL ME YOUR CREW NUMBER PLEASE.
LOOK, I DON'T HAVE AN ID SO I DON'T HAVE A NUMBER EITHER.
MAY I ASK YOU YOUR NAME?
IT'S TERURU ICHIGAYA.
IT SEEMS ACCORDING TO THE CIVIL REGISTRATIONS OFFICE, NO PERSON BY THE NAME OF TERURU ICHIGAYA RESIDES IN SIDONIA.
...

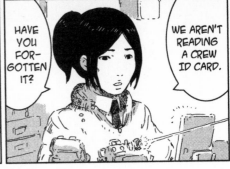

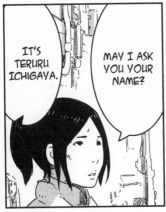

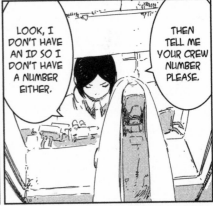

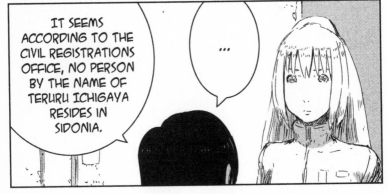

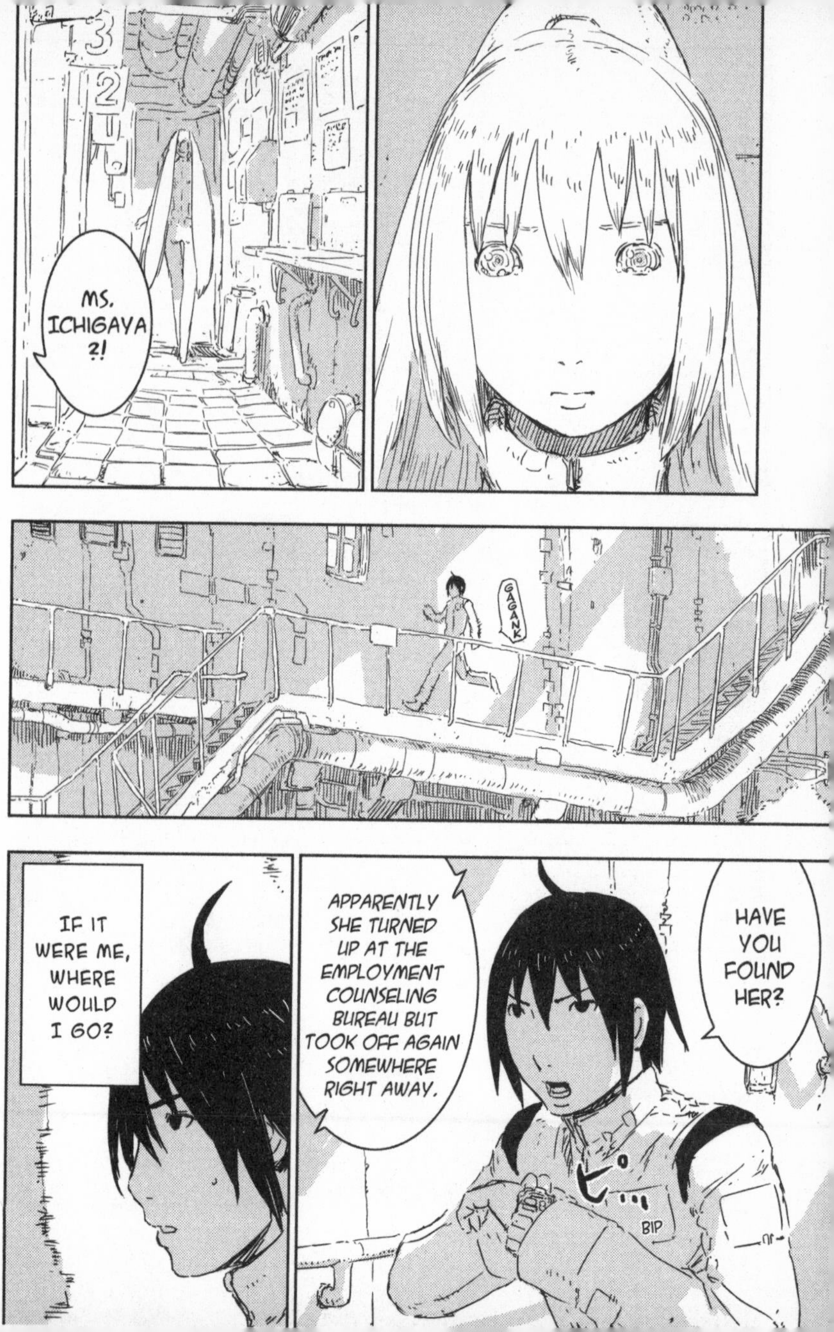
MS. ICHIGAYA ?!
GAGANK
HAVE YOU FOUND HER?
APPARENTLY SHE TURNED UP AT THE EMPLOYMENT COUNSELING BUREAU BUT TOOK OFF AGAIN SOMEWHERE RIGHT AWAY.
BIP
IF IT WERE ME, WHERE WOULD I GO?

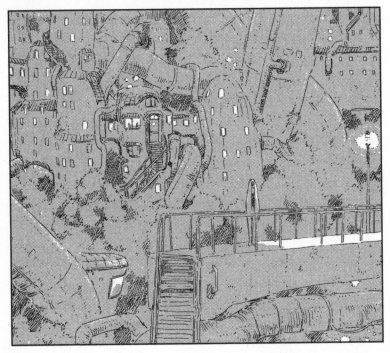

FATHER
...

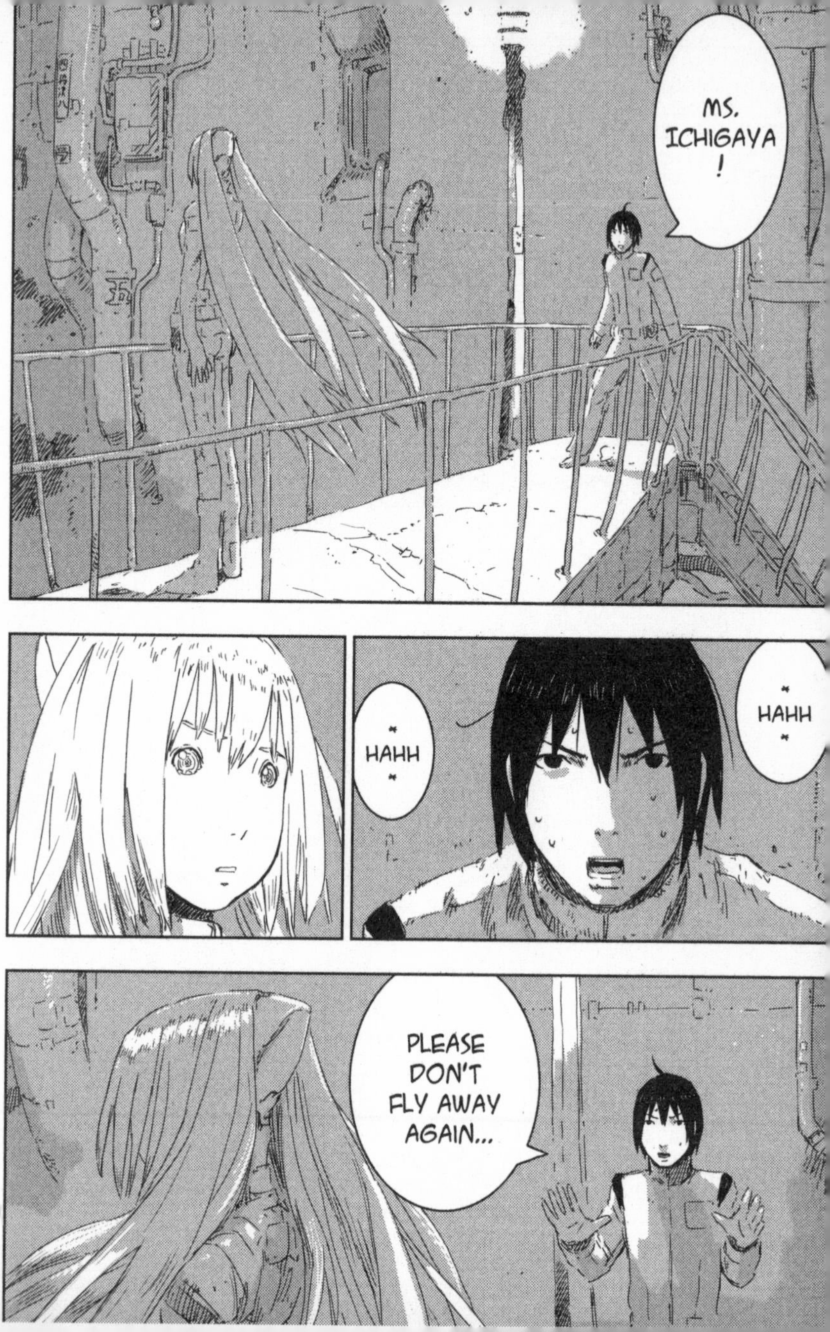
MS. ICHIGAYA!
HAHH
HAHH
PLEASE DON'T FLY AWAY AGAIN...

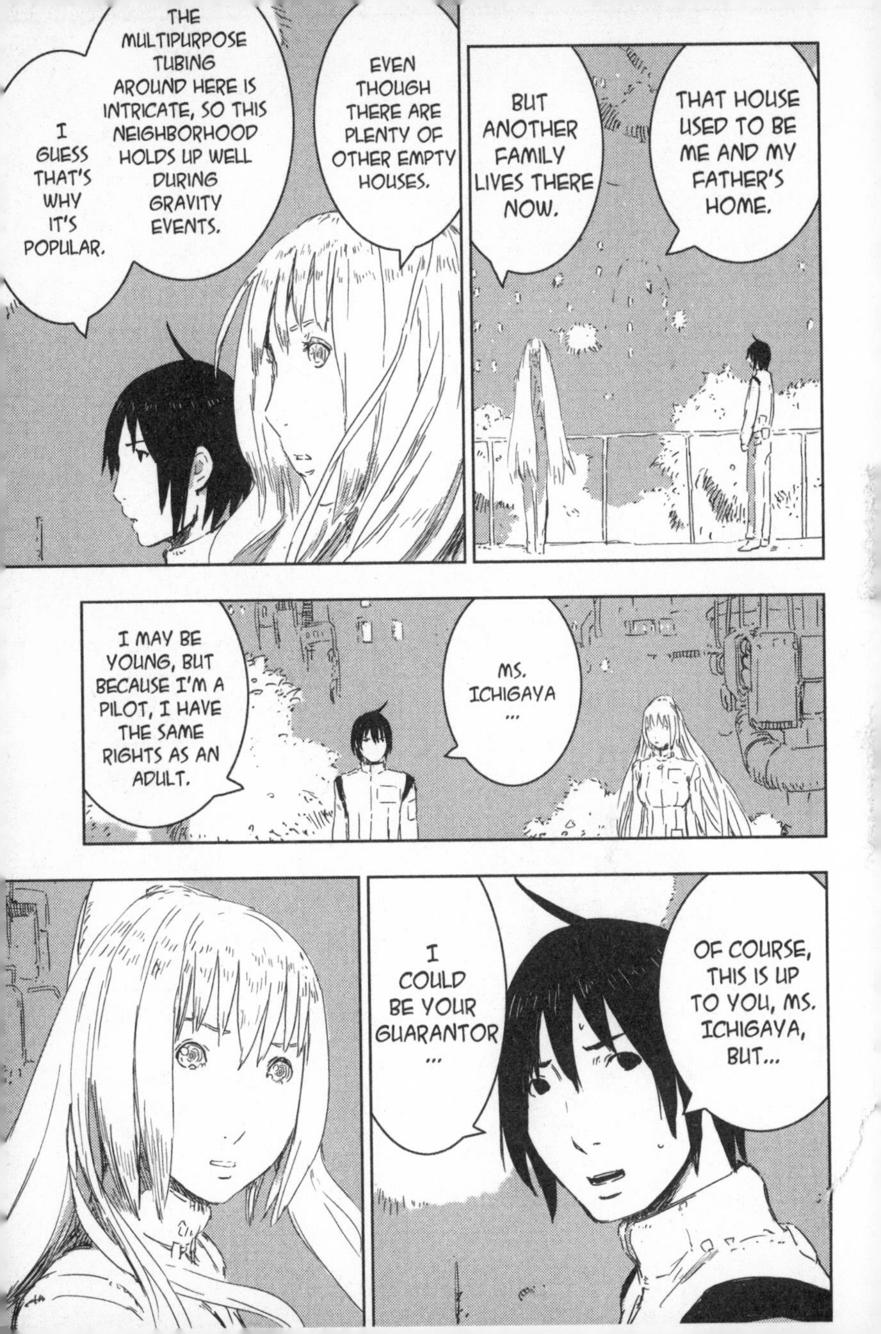
THAT HOUSE USED TO BE ME AND MY FATHER'S HOME.
BUT ANOTHER FAMILY LIVES THERE NOW.
EVEN THOUGH THERE ARE PLENTY OF OTHER EMPTY HOUSES.
THE MULTIPURPOSE TUBING AROUND HERE IS INTRICATE, SO THIS NEIGHBORHOOD HOLDS UP WELL DURING GRAVITY EVENTS.
I GUESS THAT'S WHY IT'S POPULAR.
MS. ICHIGAYA ...
I MAY BE YOUNG, BUT BECAUSE I'M A PILOT, I HAVE THE SAME RIGHTS AS AN ADULT.
OF COURSE, THIS IS UP TO YOU, MS. ICHIGAYA, BUT...
I COULD BE YOUR GUARANTOR ...

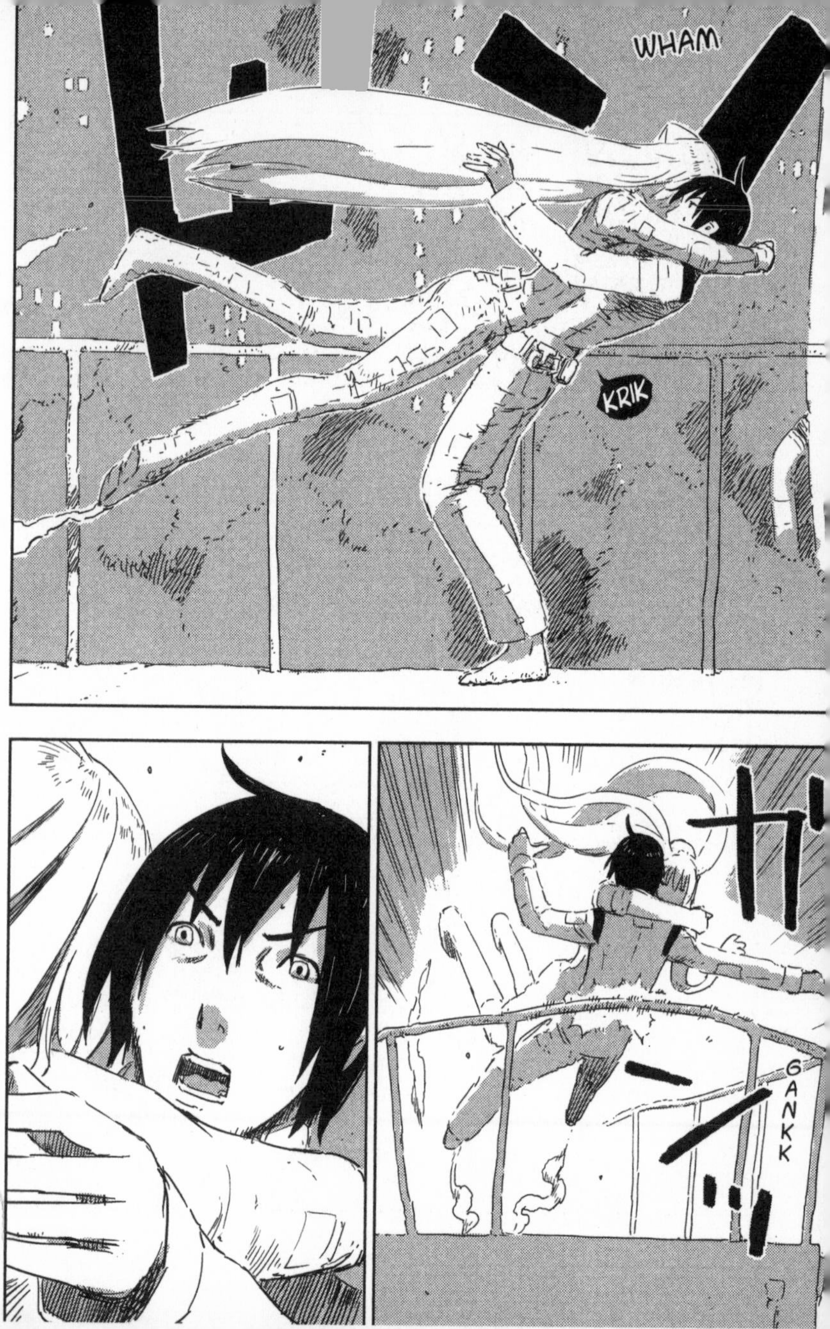
WHAM
KRIK
ガッ
GANKK

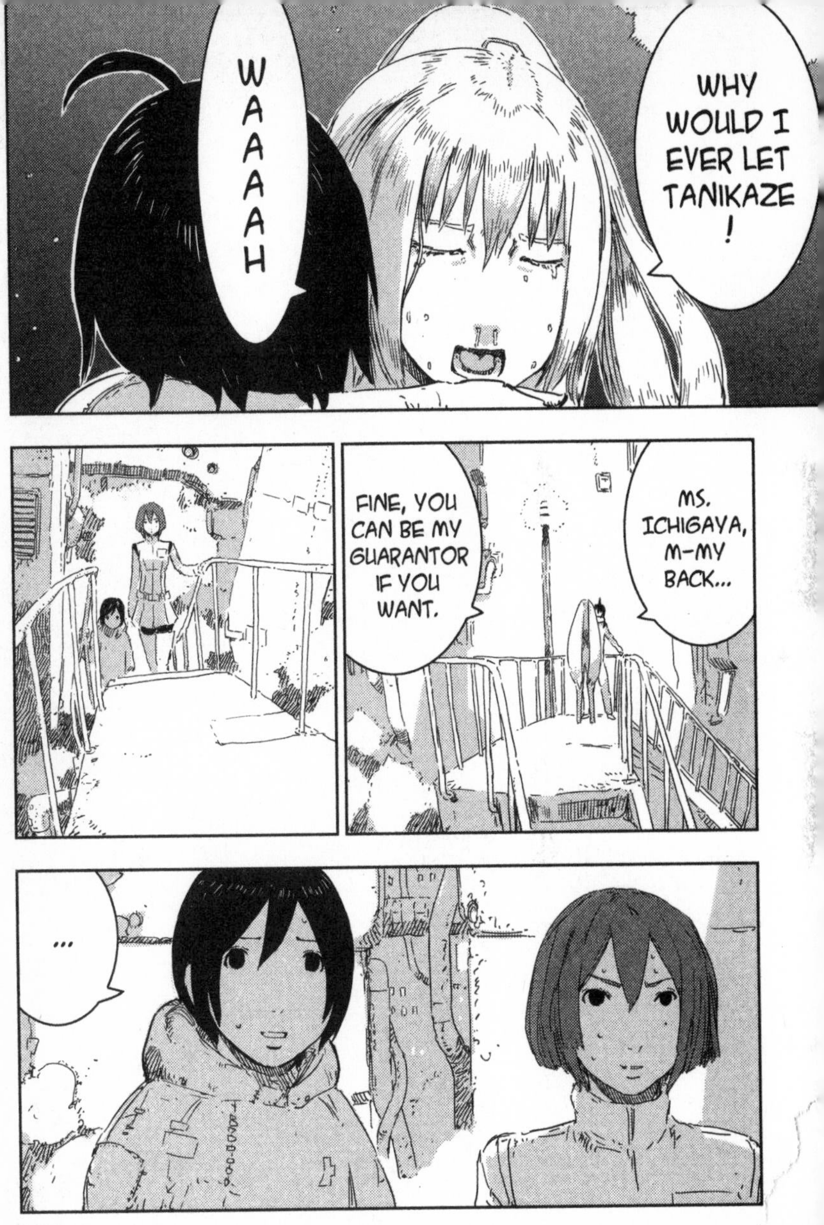
WHY WOULD I EVER LET TANIKAZE !
WAAAAAH
MS. ICHIGAYA, M-MY BACK...
FINE, YOU CAN BE MY GUARANTOR IF YOU WANT.
...

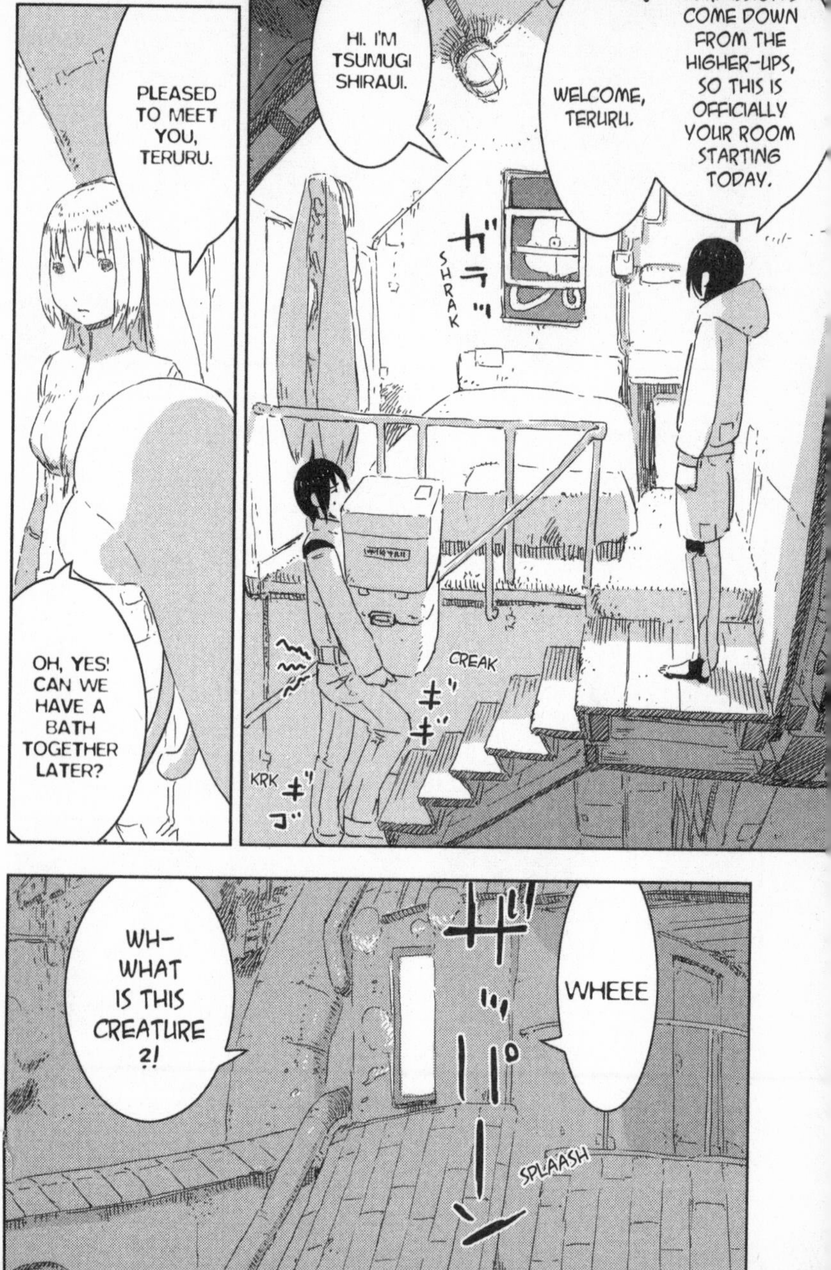
PERMISSION'S COME DOWN FROM THE HIGHER-UPS, SO THIS IS OFFICIALLY YOUR ROOM STARTING TODAY.
WELCOME, TERURU.
ガラッ
SHRAK
HI. I'M TSUMUGI SHIRAUI.
CREAK
KRK
PLEASED TO MEET YOU, TERURU.
OH, YES! CAN WE HAVE A BATH TOGETHER LATER?
WHEEE
SPLAASH
WH-WHAT IS THIS CREATURE?!

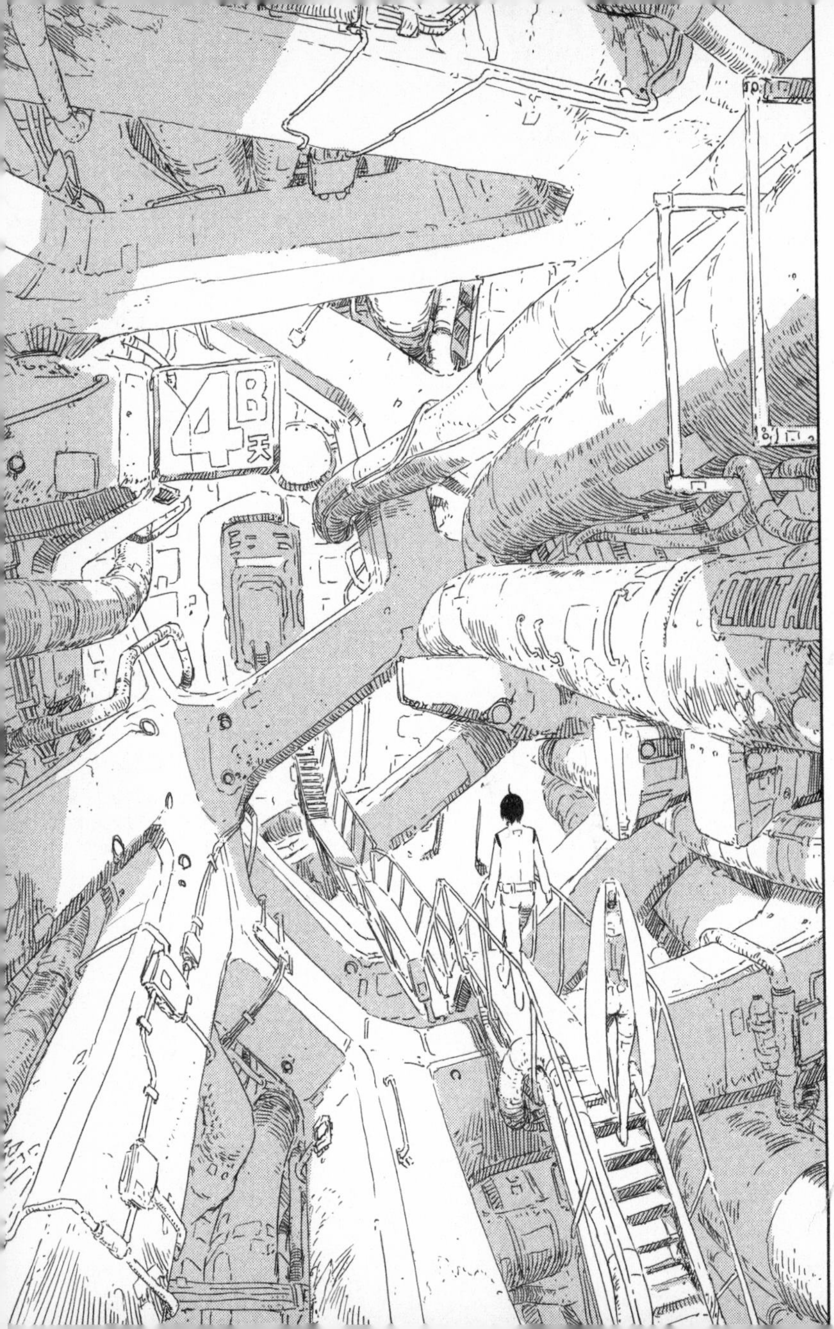
4B
天
LIMIT

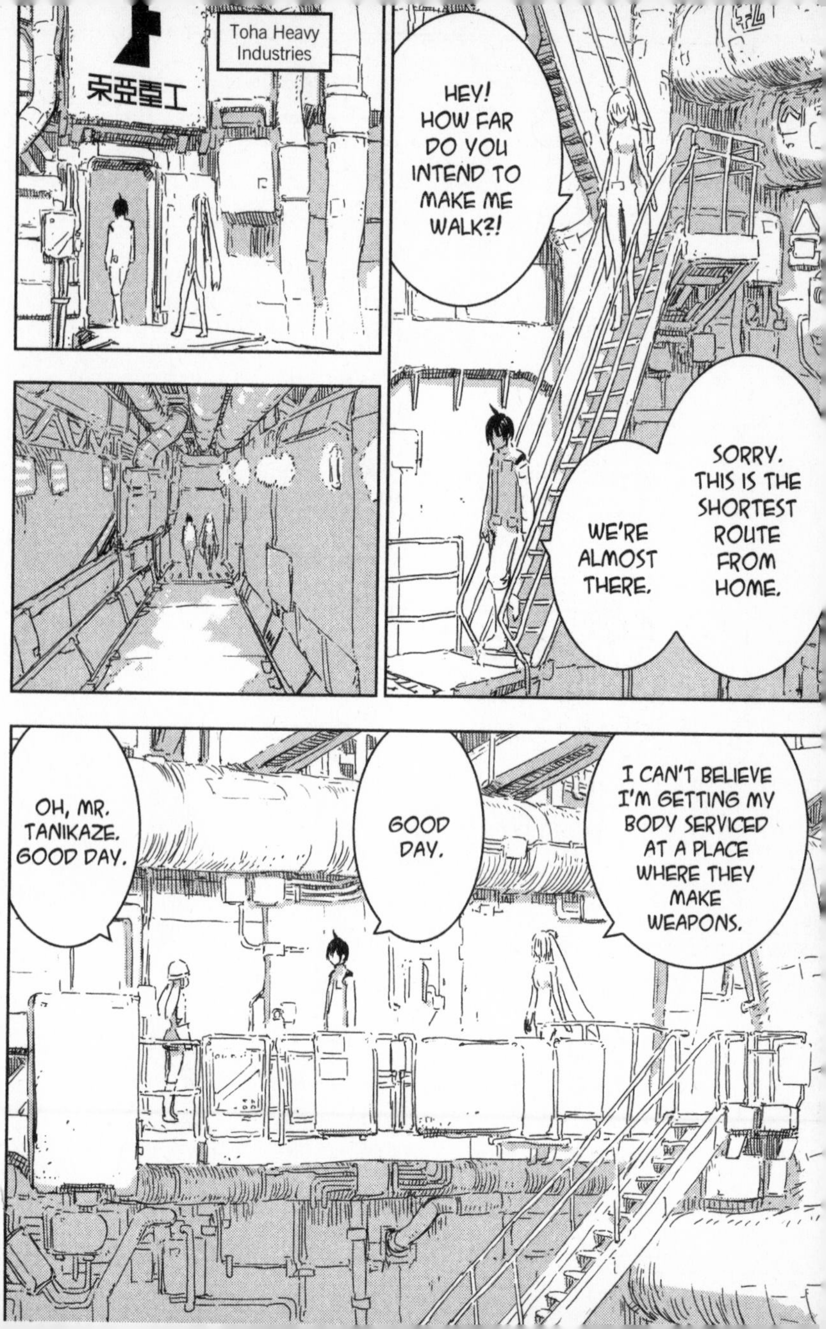
HEY! HOW FAR DO YOU INTEND TO MAKE ME WALK?!
SORRY. THIS IS THE SHORTEST ROUTE FROM HOME.
WE'RE ALMOST THERE.
東亜重工
Toha Heavy Industries
I CAN'T BELIEVE I'M GETTING MY BODY SERVICED AT A PLACE WHERE THEY MAKE WEAPONS.
GOOD DAY.
OH, MR. TANIKAZE. GOOD DAY.

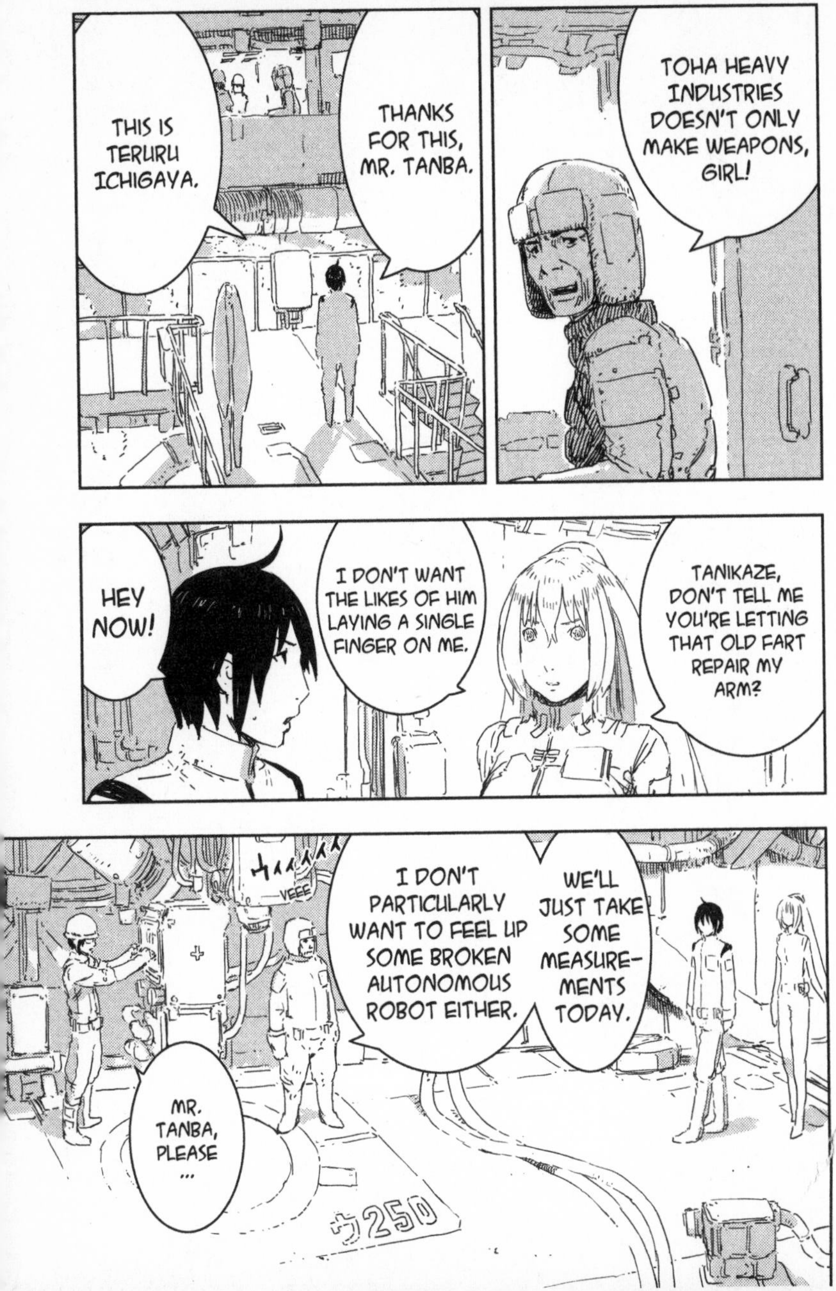
TOHA HEAVY INDUSTRIES DOESN'T ONLY MAKE WEAPONS, GIRL!
THANKS FOR THIS, MR. TANBA.
THIS IS TERURU ICHIGAYA.
TANIKAZE, DON'T TELL ME YOU'RE LETTING THAT OLD FART REPAIR MY ARM?
I DON'T WANT THE LIKES OF HIM LAYING A SINGLE FINGER ON ME.
HEY NOW!
VEEE
WE'LL JUST TAKE SOME MEASUREMENTS TODAY.
I DON'T PARTICULARLY WANT TO FEEL UP SOME BROKEN AUTONOMOUS ROBOT EITHER.
MR. TANBA, PLEASE...
ウ250

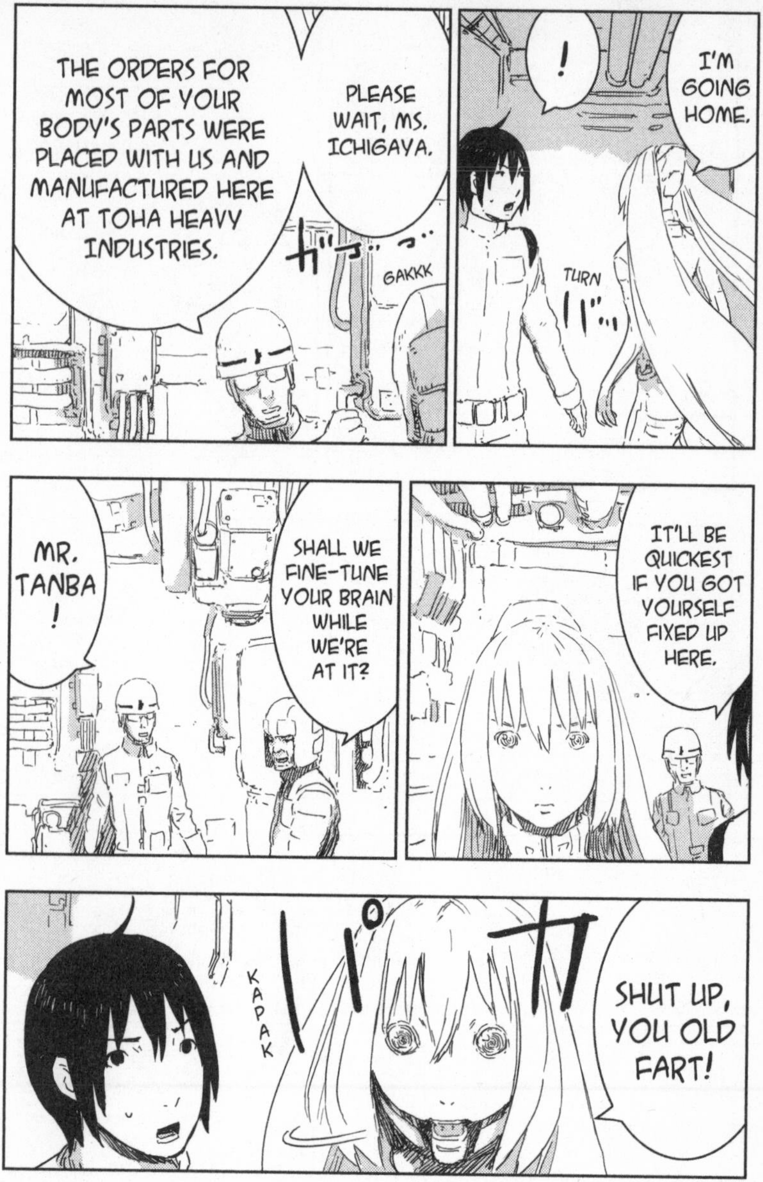

I'M GOING HOME.
!
TURN
PLEASE WAIT, MS. ICHIGAYA.
THE ORDERS FOR MOST OF YOUR BODY'S PARTS WERE PLACED WITH US AND MANUFACTURED HERE AT TOHA HEAVY INDUSTRIES.
GAKKK
IT'LL BE QUICKEST IF YOU GOT YOURSELF FIXED UP HERE.
SHALL WE FINE-TUNE YOUR BRAIN WHILE WE'RE AT IT?
MR. TANBA!
SHUT UP, YOU OLD FART!
KAPAK

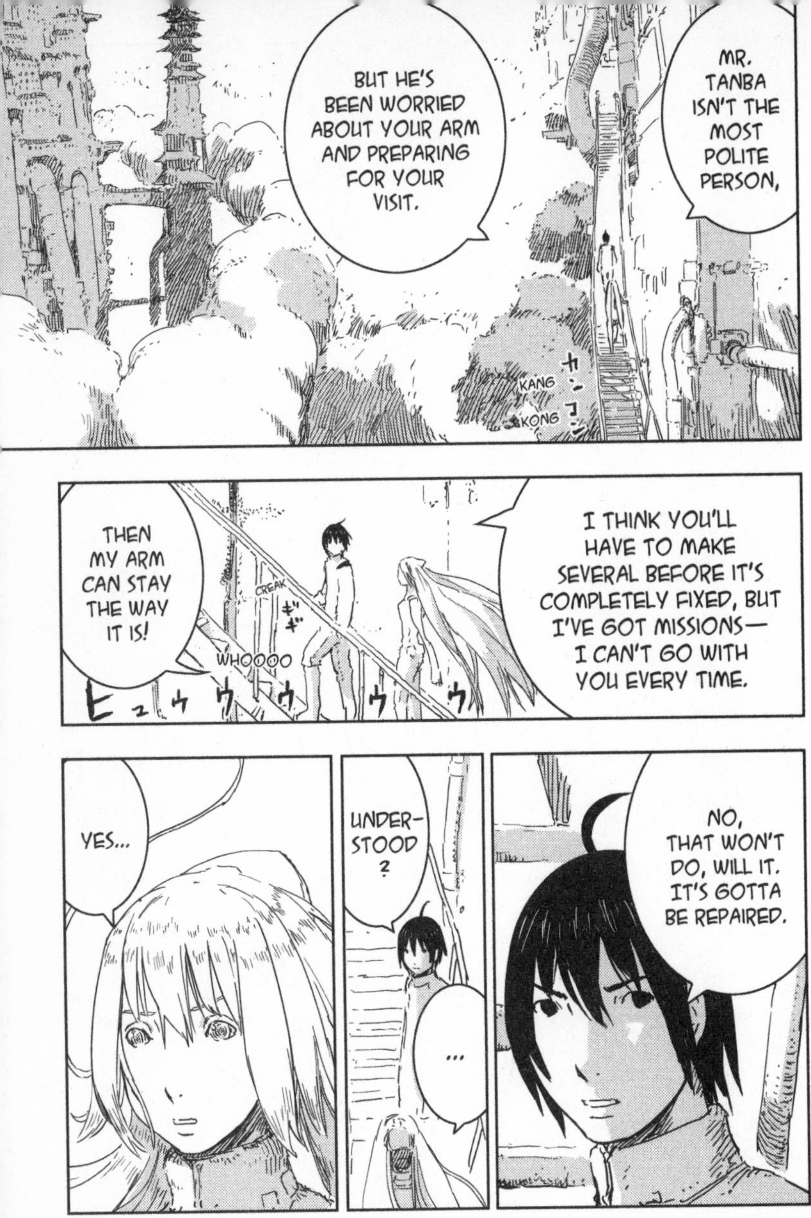
MR. TANBA ISN'T THE MOST POLITE PERSON,
BUT HE'S BEEN WORRIED ABOUT YOUR ARM AND PREPARING FOR YOUR VISIT.
KANG
KONG
I THINK YOU'LL HAVE TO MAKE SEVERAL BEFORE IT'S COMPLETELY FIXED, BUT I'VE GOT MISSIONS— I CAN'T GO WITH YOU EVERY TIME.
CREAK
THEN MY ARM CAN STAY THE WAY IT IS!
WHOOOOO
NO, THAT WON'T DO, WILL IT. IT'S GOTTA BE REPAIRED.
UNDER-STOOD?
...
YES...

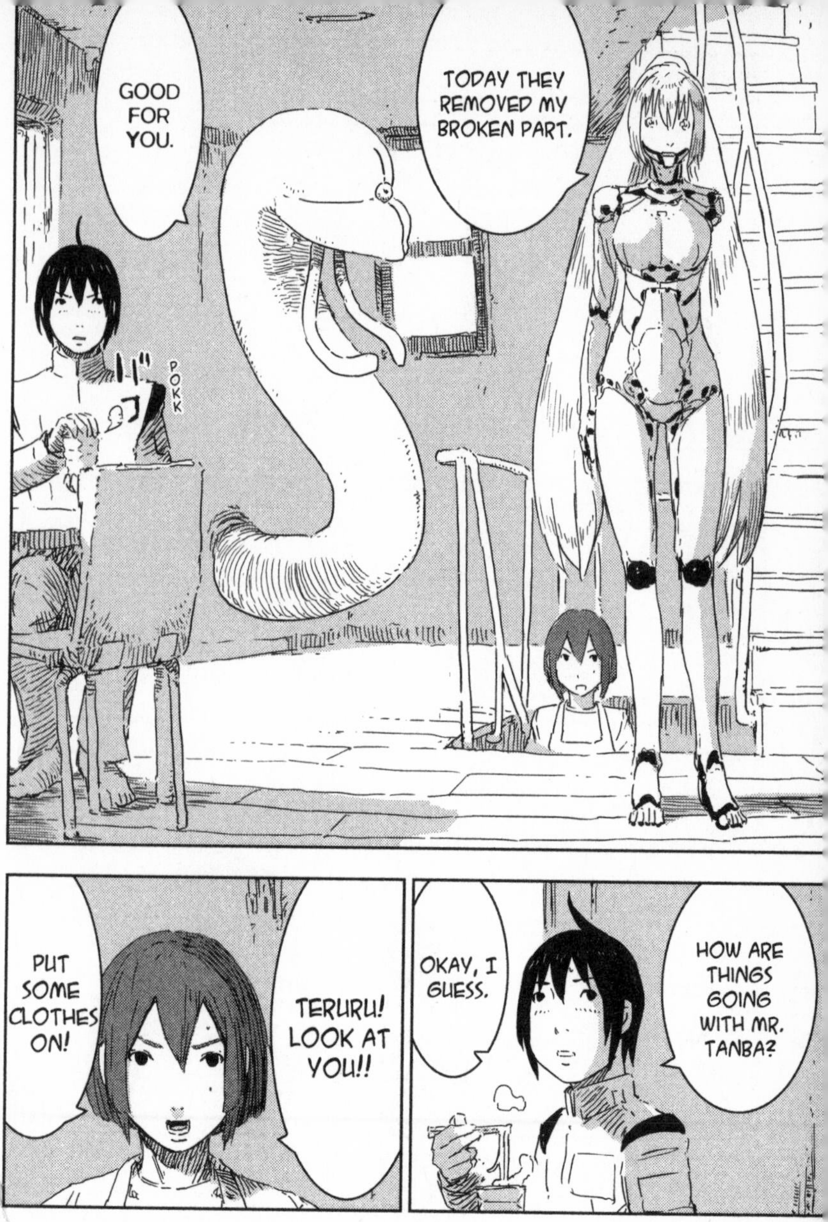
TODAY THEY REMOVED MY BROKEN PART.
GOOD FOR YOU.
POKK
HOW ARE THINGS GOING WITH MR. TANBA?
OKAY, I GUESS.
TERURU! LOOK AT YOU!!
PUT SOME CLOTHES ON!

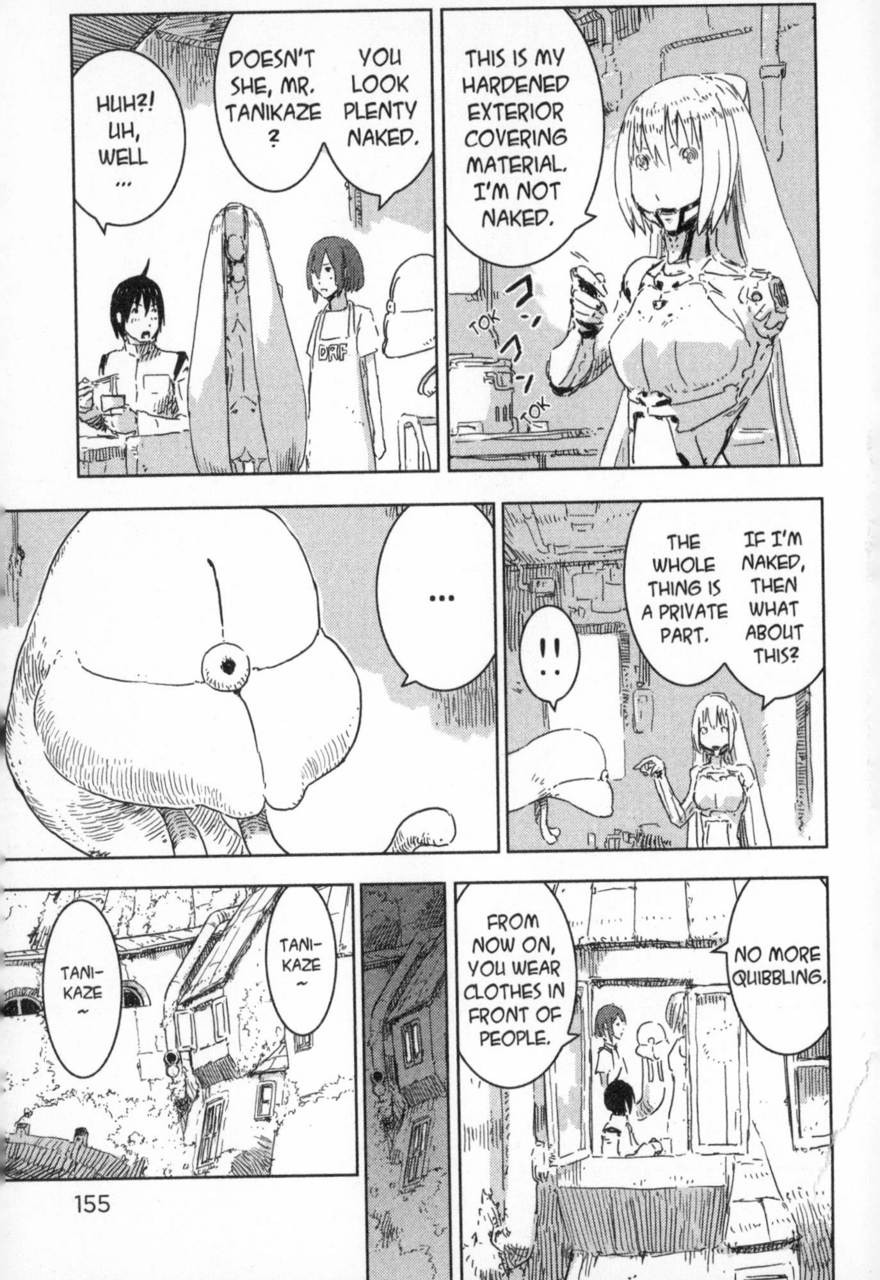
THIS IS MY HARDENED EXTERIOR COVERING MATERIAL. I'M NOT NAKED.
TOK
TOK
YOU LOOK PLENTY NAKED.
DOESN'T SHE, MR. TANIKAZE?
HUH?! UH, WELL ...
IF I'M NAKED, THEN WHAT ABOUT THIS?
THE WHOLE THING IS A PRIVATE PART.
!!
...
NO MORE QUIBBLING.
FROM NOW ON, YOU WEAR CLOTHES IN FRONT OF PEOPLE.
TANI-KAZE ~
TANI-KAZE ~

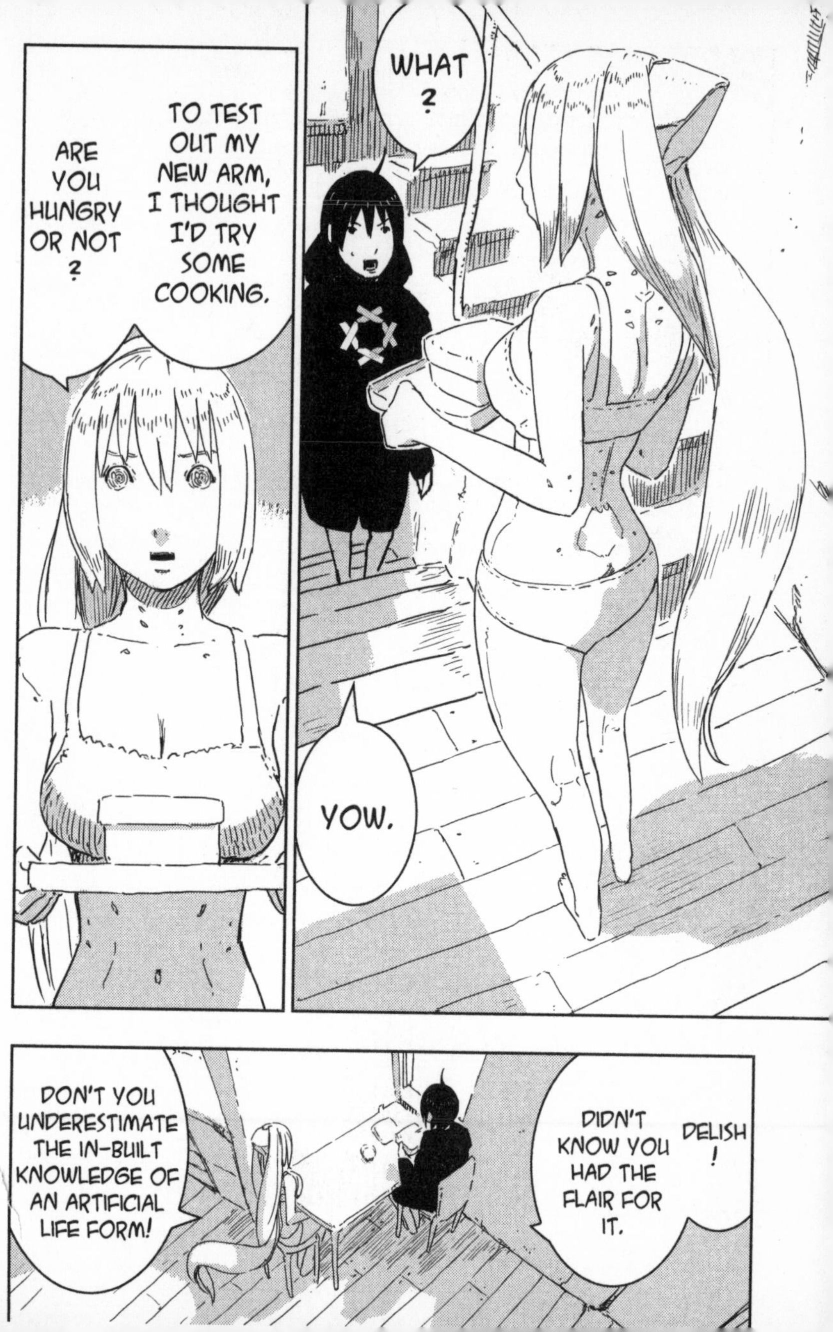
WHAT ?
YOW.
TO TEST OUT MY NEW ARM, I THOUGHT I'D TRY SOME COOKING.
ARE YOU HUNGRY OR NOT ?
DELISH !
DIDN'T KNOW YOU HAD THE FLAIR FOR IT.
DON'T YOU UNDERESTIMATE THE IN-BUILT KNOWLEDGE OF AN ARTIFICIAL LIFE FORM!

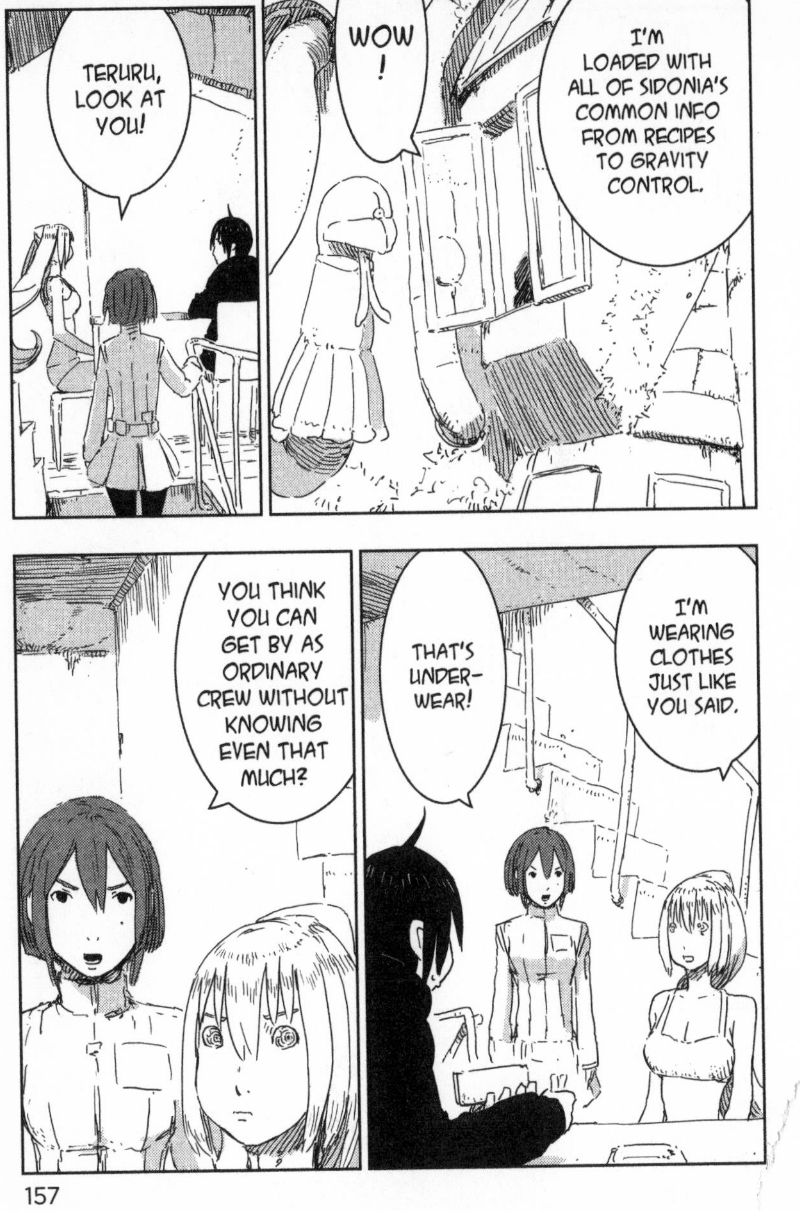
I'M LOADED WITH ALL OF SIDONIA'S COMMON INFO FROM RECIPES TO GRAVITY CONTROL.
WOW!
TERURU, LOOK AT YOU!
I'M WEARING CLOTHES JUST LIKE YOU SAID.
THAT'S UNDER-WEAR!
YOU THINK YOU CAN GET BY AS ORDINARY CREW WITHOUT KNOWING EVEN THAT MUCH?

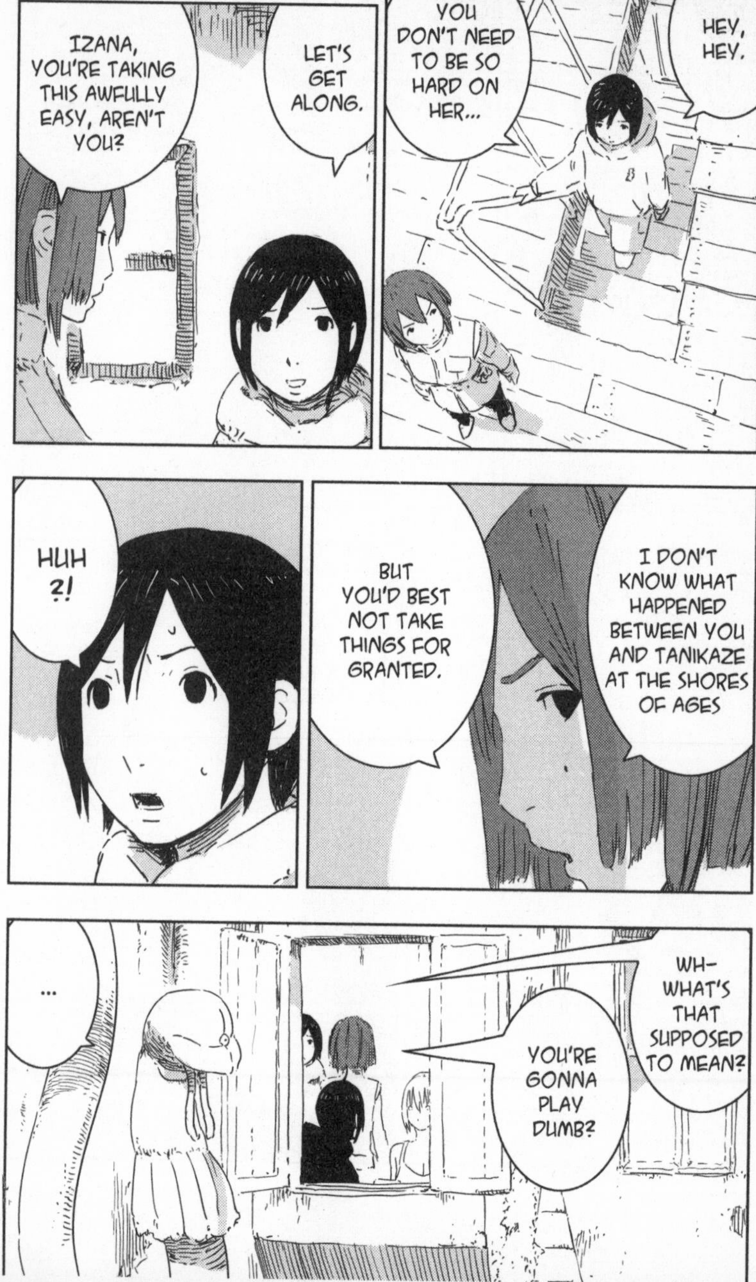
HEY, HEY.
YOU DON'T NEED TO BE SO HARD ON HER...
LET'S GET ALONG.
IZANA, YOU'RE TAKING THIS AWFULLY EASY, AREN'T YOU?
I DON'T KNOW WHAT HAPPENED BETWEEN YOU AND TANIKAZE AT THE SHORES OF AGES
BUT YOU'D BEST NOT TAKE THINGS FOR GRANTED.
HUH ?!
WH- WHAT'S THAT SUPPOSED TO MEAN?
YOU'RE GONNA PLAY DUMB?
...

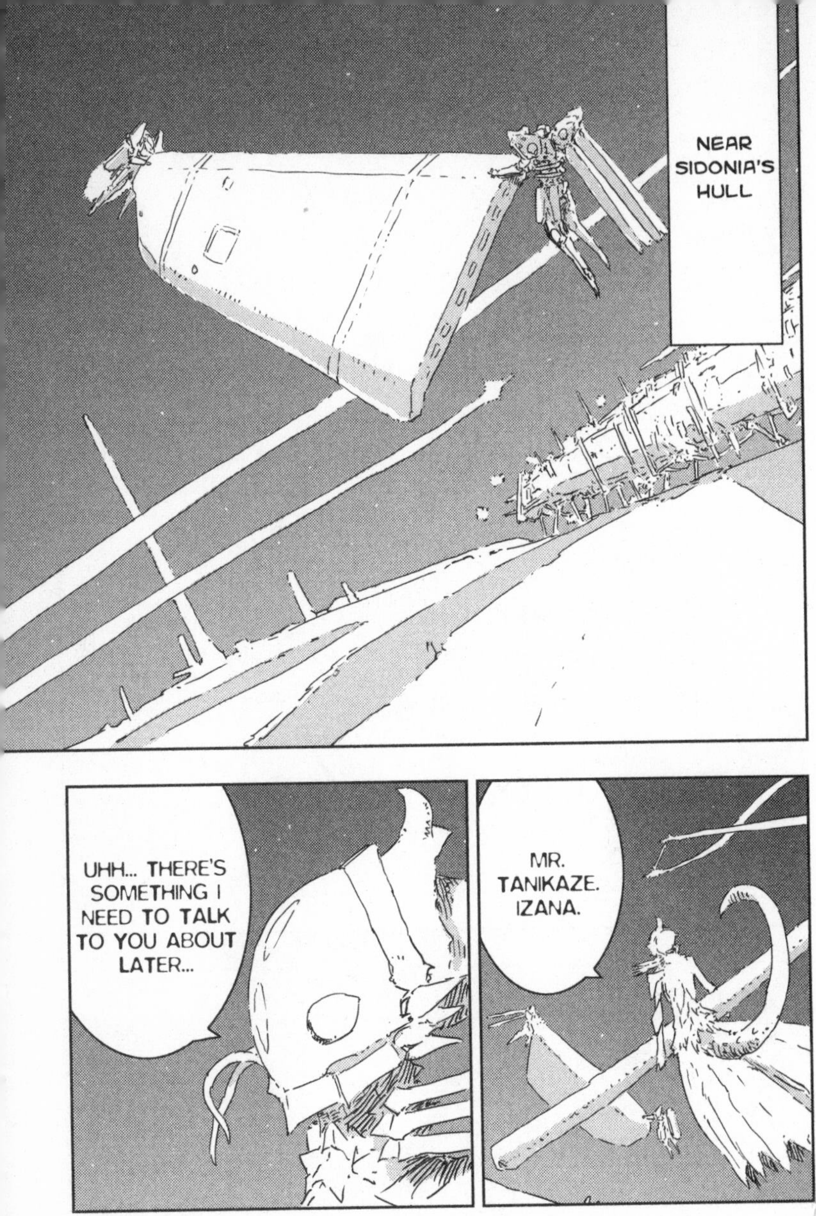
NEAR SIDONIA'S HULL
MR. TANIKAZE. IZANA.
UHH... THERE'S SOMETHING I NEED TO TALK TO YOU ABOUT LATER...

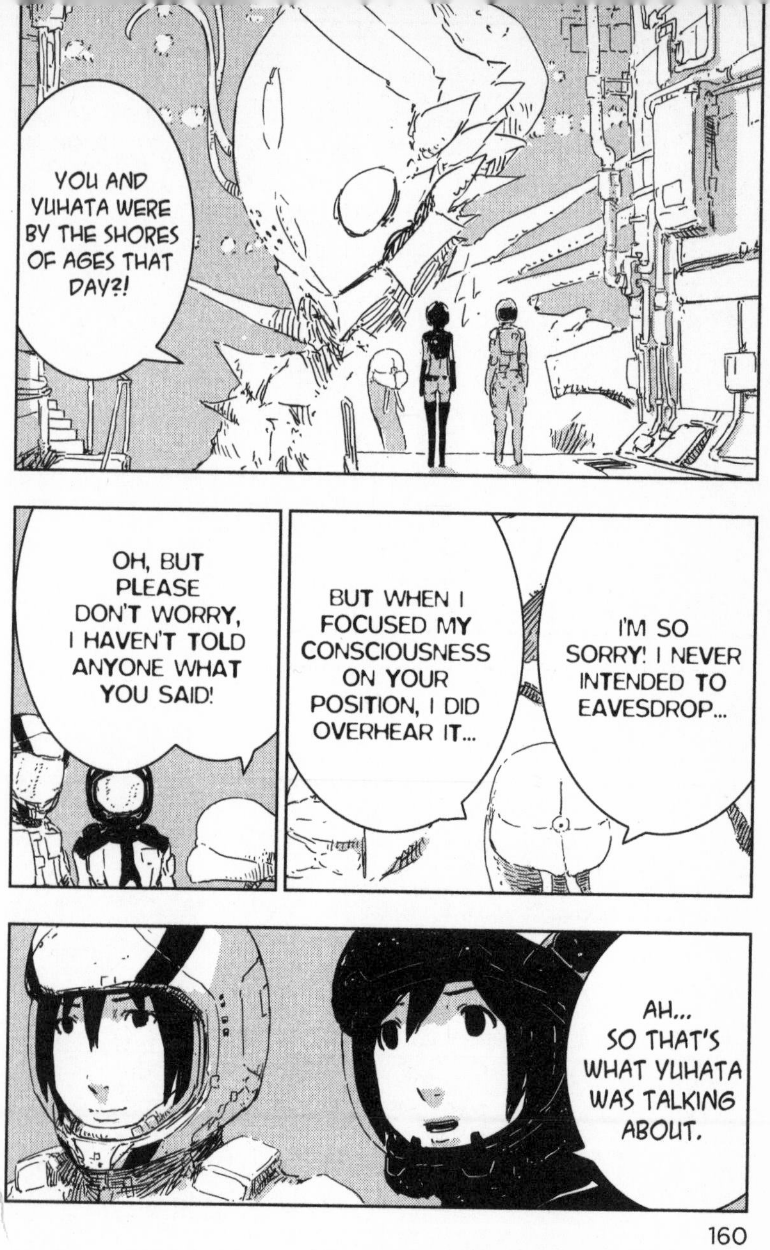
YOU AND YUHATA WERE BY THE SHORES OF AGES THAT DAY?!
I'M SO SORRY! I NEVER INTENDED TO EAVESDROP...
BUT WHEN I FOCUSED MY CONSCIOUSNESS ON YOUR POSITION, I DID OVERHEAR IT...
OH, BUT PLEASE DON'T WORRY, I HAVEN'T TOLD ANYONE WHAT YOU SAID!
AH... SO THAT'S WHAT YUHATA WAS TALKING ABOUT.

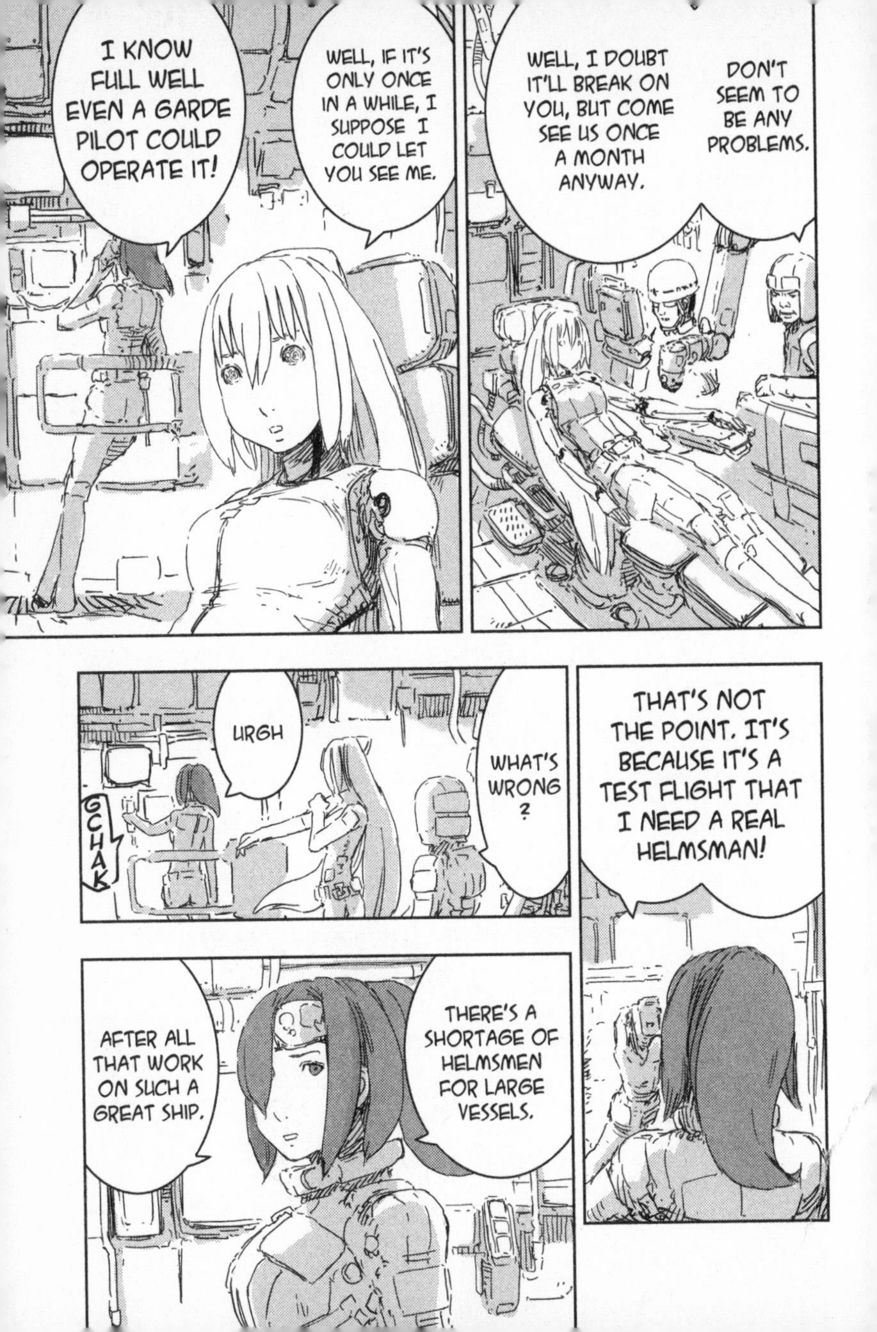
DON'T SEEM TO BE ANY PROBLEMS.
WELL, I DOUBT IT'LL BREAK ON YOU, BUT COME SEE US ONCE A MONTH ANYWAY.
WELL, IF IT'S ONLY ONCE IN A WHILE, I SUPPOSE I COULD LET YOU SEE ME.
I KNOW FULL WELL EVEN A GARDE PILOT COULD OPERATE IT!
THAT'S NOT THE POINT. IT'S BECAUSE IT'S A TEST FLIGHT THAT I NEED A REAL HELMSMAN!
WHAT'S WRONG?
URGH
GCHAK
THERE'S A SHORTAGE OF HELMSMEN FOR LARGE VESSELS.
AFTER ALL THAT WORK ON SUCH A GREAT SHIP.

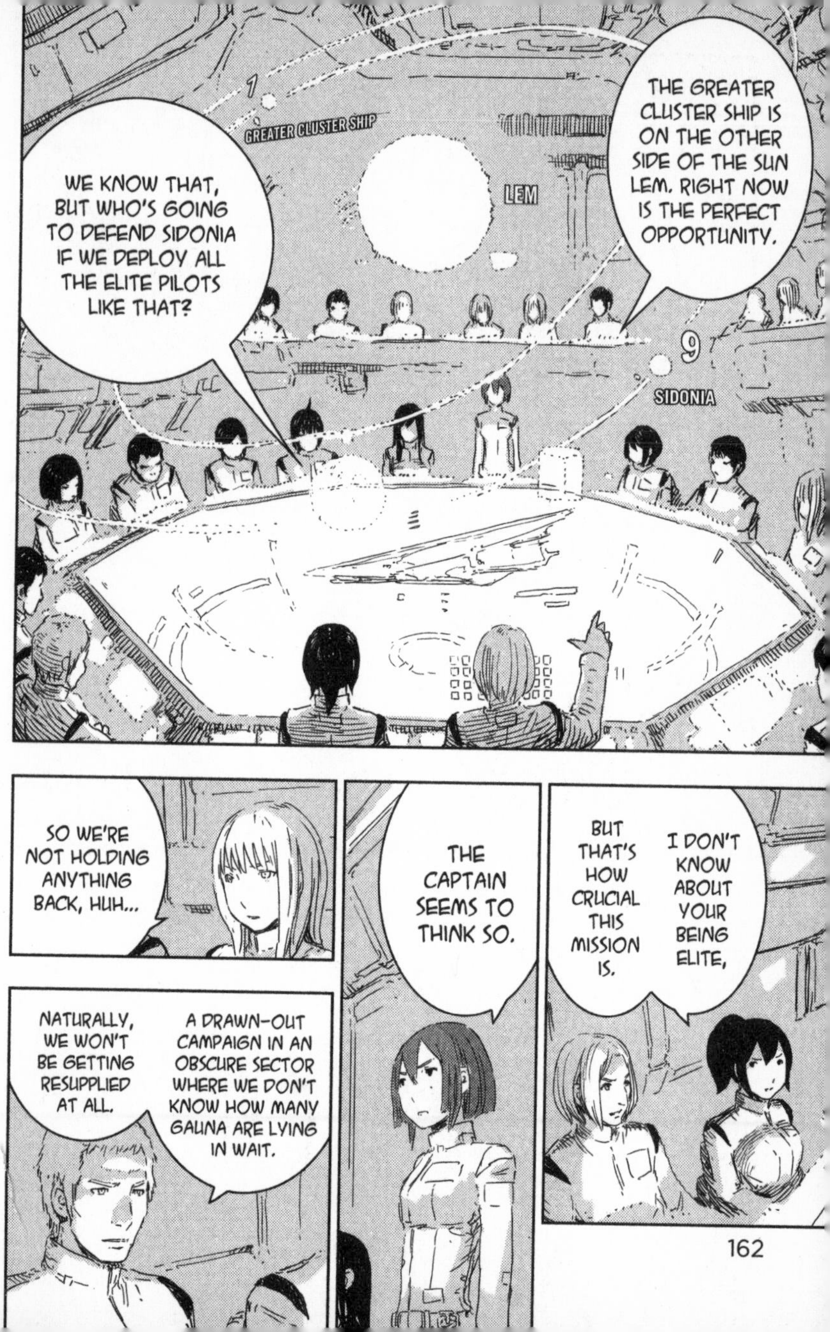
GREATER CLUSTER SHIP
LEM
SIDONIA
THE GREATER CLUSTER SHIP IS ON THE OTHER SIDE OF THE SUN LEM. RIGHT NOW IS THE PERFECT OPPORTUNITY.
WE KNOW THAT, BUT WHO'S GOING TO DEFEND SIDONIA IF WE DEPLOY ALL THE ELITE PILOTS LIKE THAT?
I DON'T KNOW ABOUT YOUR BEING ELITE,
BUT THAT'S HOW CRUCIAL THIS MISSION IS.
THE CAPTAIN SEEMS TO THINK SO.
SO WE'RE NOT HOLDING ANYTHING BACK, HUH...
A DRAWN-OUT CAMPAIGN IN AN OBSCURE SECTOR WHERE WE DON'T KNOW HOW MANY GAUNA ARE LYING IN WAIT.
NATURALLY, WE WON'T BE GETTING RESUPPLIED AT ALL.

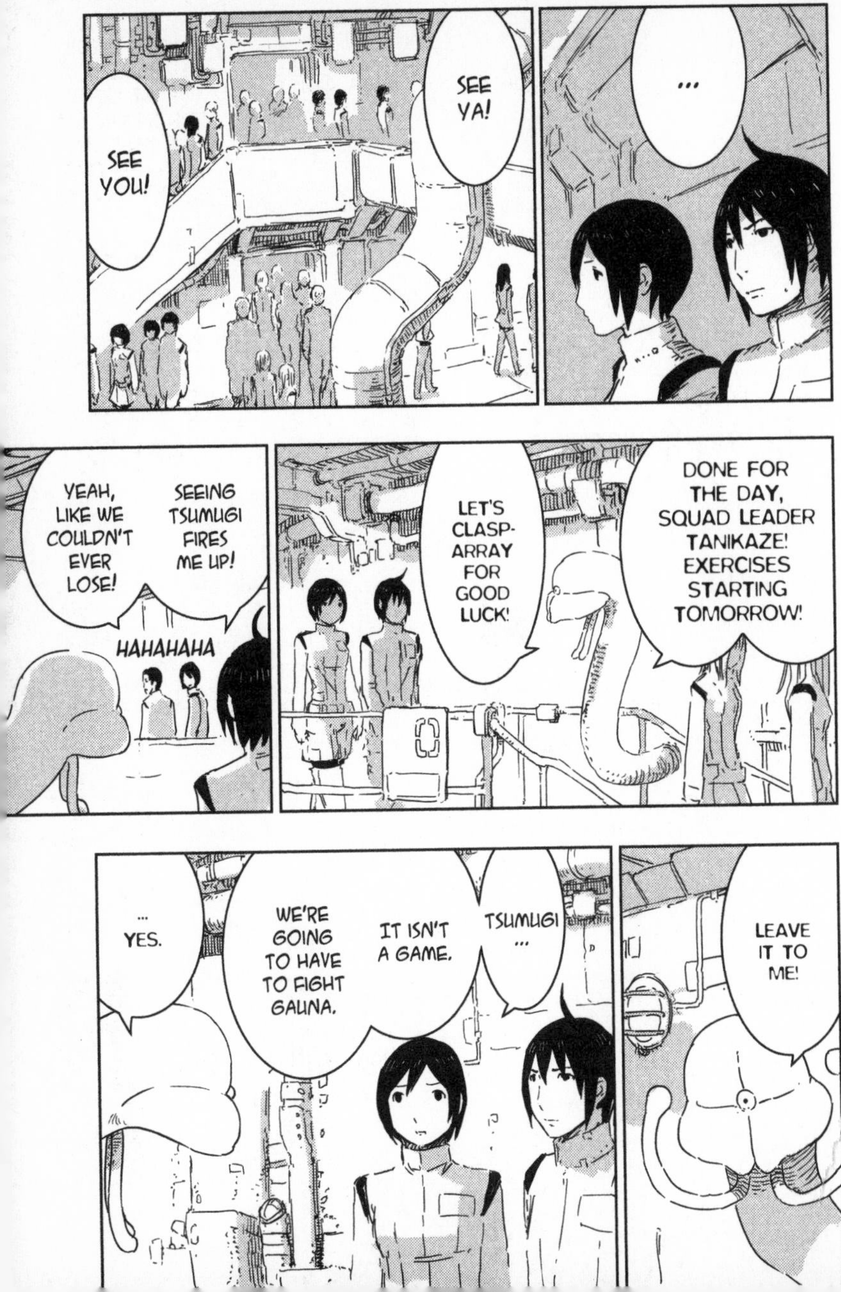
...
SEE YA!
SEE YOU!
DONE FOR THE DAY, SQUAD LEADER TANIKAZE! EXERCISES STARTING TOMORROW!
LET'S CLASP-ARRAY FOR GOOD LUCK!
SEEING TSUMUGI FIRES ME UP!
YEAH, LIKE WE COULDN'T EVER LOSE!
HAHAHAHA
LEAVE IT TO ME!
TSUMUGI ...
IT ISN'T A GAME.
WE'RE GOING TO HAVE TO FIGHT GAUNA.
... YES.

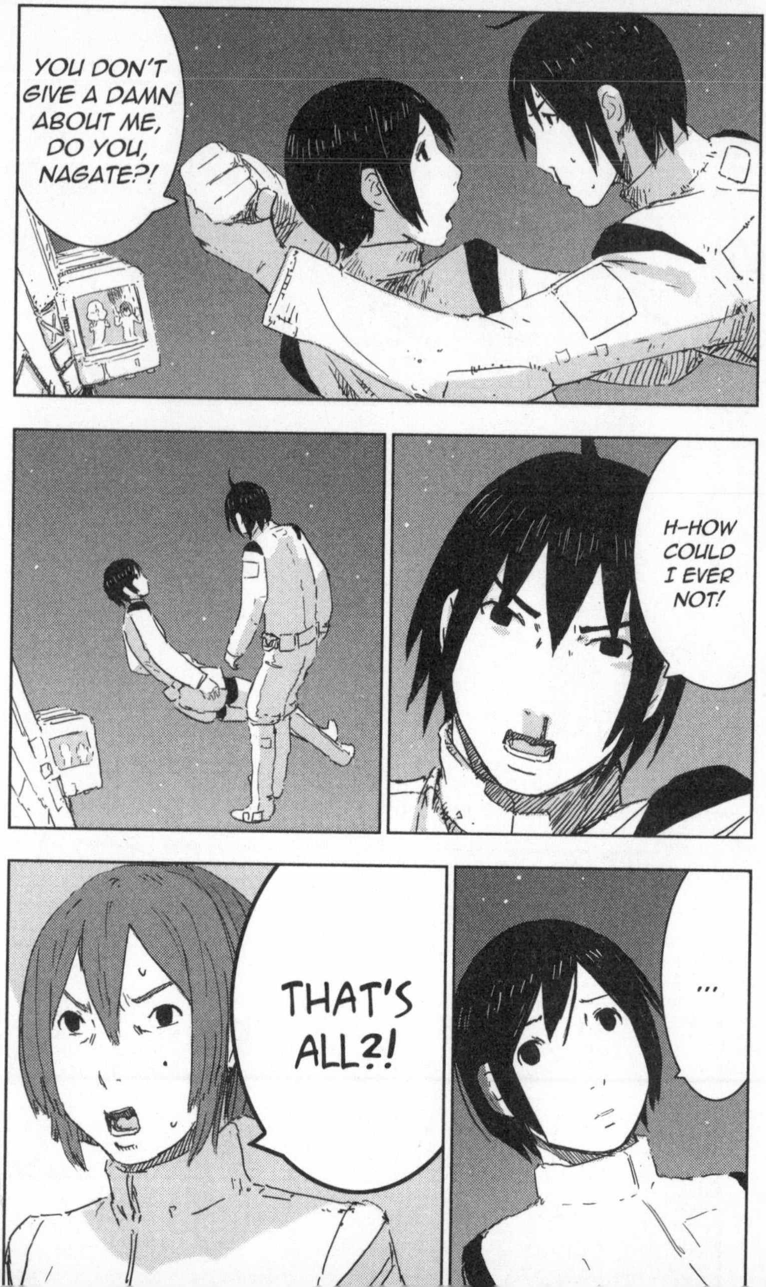
YOU DON'T GIVE A DAMN ABOUT ME, DO YOU, NAGATE?!
H-HOW COULD I EVER NOT!
THAT'S ALL?!
...

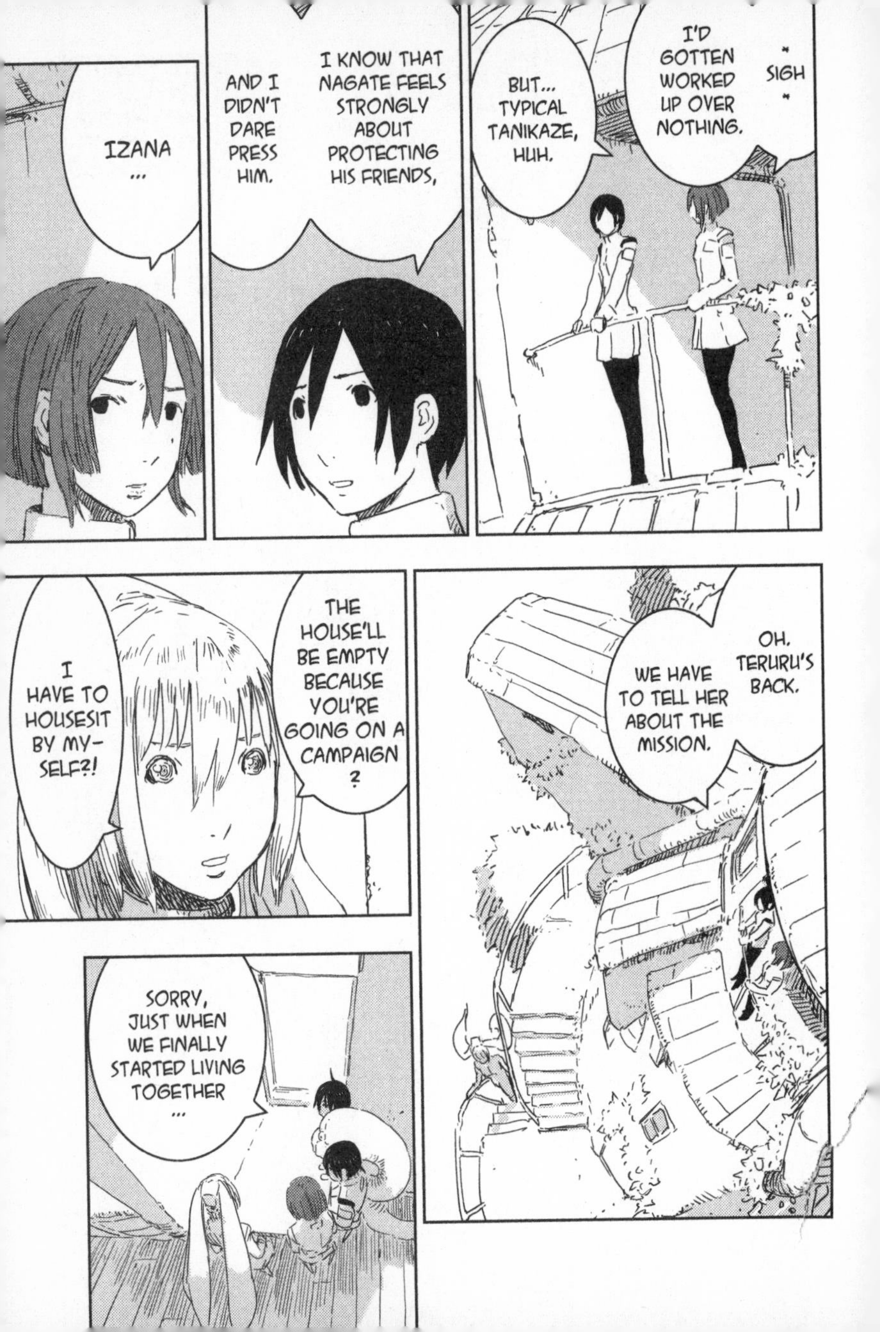
SIGH
I'D GOTTEN WORKED UP OVER NOTHING.
BUT... TYPICAL TANIKAZE, HUH.
I KNOW THAT NAGATE FEELS STRONGLY ABOUT PROTECTING HIS FRIENDS,
AND I DIDN'T DARE PRESS HIM.
IZANA ...
OH. TERURU'S BACK.
WE HAVE TO TELL HER ABOUT THE MISSION.
THE HOUSE'LL BE EMPTY BECAUSE YOU'RE GOING ON A CAMPAIGN?
I HAVE TO HOUSESIT BY MY-SELF?!
SORRY, JUST WHEN WE FINALLY STARTED LIVING TOGETHER ...

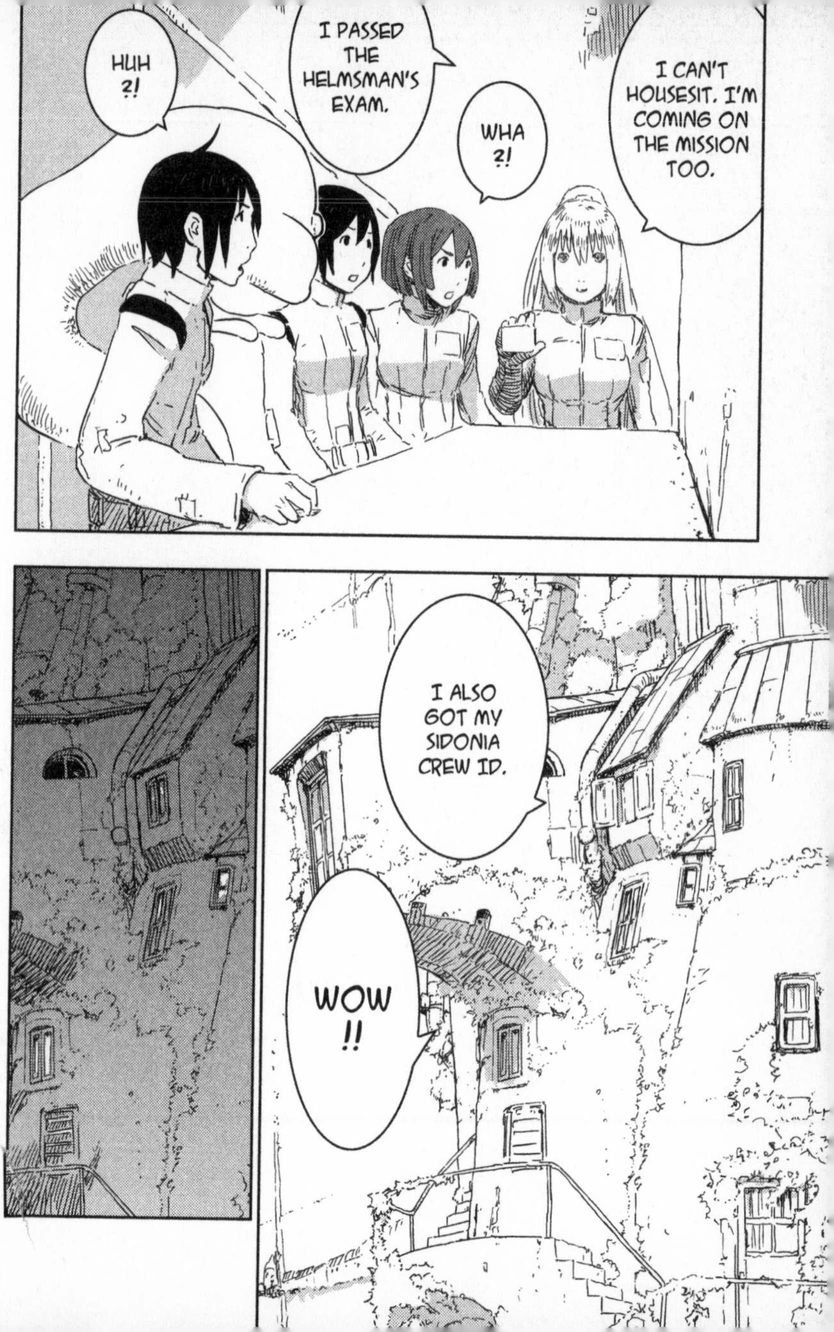
I CAN'T HOUSESIT. I'M COMING ON THE MISSION TOO.
WHA ?!
I PASSED THE HELMSMAN'S EXAM.
HUH ?!
I ALSO GOT MY SIDONIA CREW ID.
WOW !!

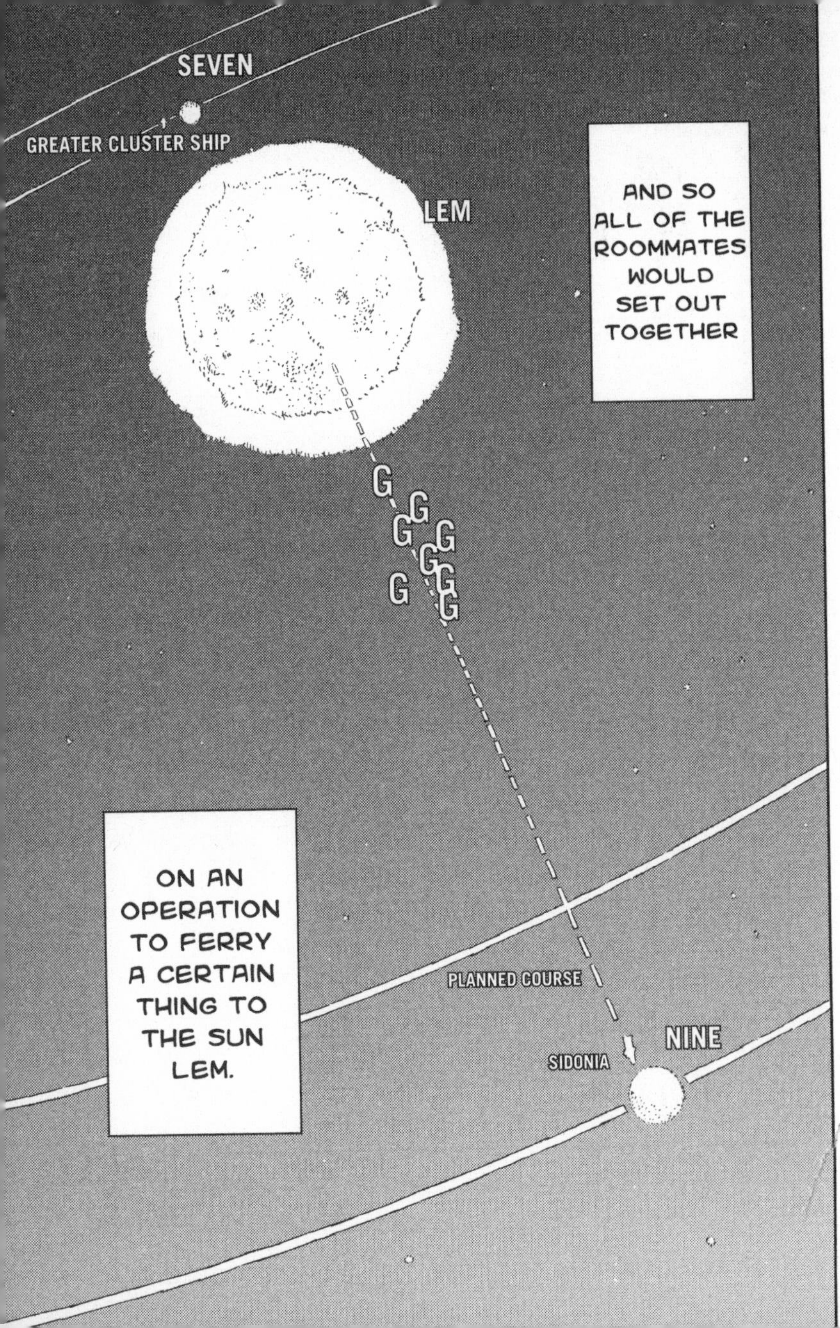
AND SO ALL OF THE ROOMMATES WOULD SET OUT TOGETHER
SEVEN
GREATER CLUSTER SHIP
LEM
G G G G G G G G
PLANNED COURSE
NINE
SIDONIA
ON AN OPERATION TO FERRY A CERTAIN THING TO THE SUN LEM.

KNIGHTS OF SIDONIA Volume ⑪ : END

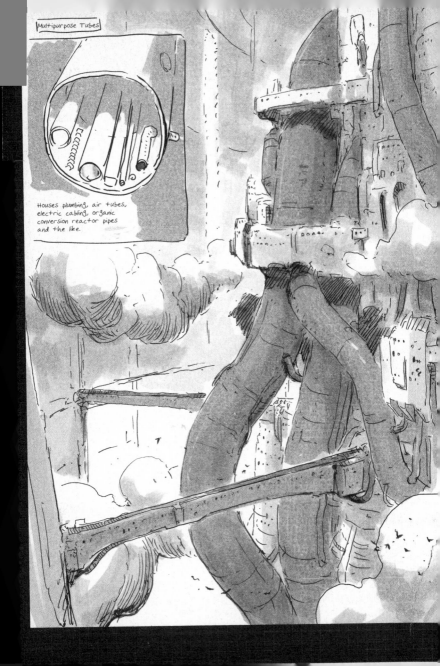

Multipurpose Tubes

Houses plumbing, air tubes, electric cabling, organic conversion reactor pipes and the like.

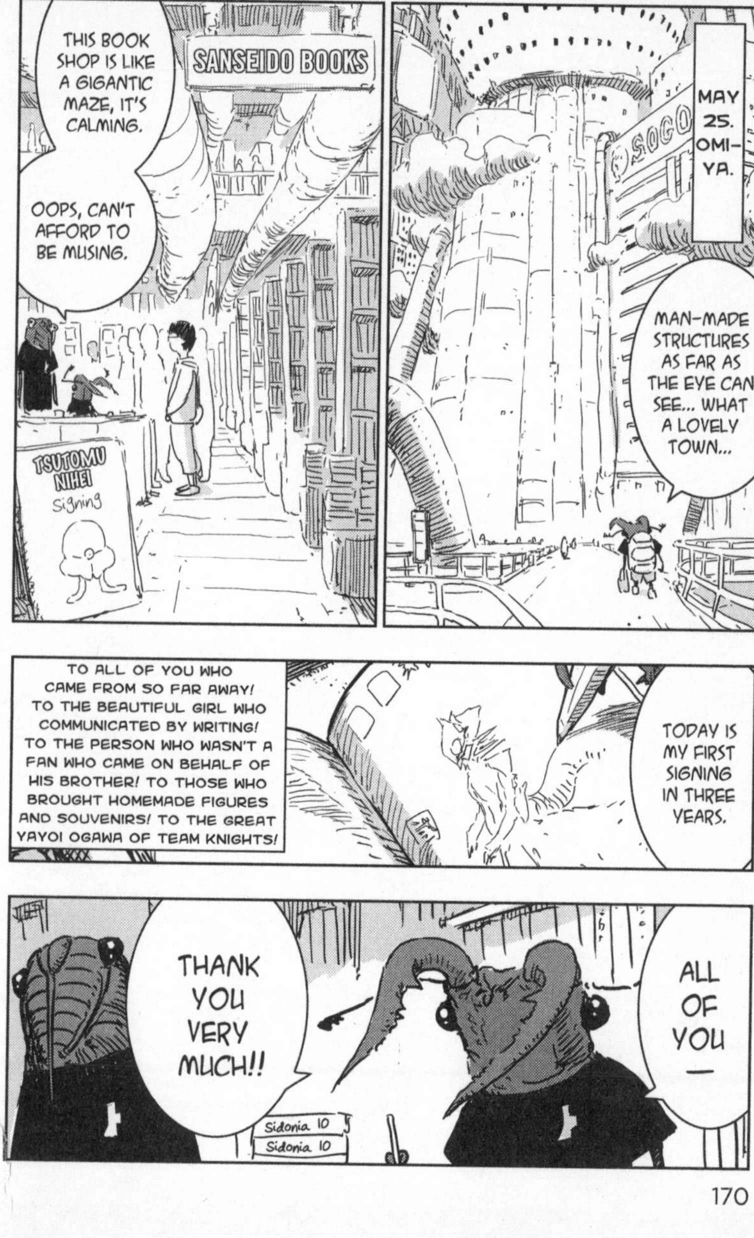
MAY 25. OMI-YA.
SOGO
MAN-MADE STRUCTURES AS FAR AS THE EYE CAN SEE... WHAT A LOVELY TOWN...
SANSEIDO BOOKS
THIS BOOK SHOP IS LIKE A GIGANTIC MAZE, IT'S CALMING.
OOPS, CAN'T AFFORD TO BE MUSING.
TSUTOMU NIHEI
Signing
TODAY IS MY FIRST SIGNING IN THREE YEARS.
TO ALL OF YOU WHO CAME FROM SO FAR AWAY! TO THE BEAUTIFUL GIRL WHO COMMUNICATED BY WRITING! TO THE PERSON WHO WASN'T A FAN WHO CAME ON BEHALF OF HIS BROTHER! TO THOSE WHO BROUGHT HOMEMADE FIGURES AND SOUVENIRS! TO THE GREAT YAYOI OGAWA OF TEAM KNIGHTS!
ALL OF YOU —
THANK YOU VERY MUCH!!
Sidonia 10
Sidonia 10

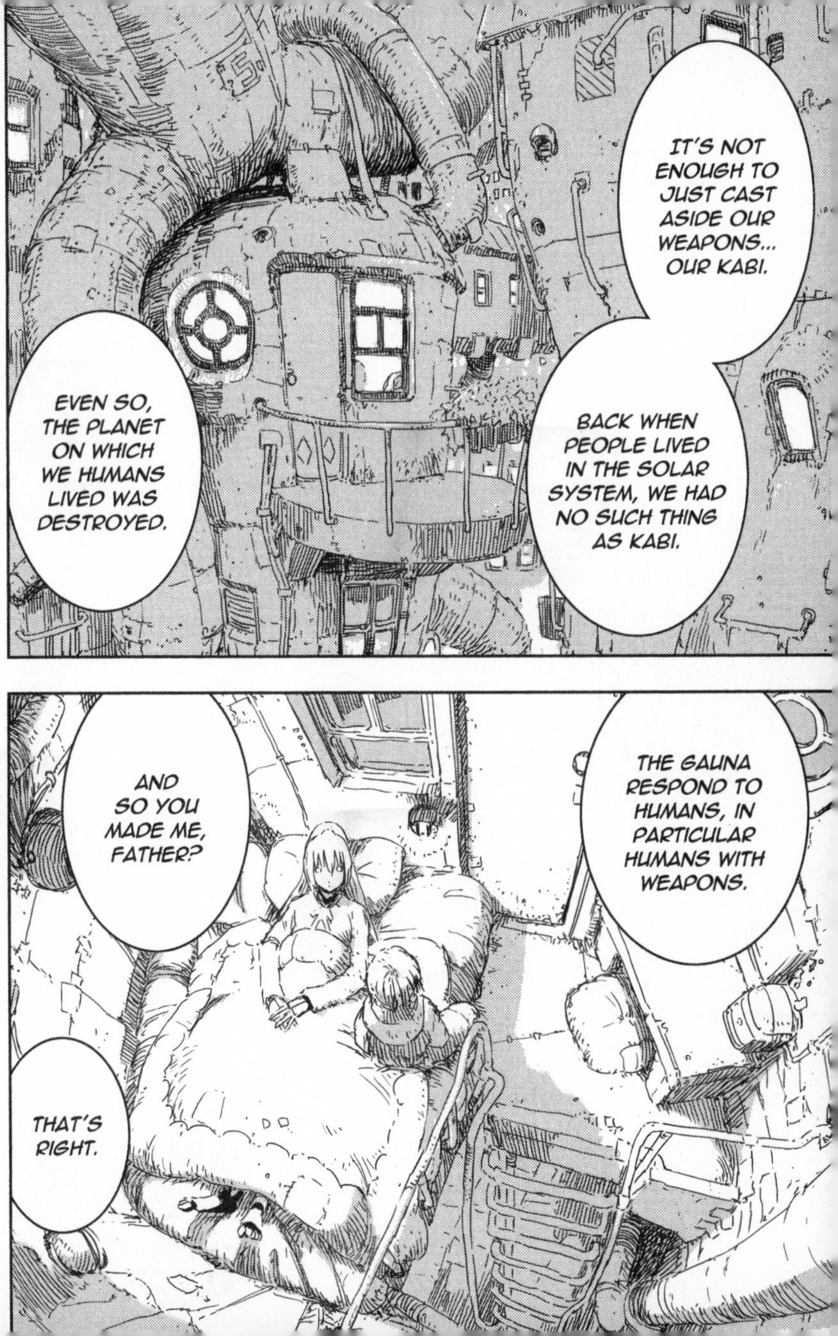
IT'S NOT ENOUGH TO JUST CAST ASIDE OUR WEAPONS... OUR KABI.
BACK WHEN PEOPLE LIVED IN THE SOLAR SYSTEM, WE HAD NO SUCH THING AS KABI.
EVEN SO, THE PLANET ON WHICH WE HUMANS LIVED WAS DESTROYED.
THE GAUNA RESPOND TO HUMANS, IN PARTICULAR HUMANS WITH WEAPONS.
AND SO YOU MADE ME, FATHER?
THAT'S RIGHT.

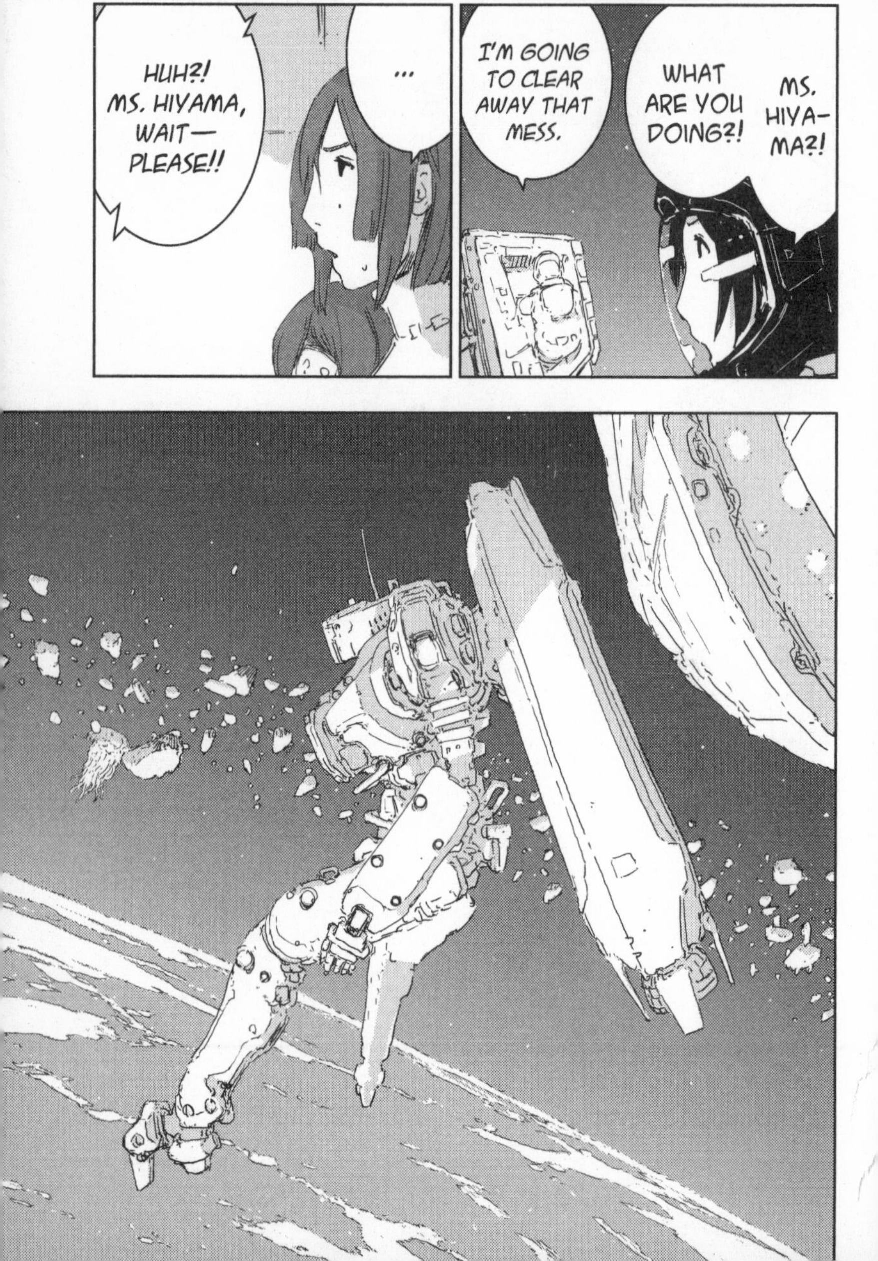
MS. HIYAMA?!
WHAT ARE YOU DOING?!
I'M GOING TO CLEAR AWAY THAT MESS.
...
HUH?! MS. HIYAMA, WAIT—PLEASE!!

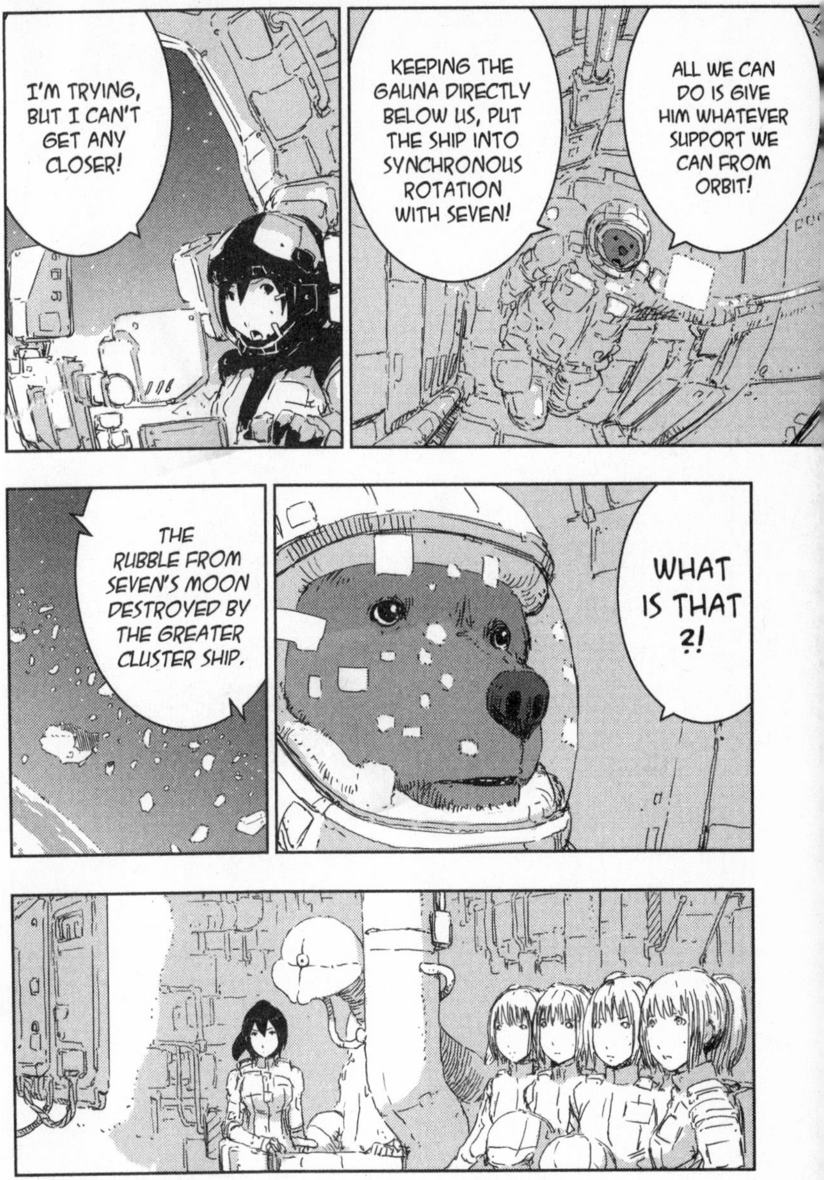
ALL WE CAN DO IS GIVE HIM WHATEVER SUPPORT WE CAN FROM ORBIT!
KEEPING THE GAUNA DIRECTLY BELOW US, PUT THE SHIP INTO SYNCHRONOUS ROTATION WITH SEVEN!
I'M TRYING, BUT I CAN'T GET ANY CLOSER!
WHAT IS THAT ?!
THE RUBBLE FROM SEVEN'S MOON DESTROYED BY THE GREATER CLUSTER SHIP.

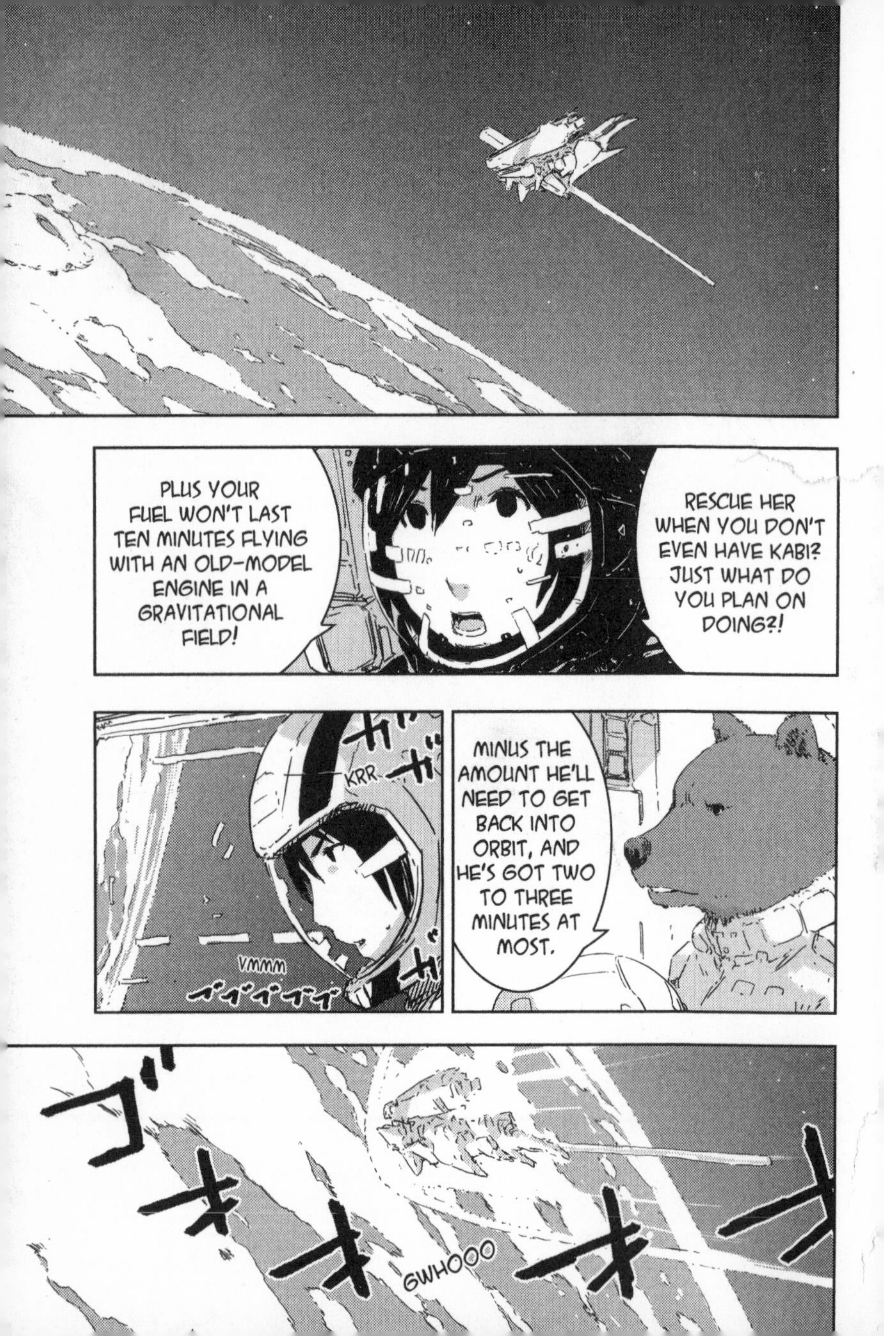
RESCUE HER WHEN YOU DON'T EVEN HAVE KABI?! JUST WHAT DO YOU PLAN ON DOING?!
PLUS YOUR FUEL WON'T LAST TEN MINUTES FLYING WITH AN OLD-MODEL ENGINE IN A GRAVITATIONAL FIELD!
MINUS THE AMOUNT HE'LL NEED TO GET BACK INTO ORBIT, AND HE'S GOT TWO TO THREE MINUTES AT MOST.
KRR
VMMM
GWHOOO